TEACHING
AT ITS
BEST

TEACHING
AT ITS
BEST

A Research-Based Resource for College Instructors

Linda B. Nilson

Vanderbilt University

ANKER PUBLISHING COMPANY, INC.
Bolton, MA

TEACHING AT ITS BEST

A Research-Based Resource for College Instructors

ISBN 1-882982-20-7

Foreign language teaching development by Christie St. John
Development and layout by Darrell L. Ray
Cover design by Deerfoot Studios

Anker Publishing Company, Inc.
176 Ballville Road
P. O. Box 249
Bolton, MA 01740-0249

ABOUT THE AUTHOR

Linda B. Nilson has been Director of Vanderbilt University's Center for Teaching since February 1993. In addition to managing the Center and its staff, she consults individually with faculty, teaches an interdisciplinary freshman seminar called "Free Will and Determinism," and designs and conducts faculty development workshops at Vanderbilt and other universities across the country. Her workshop repertoire includes comprehensive course design, interpretation of student evaluations, peer assessment of teaching for promotion and tenure, learning styles, case study design and debriefing, cooperative learning, and discussion management.

For the previous three and a half years, she directed the Teaching Assistant Development Program at the University of California, Riverside, and designed and taught a very popular graduate seminar on college teaching. In addition, she developed the "disciplinary cluster" approach to training TAs, a cost-effective way for a centralized unit to provide disciplinary-relevant instructional training. This approach received coverage in *The Chronicle of Higher Education*. She similarly structured TA training at Vanderbilt.

Since moving to the South, Dr. Nilson has been very active in the Southern Regional Faculty and Instructional Development Consortium. She has served on its Executive Committee since 1993, organized and hosted its 1994 conference, and is completing a three-year term as Chair (1995-98). She is also active in the Professional and Organizational Development (POD) Network.

Dr. Nilson entered the area of instructional and faculty development in the late 1970s while she was on the sociology faculty at UCLA. After distinguishing herself as an excellent instructor, her department selected her to establish its Teaching Assistant Training Program. She supervised it for four years, and it still follows her original organization.

In addition to *Teaching at Its Best: A Research-Based Resource for College Instructors,* Dr. Nilson has written three book-length instructional handbooks, one for each of the universities where she has worked. She has also published and presented papers on TA training, critical thinking, college teaching journals, the academic job market, and faculty workshop themes and designs. As a sociologist, she published research in the areas of occupations and work, social stratification, political sociology, and disaster behavior.

Dr. Nilson's career also included several years in the business world as a technical and commercial writer, a training workshop facilitator, and business editor of a Southern California magazine.

A native of Chicago, Dr. Nilson was a National Science Foundation Fellow at the University of Wisconsin, Madison, where she received her Ph.D. and M.S. degrees in sociology. She completed her undergraduate work in three years at the University of California, Berkeley, where she was elected to Phi Beta Kappa.

CONTENTS

PREFACE

This book is designed for use in colleges and universities with high standards of instructional excellence, especially at the undergraduate level. While the text addresses the concerns of new as well as experienced instructors, it assumes a sincere dedication to "teaching at its best" and a student population committed to learning at its best. Teaching and learning that need little or no remediation provide fertile soil for innovation. So this book focuses on state-of-the-art techniques and formats designed to elevate college teaching to its highest potential.

It is intended to be used as a toolbox. It is a concise compilation of hundreds of teaching techniques and formats, classroom activities and exercises, suggestions to enhance instructor-student rapport, guidelines for assignments and papers, and tips for teaching any material more effectively. In considering this resource as a toolbox, the reader may recall the timeless advice of some mechanical sage: "Always use the right tool for the job." But in teaching, there may be several, even many "right tools" for a given teaching "job," and this book presents alternatives wherever appropriate.

Two objectives guided the decisions regarding its content, organization, and layout: 1) to enhance the credibility of the content by grounding it in the vast body of research on college-level teaching and 2) to make the content easily and quickly accessible.

The college-level teaching literature has expanded rapidly since the late 1960s, gaining high quality and developing into a thriving field of its own. The research encompasses not only the "results" of different instructional methods--usually measured by student learning, satisfaction, and retention--but also recommendations on how to implement these methods most successfully. Of course, few instructors have the time to keep abreast of both their own area of scholarship and instructional research. This is why a concise summary of teaching options and innovations should be a particularly useful resource.

To ensure accessibility and to allow rapid reading, the writing style is concise and informal, the paragraphs are relatively brief, and the format is double-column. The thirty chapters are grouped into five major sections ordered roughly according to most instructors' chronological need for the material.

Part I: Sound Preparations addresses the tasks that need to be done before a semester or quarter begins.

Part II: Good Beginnings focuses not only on what to say and do on the first day of class but also on how to set policies, tones, and a productive learning environment for the entire term from that that first day on.

Part III: Varieties of Learning and Teaching Styles presents an extensive and varied menu of the most effective teaching techniques and formats available at the college level. Most of them appeal to a range of student learning styles and are easily adaptable to any subject matter.

Part IV: Disciplinary Differences then concentrates on methods that are discipline-specific.

Finally, Part V: Assessment/Measuring Outcomes offers guidance on, first, evaluating student learning, including testing and grading, and second, assessing instructor effectiveness, including documenting it for review.

Still, the organization of the book is flexible. The chapters need not be read in any order, and the text makes numerous cross-references to other chapters that elaborate on a given subject. In addition, the chapters are purposely short and generously divided into sections. Therefore, the reader can casually browse or quickly locate specific topics of interest.

The content is sufficiently rich and varied to offer something to instructors at all levels, from beginning TAs to seasoned full professors--a highly disparate audience. Experienced faculty can simply skip over the tools with which they have already achieved success.

Another feature of this book is that almost all of it is written in the second person. The new teaching books, including those published by major presses, are increasingly written in this form, and for good reason. It personalizes the information for the reader and makes it easier to read. In addition, certain techniques follow certain essential rules and formulae; some are even defined by a specific sequence of action (e.g., instructor does this, students do that, instructor gives a certain response). In other words, the directions resemble recipes or assembly instructions. Clearly, the second person is the most concise way to present such information.

Teaching at Its Best evolved out of an instructional handbook that I wrote initially for the faculty and TAs at Vanderbilt University, where I direct the Center for Teaching. Several people deserve special thanks for helping to make the handbook version and now this book a reality: Associate Provost John H. Venable and Associate Dean of the College of Arts and Science, George H. Sweeney, both at Vanderbilt University, who supported the development of the initial handbook; Darrell L. Ray, a Vanderbilt Ph.D. in biology and one of the Center for Teaching's first (1993) Master Teaching Fellows, who drew from the best of the Center's resource collection to first-draft many of the chapters; Christie St. John, a Vanderbilt Ph.D. in French and Italian and a 1994-95 Master Teaching Fellow, who drafted the chapter on teaching foreign languages; Melissa Penix, the Center's Secretary, who painstakingly proofread the manuscript and supervised production; Dr. A. Darlene Panvini, who also painstakingly proofread the manuscript, advised on production, and offered substantive improvements; and my late husband Brent, who graciously tolerated my long evening and weekend absences from his side. This book is dedicated to Brent's memory.

Linda B. Nilson
Nashville, Tennessee
1997

Part I.

Sound

Preparations

INSTRUCTIONAL SUPPORT SERVICES AND RESOURCES

Teaching well at the college level is a challenging endeavor, especially for those who are new to the profession. Even experienced faculty in a new institution feel unsettled as they anticipate unfamiliar policies, forms, procedures, expectations, and types of students. Every college and university is a large, multilayered organization--a few rivaling small cities in size and complexity--each with its own unique subculture, norms and values, official power structure, informal power networks, and infrastructure of services and support units.

Most colleges and universities offer a wealth of instructional support services and resources--the library and computer services being among the most obvious. But the instructional help available from some individuals and units may not be obvious from their titles or names alone. The people and campus offices described below are well worth your getting to know. The referral services they provide can save you countless hours, and the information they furnish can prevent costly, however innocent, mistakes.

Colleagues, especially senior ones, are perhaps the most conveniently located and sometimes the most knowledgeable sources of information on discipline-specific issues, including how best to teach certain material, what to expect of students in specific courses, how to motivate students in a given subject, how to locate appropriate guest speakers, how to prepare for tenure and other faculty reviews, how to obtain special services or funding, and what assistance to request from department support staff. Colleagues are also excellent sources of informal feedback on teaching; most will be happy to serve as a classroom observer or teaching videotape reviewer. (Also see the "teaching center" below).

Department chairs are special colleagues who can offer broader, departmental perspectives on the discipline-specific issues above. They are especially well informed on departmental curriculum matters and can advise on proposals to develop new courses and to revise established ones. They may also provide the best counsel on standards and procedures for promotion and tenure. Finally, since they have the opportunity to study the teaching evaluations of all the courses and sections in their department, chairs can help interpret the student ratings and written comments as well as suggest ways to improve them.

The *Dean's office* of your college, school, or division can advise you about promotion and tenure matters, student characteristics,

4

curriculum issues, and course design/development from a still broader perspective. Demographic and academic data about the student body will prove particularly valuable in helping you decide on the objectives, design, content, and techniques for each of your courses. You will also need information about curriculum policies and procedures: Do your courses satisfy general education or breadth requirements? If so, roughly what percentage of students will enroll in that course for that reason alone? How do you propose and get approval for a new course? What components and assignments must a course have to qualify for "honors," "writing," or any other special designation? Finally, the Dean's office may be the place to turn for help with classroom matters--for example, if the classroom you are assigned doesn't meet your class size, ventilation, or technological needs, or if you need a room reserved for special class activities and sessions.

A *teaching, faculty development, or instructional development center* has become an increasingly common resource on both research- and teaching-oriented campuses. It usually provides instructional consultation and training services to faculty and TAs, such as classroom videotaping, classroom observations, class interviews (often in a small-group format called a "small group instructional diagnosis"), midterm student evaluations, advisory consultations, orientations for new instructors, and teaching workshops. Often these centers also maintain a library, run lecture series, publish a newsletter and teaching handbook, and award mini-grants for teaching

innovations. Many house special language testing and training programs for International TAs.

On a number of campuses, these centers also offer consultations and training in instructional technology, such as the most effective pedagogical applications and the how-to's of available software (see Chapter 21). Certainly those with "instructional development," "technology," or "academic computing" in the title do. But such services may be found in media units, libraries, computer centers and laboratories, and distance learning facilities. Campuses that have come to rely greatly on technology often have specialized, stand-alone centers.

An *A/V or media center* furnishes classrooms with audio/visual equipment at your request. Very likely it maintains a library of instructionally useful videos and films. In some colleges and universities it also houses instructional technology equipment, training, and consultation.

A *women's center* often provides a wider variety of services than the lecture series, library, and support groups that you would expect. It is well worth asking if the one on your campus also sponsors self-development and health workshops, career planning forums, book and study groups, and writers groups. No doubt it offers legal and policy information about sexual harassment as well as emotional support for those who may have a complaint. (However, complaints are probably processed by the "equal opportunity" unit described below.)

Ethnic cultural centers similarly may be a richer instructional resource than one might expect. They usually offer symposia on cultural topics, academic materials (both print and video), art exhibits, and musical performances.

An *international center* typically provides acculturation counseling and support for international students and their families, as well as legal advice on visas, work permits, taxes, etc. It may also be the primary information source on opportunities to work and study abroad. On some campuses, the international center is also responsible for ESL testing and courses.

An *equal opportunity center* may go by any number of titles, but you should look for key words such as "opportunity development, "affirmative action," "equality," "equity," and "civil rights." Almost all American campuses have such an office. Its purpose is to coordinate state- and federally-mandated programs designed to ensure equal opportunities for minorities, women, individuals with disabilities, and other disadvantaged groups. It also serves as a source of information for students, faculty, and staff who may have questions or complaints related to equal opportunity in education, employment, and campus programs and activities. If a complaint is judged valid, it will also advise on grievance procedures.

Sexual harassment falls under the equal opportunity umbrella. Often in collaboration with a women's center (see above), an equal opportunity office disseminates information on the legal definition of sexual harassment, the institution's policy regarding it, specific types of harassment behavior, its prevalence, its prevention,

procedures for filing a complaint or a grievance, and confidential support and counseling services.

On many campuses this type of center also identifies students with learning disabilities and recommends any special accommodations that instructors should make in their teaching and testing. Most accommodations are minor (e.g., an isolated test environment and/or a longer test period), and the office may even provide special facilities for certain needs. If your equal opportunity office does not handle learning disability issues, one of the units covered below probably does.

The centers above may serve your own or your students' needs. Let's consider now the units and individuals that specialize in serving students. Students seeking general academic counsel should be referred to their academic advisers; those requesting information or assistance with respect to a specific course should be sent to the instructor or the department. At times, however, students need help with other problems, some that most instructors are ill-equipped to address. These include learning disabilities, math or test anxiety, severe writing problems, poor study and test-taking skills, weak academic backgrounds, emotional difficulties, and career planning questions. These cases call for a referral to a unit in the next group.

Almost all campuses have a facility designed to help students improve their academic skills. It is often called a *learning, learning skills, learning resources, academic assistance,* or *academic support center*, and its services typically include individual counseling in academic skills, individual and small group tutoring, workshops in learning strategies (e.g., reading skills, study skills, notetaking, test preparation, and test-taking). Some tutoring may be geared to specific courses or subject matter that are known to give students trouble, such as calculus, chemistry, physics, biology, economics, and foreign languages. This type of center may also offer ESL testing and courses.

A *writing program* may be housed in a learning center or comprise its own stand-alone unit. It is likely to provide individual and/or small-group tutoring in the mechanics of grammar and punctuation as well as the structure of exam essays, short papers, critical papers, and research papers. It may even schedule formal writing workshops. Staff are trained not to outline or edit student work, but rather to show students how to master the stages of the writing process on their own.

A *psychological* or *counseling center* is the place to refer students who manifest any type of psychological or emotional disorder. As they usually show signs of trouble only in more private environments, Chapter 9 on office hours lists the behaviors to watch out for. This type of unit gives free individual counseling for psychological, emotional, and sometimes even academic problems, and it may coordinate group programs for personal growth, self-improvement, and self-awareness.

A *career center* helps students identify and achieve their occupational goals. It typically provides assessment tests in skills and inter-ests and resources for career exploration as well as information on internship opportunities and summer jobs. Workshops on job search strategies, résumé preparation, communication and decision-making skills, and job interview techniques may also available.

All of these campus units will welcome your requests for further information and will gladly mail you their brochures, newsletters, and any other materials they furnish for students. They are well worth learning about as they are "service centers" with a service orientation. They exist to meet your and/or your students' needs, whether they be instructional, professional, or personal. Unless their resources are already stretched beyond capacity, they actively pursue and benefit from increasing usage. So if they can make your life as an instructor easier, if they can save you class and office-hour time, if they can handle any of the many student requests and problems that pass through your office door, by all means take advantage of their invaluable services.

Understanding Your Students

Whenever we prepare an oral presentation, a publication, or letter, one of the first issues we consider is our audience. The person or people to receive our message influences our content, format, organization, sentence structure, and word choice. The same holds true in teaching. The nature of our students--their academic preparation, aspirations, and cognitive development--affects our choices of what and how to teach.

Your Undergraduate Student Body Profile

If you're not already familiar with your student audience, or your recent experience tells you that its composition is changing, your institutions's admissions office can provide the type of student data you need. At a minimum, you should find out the distributions and percentages on the following variables: age; marital and parental status; race and ethnicity; full-time and part-time employed; campus residents v. commuters; native v. international; geographical mix; and special admissions. If your students are primarily young, on-campus residents, you can afford to make more collaborative out-of-class assignments.

You also need to know your students' level of academic preparation and achievement. You can assess your institution's selectivity by comparing the number of applicants each year with the number of those accepted (a 2:1 ratio or above is highly selective). For each entering class, you can find out about its average scholastic test scores (SATs and ACTs), the percentage that ranked at varying percentiles of their high school graduating classes, the percentage of National Merit and National Achievement Finalists (over 5% is high), and the percentage that qualified for advanced placement credit (over a third is high).

If your student body is largely young and traditional, ask about the high school leadership positions and activities of a given class. Your institution's career center should also have on file the percentage of students planning on different types of graduate and professional educations, as well as the immediate employment plans of the next graduating class.

No matter how bright or mature your prospective students may be, do not expect them to have reached a high level of cognitive maturity in your discipline. As the next section explains, almost all students, especially freshmen and sophomores, begin a course of study with serious misconceptions about knowledge in general and the discipline specifi-

8

cally. Only as these misconceptions are dispelled do students mature intellectually through distinct stages. As an instructor, you have the opportunity--some would say the responsibility--to lead them through these stages to epistemological maturity.

The Cognitive Development of Undergraduates

Psychologist William G. Perry (1968, 1985) formulated a theory of the intellectual and ethical development of college students. Since he introduced it, the research supporting it accumulated rapidly, making Perry's the leading theory on the cognitive development of undergraduates. While it applies across disciplines, a student's level of maturity may be advanced in one and not in another. So we shouldn't assume, for example, that a sophisticated senior in a laboratory science major has a comparable understanding of the nature of knowledge in the social sciences or the humanities.

The more elaborate version of Perry's theory posits nine positions through which students pass on their way to cognitive maturity. (Perry also developed a simpler model of four stages, which are referred to in italics below.) How far and how rapidly students progress through the hierarchy depends largely on the quality and type of instruction they receive. It is this "flexible" aspect of Perry's theory that has made it particularly attractive and useful. The schema suggests ways that we as instructors can accelerate our undergraduates' intellectual growth.

Let us begin with position 1, the cognitive state in which most freshmen arrive. (Of course, some sophomores, juniors, and seniors are still at this level.) Perry used the term *dualism* to describe students' thinking at this stage because they perceive the world in black-and-white simplicity. They decide what to believe and how to act according to absolute standards of right and wrong, good and bad, truth and falsehood. Authority figures, like instructors, supposedly know and teach the absolute truths about reality. Further, all knowledge and goodness can be quantified or tallied, like correct answers on a spelling test.

At position 2, students enter the general cognitive stage of *multiplicity*. They come to realize that there exists uncertainty and, therefore, a multiplicity of opinions. But to them the variety merely reflects that not all authorities are equally legitimate or competent. Some students don't even give these competing opinions much credence, believing them to be just an instructor's exercise designed ultimately to lead them to the one true answer. As they advance to position 3, they accept the notion that genuine uncertainty exists, but only as a temporary state that will resolve once an authority finds the answer.

Entering position 4, which marks the broader stage of *relativism*, students make an about-face and abandon their faith in authority's ability to identify "the truth." At this point, they either consider all views equally valid or allow different opinions within the limits delineated by some standard. In brief, they become relativists with no hope of there ever being one true interpretation or answer.

Students at position 5 formalize the idea that all knowledge is relativistic and contextual, but with qualifications. They may reserve dualistic ideas of right and wrong as subordinate principles for special cases in specific contexts. Thus, even in a relativistic world, they may permit certain instances where facts are truly facts and only one plausible truth exists.

At some point, however, students can no longer accommodate all the internal inconsistencies and ambiguities inherent in position 5. They may want to make choices but often lack clear standards for doing so. So they begin to feel the need to orient themselves in their relativistic world by making some sort of personal commitment. As this need grows, they pass through position 6 and into the more general cognitive stage of *commitment*. When they actually make an initial, tentative commitment to a particular view in some area, they attain position 7. Next, at position 8, they experience and examine the impacts and implications of their choice of commitment. That is, they learn what commitment means and what trade-offs it carries.

Finally, at position 9, students realize that trying on a commitment and either embracing or modifying it in the hindsight of experience is a major part of personal and intellectual growth. This process is, in fact, a life-long activity that paves the road toward wisdom and requires an ever open mind.

Encouraging Cognitive Growth

Nelson (1993), a leading authority on developing thinking skills, contends that we can facilitate students' progress through these stages by familiarizing them with *uncertainty* and *standards of comparison* in our disciplines. He and many others have achieved excellent results by implementing his ideas. (Kloss, 1994, offers a somewhat different approach tailored to literature instructors.)

Exposure to uncertainties in our knowledge bases helps students realize that often there is no one superior truth, nor can there be, given the nature of rational knowledge. This realization helps lead them out of dualistic thinking (position 1) and through multiplistic conceptions of knowledge (positions 2 and 3). Once they can understand uncertainty as legitimate and inherent in the nature of knowledge, they can mature into relativists (positions 4 and 5).

Instructive examples of such uncertainties include the following: 1) the range of viable interpretations that can be made of certain works of literature and art; 2) the different conclusions that can be legitimately drawn from the same historical evidence and scientific data; 3) a discipline's history of scientific revolutions and paradigm shifts; 4) unresolved issues on which a discipline is currently conducting research; and 5) historical and scientific unknowns that may or may not ever be resolved.

Our next step is to help students advance beyond relativism through positions 6 and 7, at which point they can make tentative commitments and progress towards cognitive maturity. To do so, students need to understand that, among all the possible answers and interpretations, some, in fact, may be more valid than others. They must also learn *why* some are better than others--that is, what criteria exist to discriminate among the options, to distinguish the wheat from the chaff.

Disciplines vary on their criteria

10

for evaluating validity. Each one has its own "metacognitive model"-- that is, a set of accepted conventions about what makes a sound argument and what constitutes appropriate evidence. Most students have trouble acquiring these conventions on their own; they tend to assume that the rules are invariable across fields. So Nelson advises us to make our concepts of evidence and our standards for comparison explicit to our students.

By the time students reach position 5, they are uncomfortable with their relativism, and by position 6, they are hungry for criteria on which to rank options and base choices. So they should be very receptive to a discipline's evaluative framework.

To encourage students to reach positions 7 and 8, we can provide writing and discussion opportunities for them to deduce and examine what their initial commitments imply in other contexts. They might apply their currently preferred framework to a new or different ethical case, historical event, social phenomenon, political issue, scientific problem, or piece of literature. They may even apply it to a real situation in their own lives. Through this process, they begin to realize that a commitment focuses options, closing some doors while opening others.

We should remind students that they are always free to reassess their commitments, to modify them, and even to make new ones, but with an intellectual and ethical caveat: They should have sound reason to do so, such as new experience or data or a more logical organization of the evidence--not just personal convenience. With a clear understanding of this final point, students achieve position 9.

Bringing Perry's and Nelson's insights into our courses presents a genuine challenge in that students in any one class may be at different stages, even if they are in the same graduating class. Most freshmen are likely to fall in the first few positions, but juniors and seniors may be anywhere on the hierarchy. It may be wisest, then, to help students at the lower positions catch up with those at the higher ones by including knowledge uncertainties, disciplinary criteria for comparison, and opportunities for students to make and justify choices in as many courses as possible.

Keep your students' cognitive growth in mind as you read other chapters in this book. If you try out the objective-centered approach to designing a course, which is outlined in the next chapter, you may want to set your students' cognitive maturity to a certain stage as a specific objective for one or more of your courses. If you'd like more suggestions for facilitating your students' advancement, Chapter 13 describes several discovery-based strategies for teaching uncertainty and alternative explanations. Finally, Chapter 22 revisits the notion of metacognitive models in greater detail as applied to teaching students to think and write in the disciplines. This chapter also summarizes some major differences in argumentation and evidence among three disciplinary groups: the sciences, history-based disciplines, and literature.

IN THE BEGINNING:
COURSE DESIGN AND OBJECTIVES

Whether you are teaching an established course for the first time, developing a brand new course, or revising a course you currently teach, it is wise to ask yourself what you are trying to accomplish. No doubt, you want your students to learn certain things, to master a body of material. But you can't assess how well you've met this goal, nor can you assess your students, unless you have them "do" something with that material that demonstrates their learning. What they do may involve writing, discussing, role playing, creating a visual work, conducting an experiment, making an oral presentation, or any other "display" of learning, as long as you can perceive it though your senses. If this line of reasoning makes sense to you, you will probably find this chapter's approach to course design very useful. Think of it as "course design by objectives."

But first let us review the components of a course, each of which requires your careful, well informed decision-making.

Elements of Course Design

Pregent (1994) presents a detailed model of course design, which starts with understanding the reason for the course. Why was the course proposed and approved in the first place, and by whom?

What special purposes does it serve? Generally, courses are developed to meet the needs of a changing labor market, to update curriculum content, or to ensure accreditation. Additionally, new ones may give the institution a competitive edge. At any rate, knowing the underlying influences can help you orient a course to its intended purposes.

Tasks. "The time necessary to prepare a new course is directly proportional to the number of tasks required to complete preparation," notes Pregent. So he advises first to evaluate the nature and the amount of prep work involved, along with other expenses and investments. Here are some tasks for which to budget time and other resources:

1) researching the subject matter of the course;
2) developing and fine tuning assignments and, if any, laboratories;
3) constructing an outline for the course;
4) writing the syllabus (see Chapter 4);
5) integrating, adapting, and/or producing *de novo* handouts, study guides, videos, demonstrations, etc.;
6) developing tests, keys, and grading scales (see Chapters 27, 28, and 29);
7) planning and conducting the ori-

12

entation and training of support staff (e.g., TAs; see Chapter 5).

Student profiles and expectations. A successful course must be relevant to the needs and level of its students. Refer to the first part of Chapter 2 for the type of student data you will need--all of which should be available from your institution's admissions office and career center--to determine the abilities, background knowledge, interests, and course expectations of your likely student population. Ask colleagues who have taught the course before about what topics, books, teaching methods, activities, assignments, etc. worked and didn't work well for them. The more relevant you can make the material to the target group, the more effective your course will be.

If you cannot gather much information in advance, plan to keep your initial course design somewhat flexible. On the first day of class, use index cards and ice breakers to find out more about your students and their expectations (see Chapter 7), then adjust and tighten the design accordingly.

Course content. The difficulty in deciding course content varies by course and instructor. If you specialize in the content area, your only difficulty may be narrowing it down. But you may have to do extensive reading before tackling a topic with which you are only marginally familiar.

Pregent advises brainstorming as many topics and themes as possible. For help, consult tables of contents of reputable texts, course catalogs and syllabi from other institutions, and colleagues. Then begin editing by assigning ranking numbers to each item, giving high-est priority to most difficult and essential topics and those that address your students' needs and expectations. Allocate time and emphasis for each topic according to these rankings.

Do not hesitate to eliminate topics entirely. Instructors, especially new ones, tend to pack too much material into a course. It is better to teach a few topics well than to merely "cover the material" with a steamroller and wind up teaching very little of anything.

Textbooks. The preceding steps will direct your search for an appropriate text. If you find one that reflects your general preferences and philosophies, you are indeed fortunate. If you don't, consider selecting the best available option for many of your reading assignments and supplementing it with handouts, reserve readings, and/or a class pack. Try to avoid making students purchase more than one expensive text.

Developing Instructional Objectives

Teaching has only one purpose, and that is to facilitate learning (Cross, 1988). Learning can occur without teaching at no loss to anyone, but teaching can and unfortunately often does occur without learning. In the latter case, the students obviously lose time, money, knowledge, and perhaps confidence in themselves and/or the educational system. But less obviously, instructors lose faith in their students and in themselves. For our own mental health as well as our students', we need to make teaching and learning synonymous sides of the same coin. An effective way to begin is to design a course around carefully considered instructional objectives.

An instructional objective is a statement that gives instructional focus and direction, establishes guidelines for testing, and conveys one's teaching intent to others (Gronlund, 1985). More succinctly, it is a statement of what your students should be able *to do* after completing your course.

There are two types of instructional objectives (Gronlund, 1985; Pregent, 1994). First, a *general objective* is a short, broad statement written from our point of view as an instructor--e.g., "This course will introduce students to the process of literary criticism." This is really a statement of what *we* want to do. *Specific objectives* describe precisely what our students must be able *to do* if we are to meet our general objective. Thus they are written from a student's point of view-- e.g., "After studying the processes of photosynthesis and respiration, the student should be able to trace the carbon cycle in a given ecosystem."

In brief, a general objective reflects the major themes and content of a course, while specific objectives detail the behavioral means to the general objectives.

Both types belong in your syllabus (see Chapter 4). If you don't share them, students may justifiably wonder what they are supposed to gain from your course, and they may wander aimlessly looking for it.

A Cognitive Hierarchy of Objectives

Bloom (1956) developed a useful taxonomy for constructing objectives. His framework posits a hierarchy of six cognitive processes, moving from the most concrete, lowest-level process of recalling stored knowledge, through several intermediate cognitive modes to the most abstract, highest level of evaluation. (Depending upon your field, you may prefer to place *application* at a higher level.) Each level is defined:

Knowledge: the ability to remember and state previously learned material

Comprehension: the ability to grasp the meaning of material and to restate it in one's own words

Application: the ability to use learned material in new and concrete situations

Analysis: the ability to break down material into its component parts so as to understand its organizational structure

Synthesis: the ability to put parts together to form a new whole

Evaluation: the ability to judge the value of material for a given purpose.

To make these terms more concrete, refer to Table I, which lists common student performance verbs for each cognitive operation. You may find it helpful to start developing specific objects from this listing; simply check the verbs that you'd like your students to be able to perform. Table II gives examples of specific objectives in various disciplines.

Bear in mind that the true cognitive level of a specific objective depends upon the material students are given in a course. If they are handed a formal definition of iambic pentameter, then their defining it is a simple recall or, at most, comprehension operation. If, however, they are only provided with examples of poems and plays written in it and are asked to abstract a definition from the exam-

Table I

Student Performance Verbs by Level of Cognitive Operation Based on Bloom's Taxonomy

1. Knowledge

arrange	order
define	recall
duplicate	recite
label	recognize
list	relate
memorize	repeat
name	reproduce

2. Comprehension

classify	locate
describe	recognize
discuss	report
explain	restate
express	review
identify	select
indicate	translate

3. Application

apply	interpret
choose	operate
compose examples	practice
demonstrate	schedule
dramatize	sketch
employ	solve
illustrate	use

4. Analysis

analyze	differentiate
appraise	discriminate
calculate	distinguish
categorize	examine
compare	experiment
contrast	question
criticize	test

5. Synthesis

arrange	integrate
assemble	manage
collect	organize
compose	plan
construct	predict
create	prepare
design	propose
formulate	set up

6. Evaluation

appraise	evaluate
argue	judge
assess	rate
challenge	score
choose	select
defend	support
dispute	value

*Depending on the use, some verbs may apply to more than one level.

Table II

Models of Specific Objectives Based on Bloom's Taxonomy

Level	The student should be able to...
Knowledge	define iambic pentameter state Newton's Laws of Motion identify the major impressionist painters
Comprehension	describe the data indicated by the graph summarize the passage from *Huckleberry Finn* properly translate into English the paragraph from Voltaire's *Candide*
Application	describe an experiment to test the influence of light and light quality on the Hill reaction of photosynthesis scan a poem for metric foot and rhyme scheme use the Archimedes Principle to determine the volume of an irregularly shaped object
Analysis	list arguments for and against gun control determine the necessary controls for an experiment discuss the rationale and efficacy of isolationism in the global economy
Synthesis	write a short story in Hemingway's style compose a logical argument on assisted suicide in opposition to your personal opinion construct a helium-neon laser
Evaluation	assess the validity of the conclusions based on the data and statistical analysis give a critical analysis of a novel with evidence to support the analysis suggest stock market investments based on company performance and projected value

ples, they are then engaging in the much higher-order process of synthesis.

As you check key verbs and construct specific objectives, think about what cognitive operations you are emphasizing. We cannot hope to foster critical thinking by setting objectives only at the knowledge and comprehension levels. While these furnish foundations for learning, they are not the end of education. Therefore, it is wise to include some higher-order objectives to challenge students to higher levels of thinking. We will revisit Bloom's taxonomy in Chapter 16 as it is also very useful for framing questions.

Elaborating a Specific Objective for Assessment

A specific objective can have as many as three parts:

1) A statement of a measurable performance. This part is essential. Objectives begin with action verbs (e.g., define, classify, construct, compute; see Table I) rather than nebulous verbs reflecting internal states (e.g., know, learn, understand, appreciate).

Example 1): The student will *classify* given rocks as igneous or metamorphic.

Example 2): The student will *describe* one difference between sedimentary and metamorphic rocks.

See Table II for more examples.

2) A statement of conditions that must be present for the student to perform the given objective. These conditions define the circumstances under which the student's performance will be assessed. If the defined skill is a simple mem-

ory exercise such as "name" or "describe," conditions may not be necessary. However, other performance verbs require conditions, as the examples below illustrate.

Example 1): *Identify* the parts of a computer system on the diagram.

Example 2): *Identify* the parts of the computer system on the bench in front of you.

3) The standards and criteria for assessing acceptable performance. These standards specify the minimum degree of accuracy that students must demonstrate to meet the objective. The first example below is too muddy to be meaningful, but the second defines a discrete task to be performed (to compute) under clear conditions (given sets of numbers) with an evaluative criterion (95% accuracy).

Example 1): State two causes of inflation with 75% accuracy.

Example 2): Compute the mean and standard deviation of given sets of numbers with 95% accuracy.

Of course, you may elaborate such standards into more refined levels designating an "A" performance, "B" performance, etc.

Course Design by Objectives

Your specific course objectives serve as a scaffolding for your course design. To design an entire course around specific instructional objectives, think of a branching-tree diagram that "grows" from three or more main "trunks" on your right and branches to your left. The main trunks on your right are your "ultimate" end-of-course objectives. Define these specific objectives first.

Then work backwards (to your left), asking yourself what your students will have to be able to do before they can accomplish each ultimate specific objective. After you determine one or more mediating specific objectives for each ultimate one, continue to work backwards to the more basic performances they must master before they can achieve these mediating objectives, and so on.

You have probably reached the beginning of your course when your specific objectives do one or more of the following: 1) entail the lowest-level cognitive operations (knowledge and comprehension); 2) involve readying your students to abandon dualistic thinking; and/or 3) requires them to identify and question the misconceptions about the subject matter that they first bring into the classroom. These are perhaps the most basic learning objectives we can set for our students. After all, they can't apply, analyze, synthesize, or evaluate knowledge that they can't summarize or paraphrase. They can't truly explore a knowledge base if they don't grasp its basic uncertainties and the field's standards for evaluating competing interpretations. And they cannot accurately map new, valid knowledge onto existing knowledge that is riddled with misconceptions and misinformation (Nelson, 1993).

Now, re-examine your ultimate specific objectives. They should suggest questions or at least foci, themes, or formats for your final exam, final paper assignment, or capstone student project. After all, these objectives delineate what you want your students to be able to do by the end of the course.

Then move backwards again through your mediating objectives.

Consider how they might suggest questions, formats, and themes for midterm exams, graded and ungraded assignments, and in-class activities. In fact, your objectives can provide a scaffolding for planning every class meeting. If you want your students to be able to write a certain type of analysis by a certain week of the term--let's say, for a grade--then structure assignments and in-class activities that will give them practice in writing that type of analysis. If you want them to be able to solve certain kinds of problems, then design assignments and activities that will give them practice in solving such problems. If you want them to research and develop a point of view, then argue it orally, then give in-class and homework assignments that give practice in each of these skills.

Put very simply, move backwards from your specific objectives to plan on how to move your students forward. Then fill in your classes and assignments with instruction, guidance, and plenty of practice in how to meet your objectives.

What if your objectives are soundly written (e.g., begin with action verbs) but don't suggest to you appropriate activities and assignments? It may be that you aren't familiar with the wide range of effective options to choose from. Explore the many dozens of teaching techniques, classroom formats, and assignment ideas in this book, especially in Parts III, IV, and V. You will find the class-by-class bricks and mortar for building a successful learning experience onto your course design scaffolding. They will help ensure that your teaching translates into learning.

18   Once you have a sound course
design, your syllabus almost writes
itself. The next chapter presents a
concise checklist of all the information that can and usually should be
included in this important course
document.

The Complete
Syllabus

A syllabus is most simply defined as a concise outline of a course of study. But it is also the students' introduction to the course, the subject matter, and *you*. In addition to providing a schedule of class assignments, readings, and activities, it should give students insight into and appreciation for the material. In a sense, then, it is not only the road map for the term's foray into knowledge but also a travelogue to pique students' interest in the expedition.

Experienced instructors consider most parts of a serviceable syllabus intuitive (Lowther et al., 1989). But some courses call for so much first-day information that it is worth reviewing all the possible components, especially for junior faculty and TAs. So here is a suggested checklist for developing a comprehensive syllabus (Nilson, 1990; Altman and Cashin, 1992; Grunert, 1997).

1) Complete course information: the course number and title; days, hours, and location of class meetings; any required or recommended pre-requisites, including permission of the instructor for enrollment; any required review sessions; and any required laboratories or recitation/discussion sections, with the same information as given for the course. If any course materials, exercises, assignments, exams, etc. are on the World Wide Web, be sure to furnish the URLs of the course and any supplementary resources.

2) Information about yourself: your full name and title (so students know how to address you), your office hours, your office location, your office phone number, your e-mail address, your home page URL (if you have one), and your department's phone number (for messages). If you decide to give students your home phone number, you may wish to limit calls to emergencies and to certain hours.

3) The same information about other course personnel, such as TAs, technicians, assistants, etc. You might encourage your section and lab TAs to develop their own syllabi.

4) An annotated list of reading materials (textbooks, journal articles, class packs, Web materials, etc.) with full citations (including edition), price, location (bookstore, library, reserve status, URL, etc.), identification as required or recommended, and your reasons for selecting them. If you do not plan to give regular assignments from the text, consider making it a recommended, supplementary source. If commercially prepared notes are available, say how helpful they might be.

5) Any other materials re-

20 *quired for the course,* including where to find them and cost estimates. For example, some science labs require students to have a personal stock of cleaning supplies and safety equipment. Art and photography classes usually expect students to supply their own expendable materials. If special types of calculators, computers, or software are called for, these too should be described in detail.

6) A complete course description, including the organization of the course and the major topics it will cover. You may even want to list topics it will *not* cover, especially if your course has too much "popular appeal" and tends to attract less-than-serious students.

7) Your general and specific instructional objectives for the course, especially what students should be able to do or do better at the end of the term. Mediating objectives are optional. Chapter 3 gives guidance in developing instructional objectives and designing a course around them.

8) All graded course requirements and a complete breakdown of your grading scale, preferably buttressed by a rationale. Nothing is so annoying as hearing half of your students bargain for points or ask for a curve after an exam. Detail the point values of all assignments, peer group evaluations, class participation, discussion, etc., as well as number and types of tests and quizzes, homework assignments, and papers. Chapter 29 examines the pro's and cons of various grading systems.

9) The criteria on which each written assignment will be *evaluated,* including your policies regarding revisions and extra credit. As with post-exam grade protests, the choral call for extra credit can be a nuisance unless your position is firmly established from the start.

10) Other course "requirements" aside from those computed in the grade. If you expect students to participate in class discussions, you must tell them. If you plan to give unannounced, ungraded quizzes to monitor comprehension, then let it be known from the beginning. It is better to make sure that all students understand your expectations from the start than to spring new rules on them later in the term.

11) Your policies on attendance and tardiness. Instructors occasionally debate whether to grade on attendance or not. As one side puts it, how can students learn and contribute to the class without being there? (As Woody Allen once put it, over 90 percent of success is just showing up.) But others argue that students are free to learn as much or as little as they choose by whatever means they choose. However you make up *your* mind, your syllabus should state your policy.

Bear in mind that some colleges and universities require instructors to report students who are excessively absent. You may have to keep attendance even if you don't intend to grade on it. Check the section on academic regulations in your institution's catalog.

12) Your policies on missed or late exams and assignments. Students do occasionally have good reasons for missing a deadline or a test. State whether they can drop one quiz/grade during the term or if a make-up is possible. If you assess penalties for late work, describe them precisely to put to rest any later disputes. Find out how you may and may not penalize students by reading the section on academic regulations in your institution's catalog.

13) A statement of your and your institution's policies on academic dishonesty, as well as their applications to your course. Cheating and plagiarism are all too common on today's college campuses, as Chapter 10 documents. Unless you make a strong statement about your intolerance of them, your students may assume that you are naive or will look the other way. If your institution has an honor code, state that you will strictly adhere to and enforce it.

Another reason to address academic honesty policies is spell out how you will apply them to cooperative learning activities and products. Instructors have to devise their own rules on small-group work. If you don't detail your rules, one of two things are likely to happen: Your students may inadvertently violate your and your institution's policies, or they may not work as cooperatively as you'd like.

14) Proper safety procedures and conduct for laboratories. While you would hope that students would have the common sense to apply good safety habits to their work, you cannot assume that these habits are intuitive. Specify strict rules for lab dress and procedures. If you threaten to exact penalties for safety violations, then stand ready to make good on your word. Remember, it is better to take away a few lab points than to risk the safety of the entire section.

15) Relevant campus support services and their locations for assistance in mastering course software, doing computer assignments, writing papers or lab reports, learning study skills, solving homework problems, etc. Chapter 1 gives tips on identifying such resources on your campus.

16) Other available study or assignment aids. If you plan to distribute study guides, practice problems, or practice essay questions, students find it helpful to know about them from the start. If you assign papers, you may wish to suggest possible topics and give specific guidelines for writing papers in your discipline (see Chapter 22).

17) A weekly or class-by-class course schedule with as much of the following as possible: topics to be covered; class activities and formats (lecture, guest speaker, class discussion, cooperative group work, demonstration, field trip, role play, simulation, debate, panel discussion, film or video, slide show, computer exercise, case study, review session, etc.); dates of announced quizzes and exams; and due dates of all reading assignments, handed-in homework assignments, papers, and projects. Be sure to accommodate holidays and breaks.

18) A concluding legal caveat or disclaimer. In our litigious society, a few students have sued professors for failing to conform to the syllabus schedule. Although you may not intend your syllabus to be a legally binding contract, students may think they are not getting their dollar's worth if

22

the syllabus isn't completed by the end of the term. Therefore, for your own protection, you might append a brief message to the effect: "The above schedule, policies, and assignments in this course are subject to change in the event of extenuating circumstances or by mutual agreement between the instructor and the students."

Two other optional syllabus components are recommended:

19) Requirements your course satisfies, such as general education, writing- across-the-curriculum, majors, and any other graduation requirements that your institution or department maintains.

20) Background information about yourself, such as your degrees, universities you have attended, other universities where you have taught and/or conducted research, and your areas of research. Students appreciate knowing something about you as a professional and a person. A little knowledge about you can help inspire a sense of personal loyalty to you.

A comprehensive, well-constructed syllabus may easily run four, five, or even more pages. Even ten pages may not be too long. The more information you include, the less you have to improvise or decide on-the-run, and the fewer questions you have to answer.

In addition, a solid syllabus says a lot of good things about you to your class. Among them, it says that you understand students, how they abhor surprises and last-minute assignments, and how they

appreciate a tightly organized, explicit course structure around which they can plan the rest of their lives. It says that you respect *them*, as well as the subject matter of the course.

Even so, you can't expect students to carefully read every work of your carefully constructed document. You should plan on reviewing every point with them during your first class meeting. In fact, that first meeting so affects the entire course flow that it merits its own chapter (Chapter 7).

COURSE COORDINATION
BETWEEN FACULTY AND TAS

On the surface, the faculty-TA relationship seems simple and clear-cut. The professor receives an invaluable staff member in return for supervising a graduate student's apprenticeship in college teaching. The TA in turn performs an array of vital support services, under the professor's direction, while preparing for his or her future career. Through the TA, the students benefit from the opportunity for personalized consultation and additional, often more participatory instruction than is possible in a large class with a single faculty member. It is an all-around win-win arrangement.

But often the faculty-TA relationship isn't as productive and mutually rewarding as it can be. Few professors are trained in supervisory techniques, and TAs may be afraid to reveal their ignorance by asking too many questions.

Like all professional relationships, the successful TA-faculty team thrives on respect, trust, cooperation, and communication. This chapter suggests specific ways for both parties to foster these qualities in their working relationship.

Before the Term:
Course Review and
Role Specifications

First, TA assignments should be made as early as possible, preferably well before the start of the term. Early assignments allow time for the faculty and TAs to discuss the course and their mutual responsibilities, as well as to prepare to meet them. This extra time is crucial for first-time TAs and for experienced TAs taking on new assignments. TAs also need the assurance that they will have support and guidance when the need arises.

If you are faculty, hold an introductory staff meeting at least a few days before classes begin. Hand out your syllabus and present your course objectives, organization, and schedule. Review general mechanics, such as grading policies and grade complaint procedures, even if TAs will not be conducting sections. Students' opinions of the course are influenced greatly by the efficiency and proficiency of the instructional staff.

Next, firmly establish the roles that you and your TAs will play. TAs must know what is expected of them, as well as what they can expect of their faculty supervisors. To ensure clarity, issue a written statement of mutual responsibilities, and make sure everyone understands and agrees.

When allocating course duties, try to divide tasks fairly, equitably, and efficiently. TA responsibilities may include assisting in course preparation, preparing and/or instructing in laboratories, leading discussions, conducting help/review sessions, attending lectures, guest lecturing, taking roll, assisting in assignment and test preparation, being available during tests, grading, calculating grades, and holding office hours. Faculty responsibilities typically involve supervising and participating in test construction, advising TAs on discussion section or laboratory content and methods, coaching them in presentation and teaching skills, providing them with feedback on their teaching effectiveness, scheduling and directing TA staff meetings, and ensuring TAs have whatever supplies they need.

Depending on the size of the class and the number of TAs involved, you may wish to assign an experienced TA to act as a "head TA" in charge of facilitating communication among all course TAs. Strong interpersonal skills are essential here as the head TA must maintain a good rapport with both you and his fellow TAs.

Finally, try to give realistic estimates of the expected time and effort required of the TAs to perform their job well. While these estimates will vary from person to person and from week to week, they will allow TAs to plan their schedules more efficiently. Be sure you know the number of hours per week that each TA assignment involves.

During the Term: Regular Meetings and Teaching Feedback

Once you and your TAs reach a clear understanding on duties and expectations, all parties must first and foremost maintain open lines of communication. If a TA cannot approach you or the head TA with a problem, it may very well worsen and sour the students' learning ex-

perience. You and the head TA should actively invite TAs to seek your problem-solving advice.

Of course, communication is a two-way street. If you are a TA, and you fail to seek and/or follow good counsel, openly disagree with your supervising faculty in front of your students, or otherwise are insubordinate, you are liable to get in trouble with the class and eventually your faculty. Clear, open communication is *everyone's* responsibility and is vital to the success of the course.

The easiest and most reliable means of maintaining good communication is the regular, usually weekly staff meeting. Scheduling these meetings is the faculty's or head TA's charge. They are essential to the smooth coordination of multi-section courses, which are so common at the introductory levels of the laboratory sciences, mathematics, English, and the foreign languages. These meetings should follow a fairly standard agenda of reviewing current and upcoming material, discussing the TAs' lesson plans, and assessing students' learning. Let us take each major topic in turn.

Agenda item #1: Course content. If you are faculty, you must ensure that your TAs have enough background in the upcoming course material to teach or tutor it. If you don't require them to attend your lectures, you might give them copies of your lecture notes. Some TAs may benefit from supplementary readings as well. You should also provide your TAs with leads on the student trouble spots they can anticipate and should address in section and office hours. Especially in the lab sciences, TAs must be well versed in the principles, procedures, hazards, and typical pitfalls of the next laboratory. In addition to your TAs' reputation with students, safety may be at stake here.

If you are a TA, you are in turn responsible for coming to these weekly meetings having read the upcoming readings, including the lab manual section, where applicable. Raise *all* your questions; reserve the "dumb" one for your fellow TAs, if you prefer. You too should anticipate student stumbling blocks and ask for help in leading your students over them. Whether or not your supervising faculty requires it, do attend all lectures. Students often complain on their teaching evaluation forms about TAs who do not. *Always* rehearse a lab you've never done before, preferably with a TA who has.

Agenda item #2: TAs' lesson plans. The second major item is what the TAs should do with the upcoming material in their discussion sections, labs, or help sessions. What teaching techniques and formats will give students the most productive chance to actively *work with* and *play with* the material? Should the TAs start off with a warm-up writing exercise on the major points of the reading, the lab procedures, or the last lecture? If discussion is appropriate, what questions should the TAs pose, and in what order? Should they be written on the board, on an overhead transparency, or in a handout? Or should they be handed out in advance and serve as a study guide? If reviewing homework problems is scheduled, should the TAs have students present their solutions on the board? Should the TAs have new problems for the students to solve in small groups? How about a short simulation, a

case study, or role playing to actively engage students in the material? If a pre-exam review session is planned, would review questions be helpful? How should the students cover them? By writing practice answers individually, or by outlining them in small groups? In any case, the TAs should not be giving the answers themselves.

The options are more numerous than the techniques and formats covered in this book, and appropriate ones deserve discussion. This way, the weekly meetings can function as a teaching methods seminar for the TA staff.

The purpose that supplementary sections and help sessions should *not* serve is to introduce totally new material. As this book emphasizes throughout, few students can master material only through passive activities like reading and listening, even when supplemented with note-taking (see especially Chapters 12, 13, and 14). Students must also talk about it, write about it, apply it to problems, use it in experiments, act it out, see it demonstrated or demonstrate it themselves--in essence, *do* something with it. The TA's most important role is to design and facilitate opportunities for students to work *actively* with material already introduced.

In addition to covering teaching techniques and formats for the coming week, these TA meetings should review what did and didn't work last time. TAs need not repeat one another's mistakes, and they can help each other solve their problems. Occasionally, too, a classroom failure may call for some damage control, while a genuine success merits recognition, even imitation.

26

Agenda item #3: Students' learning. The final item of business, assessing students' learning, has two parts. The first part is openly discussing how well students are learning the material. This information may come from homework assignments, quizzes and tests, classroom participation, classroom assessment exercises, consultations with students, and general impressions. By identifying areas of student weakness, all parties know what to review before proceeding to new material.

If you're a TA, you probably have an inside track on how the students are doing. Generally students talk more often and more candidly with you than with faculty. So you have a clearer picture of their involvement and difficulties with the material. You are also probably better positioned to identify individual students who are having academic or emotional trouble. When such cases arise, advise your supervising faculty. But for the students' sake, tell them about the campus units that can help them (see Chapters 1 and 10).

The second part of assessing students' learning is planning the next stage of assessment and testing. Whether you are faculty or a TA, have other members of the course staff review a draft of any assignment, quiz, or test you've written. It is amazing what another set of eyes can pick up--not just typos but also double-barreled multiple choice items, ambiguous essay questions, awkward sentence structure, confusing word usage, and all the other verbal land mines that are so hard to avoid. Sometimes, too, instructors forget to model their test questions on the homework and in-class exercises to which they accustomed their stu-

dents. It is also easy to overlook important material covered just a few weeks ago. Assignments, quizzes, and exams are important enough to ask others to review.

If you are a supervising faculty member fortunate enough to have all experienced TAs for a particular course, you may be tempted to shorten or forego the weekly staff meetings. But resist the temptation! Your holding these meetings demonstrates your commitment to teaching excellence and staff morale.

One more faculty responsibility-- an essential facet of supervision--is to observe and give constructive feedback to each of your TAs who ever appear before a class. The fact that you care enough to do so reinforces your TAs' loyalty and morale, along with the value of teaching in general. It is best to follow up each observation with a one-on-one consultation focusing on strategies for professional growth and improvement. For obvious reasons, do not delegate this task to a head TA.

Extending Managing to Mentoring

Beyond supervising TAs, you will no doubt become a mentor to certain graduate students. The mentoring relationship is complex enough to deserve discussion.

The role of the mentor is a multi-faceted one that extends beyond the "role model" (Murray, 1991). For example, the mentor serves as a source of information about the profession and she tutors the protégé (or mentee) in specific professional skills. During times of personal turmoil, the mentee seeks advice and a sympathetic ear, casting the mentor in a confidant role. The mentor also helps the protégé plot a suitable career path.

However, the mentoring relationship is a two-way street. As such, the protégé must accept responsibility for and be willing to actively advance his own growth and development. Additionally, he must test his abilities against new challenges and honestly evaluate them in view of career options. Finally, he must be receptive to the mentor's instruction, coaching, and constructive criticism.

Faculty who lament the quality of graduate students entering their disciplines or departments can take heart in knowing that, in both industry and education, mentoring can improve the quality of recruits. For example, General Electric's Power Generation Division uses its mentoring program to impress on potential employees that they are carefully prepared for their jobs, not thrown into a sink-or-swim situation. Universities with alumni mentoring programs, such as Trinity College, have raised their students' academic achievement by arranging opportunities for them to explore career options with successful alumni (Kirby, 1989).

Studies of the public service professions and industry indicate that mentoring can also be an effective staff development tool. Police officers who participate in a formal mentoring program show greater productivity and discipline during their careers (Fagan, 1986).

The mentoring relationship reaps returns for the mentor as well. According to some mentors, it heightens their motivation. While some senior personnel face burnout, mentors are constantly reminded of what they first found interesting and exciting about their

profession. They become more inspired leaders, enhancing overall group and organizational productivity.

Here are some practical guidelines for both faculty and graduate students (Cameron, 1993):

- *Mentors*, reasonably pace your training and advising. Remember that you didn't learn everything at once or the first time through.
- *Protégés*, regard your relationship as a college teaching tutorial, and budget time for it. If you feel overwhelmed, let your mentor know.

- *Mentors*, be aware that your protégé is probably unfamiliar with various university and department regulations, office procedures, routine deadlines, and endless other professional protocols that are now second nature to you. Remember to convey this information explicitly.
- *Protégés*, take what your mentor tells you seriously, even if some of it sounds silly or strange.

- *Mentors*, give fair, encouraging, and caring feedback on your protégés' job performance on a regular basis. They may not know when they've done well and when they haven't, and they need to know, for both your and their sakes. Critical remarks can evoke a defensive, even fearful reaction. So couch them in terms of ways to improve and expectations for future success.
- *Protégés*, ask for regular feedback, and don't expect to hear you're doing a perfect job. There is always a lot to learn and plenty of room for improvement. If you find it hard to believe,

28

just trust for now that your mentor's constructive criticism has nothing to do with her not liking you as a person or not believing in you as a junior professional. In fact, it's a compliment; it means she considers you strong enough to hear the truth and to make improvements. If your mentor's counsel sounds inappropriate, ask for clarification, ponder it for while, and pass judgment later.

- *Mentors*, cultivate an environment where temporary lapses and setbacks, fears, and failures can be shared, forgiven, overcome, and filed away as learning experiences. Give your protégés as many chances as your course can afford. Whenever appropriate, counsel them on how to avoid or conquer the problem. For instance, advise an anxious protégé to visualize a worst-case classroom scenario, and together brainstorm ways to defuse the situation. (Your campus' teaching center can help.)
- *Protégés*, bring your performance fears out in the open. Your mentor can help you calm your adequacy anxieties, control your stage fright, and feel capable of handling your worst-case teaching nightmare. Remember, your mentor faced similar fears at one time. She hasn't forgotten and she wants to help you.
- *Mentors*, resist the natural temptation to mold your protégés into your clones. Each must find and explore his own potential.
- *Protégés*, "try on" and borrow elements of your mentor's teaching and testing style that fit you, but shop around. Great teaching takes many forms. Developing your own unique excellence is a creative, long-term process.

- *Mentors*, expect to feel occasionally that your time and wisdom are going unappreciated. Your protégés probably lack the experience to put your good counsel and training into perspective at the moment. Know that they will acquire that perspective and gratitude over time.
- *Protégés*, thank your mentor for her time, advice, instruction, and caring. Credit her when appropriate. Don't forget that while supervising a course is an assigned task, the more personal attention your mentor is giving you is purely voluntary and its own reward.

- *Mentors* and *Protégés*, review your relationship periodically. Bear in mind that, if it should endure, it is designed to self-destruct over the long run as the protégé evolves into a colleague. In the meantime, expect occasional tensions and imbalances. Mentors can find it hard both to accept and to relinquish their superior role; protégés can vacillate between dependency and the desire to break away. Talking about these stresses informally can resolve them.

These same principles apply to mentoring relationships between faculty and undergraduates and between senior faculty and junior colleagues. At any level, the positive effects of the relationship are mutually substantial and the material costs minimal. An active mentoring program then can greatly enhance a course, a department, and an entire institution.

COPYRIGHT GUIDELINES FOR THE CLASSROOM

Welcome to the through-the-looking-glass world of "fair use," "educational purposes," and other such Cheshire categories that make most of us instructors think twice before we press the start button on our copying machine or even consider showing a videotape in class. This is the unwieldy wonderland in which the only legally correct answer to your simplest query may be "probably," "unlikely," and "it depends upon the specific case." For example, Q: Is a classroom a public place? (This issue may affect the legality of showing a videotape in class.) A: Experts disagree and the courts have not yet settled the issue.

In the absence of simple, clear rules of thumb, it is little wonder that we tend to pick up copyright law by word of mouth--and wind up swapping myths and misconceptions. The legal ambiguities only feed our fears of what might happen to us if we were actually caught by the copyright enforcers (whoever they may be) violating their law, even unknowingly.

The laws, guidelines, and enforcement policies are not well publicized in the academic world and may surprise you. Many of them are highly technical, make questionable sense, and are frankly difficult to absorb and remember. Much of the information here comes from a rare session on copyright law (Jordan, 1996) conducted at a faculty and instructional development conference.

Copying Print Media

Let us begin with what we as instructors are allowed to copy without having to request permission or obtain a license from the copyright holder. Like many of the "fair use" provisions for educators, the guidelines below are only guidelines, and they apply only to printed works. They were agreed upon and written by educators, authors, and publishers and are not actually "law," although they are part of the legislative history of the Copyright Act. They do not cover all situations, nor do they claim to. In fact, they are prefaced by the statement: "There may be instances in which copying which does not fall within the guidelines stated below may nonetheless be permitted under the criteria of fair use."

Single Copying. As an instructor, you may make single copies, including a transparency, of the following for teaching purposes: a chapter of a book; an article from a periodical or newspaper; a short story, essay, or poem; a chart, graph, diagram, drawing, cartoon, or picture from a book, periodical, or newspaper.

Multiple Copying. You may make multiple copies -- that is, one copy per student in a course -- if the work meets the criteria of brevity, spontaneity, and cumulative effect and if each copy contains a copyright notice.

The guidelines define the "brevity" criterion in this way: 1) an entire poem printed on no more than two pages or an excerpt from a longer poem, not to exceed 250 words copied in either case; 2) an entire article, story, or essay of less than 2,500 words or an excerpt of fewer than 1,000 words or less than 10% of the work, whichever is less, but in either event a minimum of 500 words to be copied; 3) one chart, graph, diagram, drawing, cartoon, or picture per book or periodical issue. Multiple copying meets the "spontaneity" criterion when you do not have a reasonable length of time to request and receive permission to copy. (What "a reasonable length of time" may be is not specified.)

The "cumulative effect" is considered acceptably small when your copying is only for one course, and you do not make multiple copies in more than nine instances per course during one term (semester, trimester, or quarter). Furthermore, you may not make multiple copies of more than one short poem, article, story, essay, or two excerpts from the same author, or more than three from the same collective work or periodical volume during one term.

Copying Short Works. Short works such as children's books are often less than 2,500 words, and you may not copy these works as a whole. All that you may reproduce is an excerpt of not more than two published pages containing not more than 10% of the total words in the text.

Prohibitions to Single or Multiple Copying. Notwithstanding the guidelines above, your in-tentions and the specific work also come into play. You may not make copies under these conditions: to create, replace, or substitute for anthologies, compilations, or collective works; to substitute for replacement or purchase; of "consumable" works such as workbooks, exercises, standardized tests, or answer sheets; of the same item term after term; if you charge students beyond the copying cost; or on direction of a higher authority.

Videotaping Broadcast Programming

These guidelines specify what educational institutions can videotape off-the-air for educational purposes without obtaining a permission or license from the copyright holder. Again, they are not part of the law but the authoritative products of a Congressional committee. They were written for and directed to campus media units, which typically videotape a program at an instructor's request.

1) These guidelines apply only to off-the-air recording by non-profit educational institutions.
2) Videotapes may be kept for only 45 calendar days after the recording date. After this time the tapes must be erased.
3) The videotape may be shown to students only during the first ten class days after the recording date and may be repeated only once for reinforcement. (Points 2 and 3 are called the "45-10 rule.")
4) Off-air recordings may be made only at the request of an individual instructor and not in anticipation of an instructor's request. The same instructor can request the program be

recorded only once.

5) Duplicate copies may be made if several instructors request the recording of the same program.
6) After the first ten class days allowed for showing, the recording may only be used only for evaluation purposes (e.g., an exam).
7) Off-the-air recordings may not be edited or combined with other recordings to create a new work or an anthology.
8) All videotapes, including copies, must contain a copyright notice when broadcast.
9) Educational institutions are responsible for ensuring compliance with these guidelines.

No guidelines or laws have been written for instructors who wish to videotape a program off-the-air at home, then show it in class. But legal experts recommend that they demonstrate compliance with the spirit of the law by following the same guidelines.

Public Broadcast Programs. The Public Broadcasting Service, the Public Television Library, the Great Plains National Instructional Television Library, and the Agency for Instructional Television have somewhat less restrictive rules for off-the-air videotaping for educational purposes:

1) Recordings may be made by instructors or students in accredited, nonprofit educational institutions.
2) Recordings may be used only for instruction in a classroom, lab, or auditorium but are not restricted to one classroom or one instructor.
3) The use of recordings is, however, restricted to one institution and may not be shared out-

side of it.

4) Recordings may be used as often as needed for seven days. Then they must be erased.

Commercially Rented Videotapes. If a videotape carries the warning "For Home Use Only," the law is unclear on whether you may show it in your classroom. If the classroom is considered a "public place," you may not, but the courts have not resolved this issue. Legal experts reason that you probably can because instructors are clearly permitted to display or perform works in face-to-face teaching situations. However, the videotape must serve a purely instructional objective. Even the hint of entertainment purposes, such as the presence of non-students in the classroom, can raise a legal flag. (Of course, you may show any rented videotape that has been cleared for public presentation in the classroom.)

Movie studios have built the home video industry into a $14 billion business, in part by enforcing the distinction between instruction and entertainment very strictly. To illustrate, in early 1996 the Motion Picture Licensing Corporation (MPLC), a Los Angeles copyright policing agency representing the Hollywood studios, sent threat letters to 50,000 day care centers across the nation. The letters demanded up to $325 per year for what they termed "a public-performance video license" for showing children's videos (e.g., Pooh and Scrooge) to their "public" of toddlers. Apparently Hollywood does not regard its standard products as educational and therefore exempt from licensing fees under the fair use provisions (Bourland, 1996).

Showing Multimedia Productions

As this book goes to press, the copyright guidelines and law governing multimedia productions are being negotiated by a committee composed of representatives of the academic community (e.g., leaders of national professional associations) and copyright lawyers representing the electronic publishers. Among the issues under discussion: To what extent will online service providers, including universities, be held liable for the copyright violations of their customers? While instructors will be allowed to show multimedia programs in their classrooms with students present, to what extent will cost-free student access be granted afterwards (e.g., in self-paced computer instruction and electronically based distance learning)? What charges, if any, will simple access to instructionally rich Web sites incur, and what will downloading cost?

At this point the degree to which fair use will extend into cyberspace is not at all clear. Instructors with a special interest should stay tuned to the news media, especially *The Chronicle of Higher Education,* to keep abreast of the latest legal developments. In the meantime, the same fair use provisions that govern printed material protect educational uses of Internet resources.

Permissions to Reprint and Licenses

When you wish to reproduce or show a work or portion of a work in a manner that violates the above guidelines, you may do so legally in one of two ways:

1) You can request in writing (e-mail okay) the permission of the copyright holder to reprint, in which case you must identify the exact portion of the work, the number of copies you wish to make and distribute, and the purpose or planned use of the copies (e.g., instruction in a given course for specific term at a given institution). You may or may not be charged a fee, depending mostly on the number of copies you wish to make. A permission granted for classroom use applies only to one course during one term.

2) You can request a license of the copyright holder in the same way, giving the same precise information. Licenses are usually required to show a work or portion of a work, or to include some nontrivial portion of it in your own work, including your own multimedia production. Licenses always entail fees and may be negotiable.

Whether a given case requires a simple permission or a license depends on three sometimes grey criteria. In general, a permission will do if: 1) your use qualifies as fair use; 2) the material you wish to use is factual or an idea; or 3) the work you wish to use is in the public domain.

In general, fair use means use for noncommercial purposes and specifically for purposes of teaching, scholarship, research, criticism, comment, and news reporting. The courts are most likely to find fair use where the copied work is a factual as opposed to a creative work, as well as where the new work does not pose market or readership competition for the copyrighted work. The amount and the significance of the protected work used also figures into the determination. Use of a tiny amount of the work should not raise concerns, but it will if the tiny amount is substantial in terms of importance-- for instance, the heart of the copied work.

To illustrate this last criterion, a magazine article that used 300 words from a 200,000-word autobiography written by President Gerald Ford was found to infringe the copyright on the autobiography. Even though the copied material comprised only a small part of the autobiography, the copied portions were among the most powerful passages in the autobiography.

No legal guidelines are given to distinguish factual material or an idea from something else. Determinations are made on a case-by-case basis.

Public domain is a clearer legal concept but may be redefined with a longer time line. As this book goes to press, a work goes into the public domain 50 years after the author's death, but only if the author never relinquished the rights. Often corporations and universities own the rights, and their rights extend even longer to 95 years from the date of first publication or 100 years from the date of creation, whichever comes first. However, by the time you read this, federal legislation may have extended both author-owned and organization-owned copyright terms for yet another 20 years.

Common Copyright Misconceptions

Before we close the topic of copyright laws and guidelines, let us dispel some popular misconceptions. First, giving credit to the author(s) of a work is not a way around or substitute for copyright law compliance. All a citation exempts you from is plagiarism. Sec-

ond, the absence of a copyright notice does *not* mean the work is not protected. While most works have a notice, those published on or after March 1, 1989 are protected even without one. Third, changing someone else's copyrighted work here and there will *not* make it legally yours. In fact, such action may make you *doubly* liable -- for infringement of copying right *and* of the copyright holder's modification right.

Finally, flattering or showcasing a work is *not* likely to allay the copyright owner's objections to your free use of the work. This is especially true of multimedia works; their producers view licenses as a new source of income. Freelance writers, music publishers, and musical performers have successfully sued major companies like *The New York Times* and CompuServe for the unauthorized publication and/or distribution of their work on online computer services.

How Copyright Violations Are Actually Handled

So what if you forget to insert an important article in your course pack, and you're tempted to make copies and hand them out to your students in class? What penalties might you face?

The law states that you face fines of $250 per copyright violation, and that means *per copy*. For a class of 100, that multiplies out to $25,000, a daunting price to pay for your students' intellectual enrichment.

However, the law doesn't usually operate by the law. In the educational arena, individuals have never been sued. Only educational institutions have been, and very few of those over the past 20 years.

34   Obviously, colleges, universities, school systems, and private schools have much deeper pockets than their professional employees. But there are other reasons why the educational world is treated so gently.

The fair use copyright provision, which took effect in 1978, contains an ignorance clause designed especially for instructors. Therefore, all an accused instructor must do in his or her defense is to prove ignorance of the law. Given the ambiguities of the law, ignorance, or at least misunderstanding, might not be difficult to show.

Copyright enforcers prefer to aim for the top and send threatening letters to school superintendents and college and university presidents and chancellors. Most are just routine reiterations of the law and the potential penalties. However, sometimes a threat is based on a tip that violations have occurred. (Some enforcement agencies maintain tip hotlines.) But even in this case, the designated agent-for-service receives not a summons but a cease-and-desist order. Educational institutions have generally induced its violators to cease and desist immediately and have avoided further legal action.

Historically, the most aggressive copyright enforcer has been the Software Publishers Association, which patrols software pirating (installation or reproduction without site licenses), and *even it* confines its efforts to organizations and stays out of people's at-home offices.

Corporations, which can rarely claim fair use protection, have never enjoyed such privileged treatment. But then they have the most to gain financially by copyright violations. The copyright cops have ensured that they also have the most to lose.

For More Information

This chapter scratches only the surface; copyright law and guidelines, even those just on fair use, comprise an entire legal specialty. More information is available by writing the U.S. Copyright Office, Library of Congress, Washington, D.C. 20559 or by calling one of its three lines: for public information, (202) 707-2100 (answering machine only) or (202) 479-0700 (person answers, but line is often busy); for ordering circulars and forms, (202) 707-9100 (answer machine takes order). Some circulars are free, such as Circular #2:"Publications on Copyright," which is a excellent place to start, while others entail a charge.

Another source of information is Copyright Information Services, an imprint of the Association for Educational Communications and Technology (AECT), also in Washington, D.C. This publisher specializes in books for educational institutions on fair use provisions.

Part II.

Good

Beginnings

YOUR FIRST DAY OF CLASS

Whether you are teaching for the first time or are a seasoned classroom veteran, the first day of class can evoke anxiety as well as excitement. Like no other day, it affects the tenor of the entire term. It may also represent innovations and experiments in course content, organization, and design, teaching formats and techniques, and assessment methods. Not to mention all those new student faces. This chapter suggests ways to reduce the anxiety, heighten the excitement, and start off the course on a positive, professional, and participatory note. It should be particularly useful to newer instructors.

First Impressions

What you do and do not do the first day of class will affect your students' and maybe even your own expectations and behavior for the rest of the term. So think in advance what expectations and behaviors you want to establish in your classroom for the next ten to 15 weeks. Plan to set these expectations and organize class activities that model the level of student involvement you have in mind for the rest of the course. For example, if you hope for considerable discussion, engage your students in discussion, perhaps about their expectations of the course or their current conceptions of the subject mat-

ter. If you intend to have a number of in-class writing exercises, start with a short one that first class. If you plan on using cooperative learning, have a small-group activity the first day.

No doubt you want to establish a serious, professional classroom atmosphere, and you communicate this tenor in several ways. First, have a comprehensive, well structured syllabus ready to distribute (see Chapter 4). It tells your class that you are careful, well organized, conscientious, and serious about teaching. Mark on your copy the points you want to elaborate, clarify, and emphasize. Make extra copies for last-minute enrollees, and bring some with you during the first two weeks of class.

Second, say a few words to market the course and the material. Enthusiasm is contagious. Your showing some of yours for the subject matter and the opportunity to teach it will motivate your students' interest in learning it and inspire their respect for you as a scholar.

Third, dress a little more formally than you normally would, at least if you're inclined to more casual attire. A touch of formality conveys professionalism and seriousness. It also gives instructors who are female, youthful-looking, and/or physically small an aura of authority and a psychological edge

38

that help separate them from their students. Of course, with time and experience, these benefits fade.

Since you expect students to be prompt, you might set a good example from the start. Arrive in the classroom early and set a welcoming tone by chatting with students informally as they arrive. Make students feel comfortable with you as a person as well as an instructor, but don't confuse your roles; remember the difference between being friendly and being friends.

Finally, make productive use of the entire class period. The rest of this chapter suggests several social and content-oriented activities that you can organize, even if the students have no background in the subject matter. The most important point is not to "waste" the first class--not to treat it as a throw-away day or to dismiss it early. Only if you treat class time like a precious commodity will your students do likewise.

If you are new to teaching, prepare to combat any sudden case of stage fright by practicing your first-day presentation in advance. As you begin class, take a long, slow, deep breath--extra oxygen works wonders for shaky nerves--and try to focus on some spot on the wall or an inanimate object to balance yourself. Or try looking just over the heads of your students for the first few minutes. Or try visualizing the situation as conducting a one-to-one tutorial instead of talking to a class. Always feel free to take a moment to collect your thoughts. Remember that many students are impressed by anyone with the courage to speak in public and

are forgiving of the occasional lapse of continuity.

Exchanging Information

Information flow should be a two-way street, even (perhaps especially) on the first day. But you as the instructor initiate the exchange, first by writing the following information on the board or an overhead before class convenes: the name and number of your course, the section number (if appropriate), the meeting days and times, your name, your office location, and your office hours. This information assures students that they are in the right place.

The next several activities need not come in the order presented, but they are strongly recommended for setting an open and participatory as well as professional tone for the rest of the term.

Student information index cards. Get to know your students, and let them know you are interested in them personally, by passing out blank index cards and asking them to write down this information for you: their full name, any preferred nickname, their year in school, their major, and their previous coursework in the field. Additional information such as hometown, outside interests, and career aspirations may help you relate class material to your students on a more personal level. Consider also asking them to write out what they expect from this course, why they are taking it (aside from breadth requirements), and/or what topics they would like to see addressed. You may be able to orient the material towards some of their interests and to advise those with totally erroneous expectations to take a more suitable course.

Your background. Since you're asking students about themselves, it's only fair to tell them something about yourself. (They *are* interested.) You needn't divulge your life history, but giving them a brief summary of at least your educational and professional background helps reinforce your credibility as an instructor and your "humanness" as a person. A bit of openness also enhances your students' sense of personal loyalty to you.

Include some information about your own research and interests, what attracted you to the field, why you love teaching it, and the implications and applications of the subject in the world. See this as an opportunity to make the material more relevant to your students.

Course information. Of course, you distribute your syllabus and perhaps other course information, but don't expect students to read these materials carefully. Review each page orally, line by line, elaborating, clarifying, and emphasizing the points you marked. When you mention your office hours, urge students to seek your help outside of class, and promise them a warm reception (see Chapter 10).

As you review the course schedule and requirements, point out and explain the teaching techniques you plan to use. Say why you've chosen them and what benefits they have over other reasonable options, especially if your methods are innovative and/or student-active. Your explanation will not only reassure students of your commitment to teaching effectiveness but also help overcome any resistance they may have to unusual formats.

Also explicitly state your expectations of them and their responsibilities for preparing for class and participating. For example, if your course calls for considerable discussion, emphasize the importance of their preparation, your rules for calling on students, your procedure of asking students to summarize at the end, etc. Also, offer them some advice on how to take notes on discussion; this remains a mystery even to the most verbal students (see Chapter 15). If you plan to lecture at all, give students some pointers on your lecture organization and good note-taking strategies (see Chapter 11). You might also share some helpful reading/study skills and/or problem-solving strategies appropriate to your particular subject matter (see Chapters 12 and 24).

You cannot possibly anticipate all the questions that students will have, especially about your testing and grading procedures. But here are some likely ones that you should be prepared to field: How will you make up the tests? What types of questions will they have? What kinds of thinking will you be testing? How should students best prepare for them? Will you distribute review questions? Will you hold review sessions? On what dimensions will you evaluate papers and other written assignments? How many A's, B's, C's, etc. do you usually give? How possible is it for all students to get a good grade?

Learning students' names. Most students expect their instructors to learn their names, unless the class is very large (near or over 100). This is especially the case at smaller and private colleges and universities. To borrow an old cliche, learning your students' names shows you care. So begin learning and using them to call on students early. If you have trouble remembering names, the strategies below may help you.

You can seat students in specific places and make a seating chart. Students may not prefer a seating chart, but they will tolerate it graciously if you say the reason is to learn their names. Seating them alphabetically before launching into small-group work is also a way to ensure randomly mixed groups.

Some instructors learn names by jotting down notes about each students' physical appearance on the class roster--information such as body shape and size, hair color and length, age, dress style, and any distinguishing physical characteristic. However, it is best to keep such notes concealed from your students' view.

Taking roll in every class helps you learn the names and is especially useful if you grade on attendance. You can also use the roll, while learning names, to call on students more or less randomly, as long as you inform your class in advance what you'll be doing. Or you may use the index cards to call on students.

Still another strategy is to have students wear name tags or to have name cards on their desks. To get around the hassle of bringing in new name tags/cards and markers to every class, make up "permanent," convention-style tags or name cards, distribute them at the start of each class, and take them up at the end of each session for the next class meeting. This is also a subtle way to take attendance.

If you really want to make an impression on a large class, take a quick-developing photograph of each student (or have your TAs do so) with his or her name printed right below the face. Then use the photos to call on students. (While this effort may sound extreme, at least three professors at Vanderbilt University do this routinely in their large classes and successfully master the names of over 100 students within several weeks.)

Social Icebreakers: "Getting to Know You"

If your class size allows it, try to incorporate one or two ice-breaker activities on the first day. There are two general types: the social or "getting-to-know-you" variety, which gets students acquainted, and subject matter icebreakers, which motivates students to start thinking about the material. Feel free to move beyond the popular examples given here and devise your own.

If you plan on discussion or group work, social ice-breakers smooth the way for broad participation and cooperative group interaction. Freshmen, in particular, appreciate the opportunity to meet their fellow students, including more senior ones, who can serve as role models.

Simple self introductions. Perhaps the simplest version is to have students take turns introducing themselves to the class by giving their name, major, and perhaps a reason for taking the class (once again, aside from fulfilling breadth requirements).

This activity may work best in a smaller class, however, as the prospect of speaking in front of a group of strangers can mildly terrify some students. On the other hand, if you will have your students make speeches or oral presentations in front the class later on, this first-day exercise can help them get used to the assignments to come.

Three-step interviews. Alternatively, students can share the same type of information with a neighbor. Then, without knowing beforehand the second part of the task, each partner can introduce his or her counterpart to another pair or to the class. This exercise has the added benefit of teaching careful listening skills (Kagan, 1988).

Class survey. In taking this informal survey of the class, you moderate a brief questioning period. Begin by asking your students to raise their hands in response to some general questions: How many students are from [various regions of the country]? East/west of the Mississippi? Freshmen, sophomores, etc.? How many work full-time? How many are married? How many have children? How many like golf? Tennis? How many have traveled abroad? To Europe? To Asia? Then you may venture into opinion questions, perhaps some relevant to the course material.

Students soon begin to form a broad picture of their class and to see what they have in common with each other. They will find it far easier to interact with classmates who share their interests and backgrounds.

"The Circles of _____." In this more structured activity, you give each student a sheet of paper with a large central circle and other smaller circles radiating from it. Students write their names in the central circle and the names of groups with which they identify (e.g., gender, age group, religious, ethnic, racial, social, political, ideological, athletic) in the satellite circles. Then ask students to move around the room to find three classmates who are most and/or least similar to themselves. This exercise makes students appreciate the diversity in the class, as well as meet their fellow students. It also gives you homogeneous or heterogeneous groups of four if you need them for the next class activity.

Subject-Matter Icebreakers

Chapter 26, "Assessing Students' Learning in Progress," describes several classroom assessment techniques that are designed to be administered on the first day of class or the day you introduce a new topic. ***Background Knowledge Probe***, ***Focused Listing***, and ***Self Confidence Surveys*** are particularly useful and appropriate for the first class. The products are not to be graded. They are meant to inform you about your students' level of cognitive and psychological preparation for your course and to orient them to the subject matter.

Problem-posting. To whet students' appetites for the material, one particularly useful first-day activity is problem-posting (McKeachie et al., 1994). First, ask students to think about and jot down either: 1) problems they expect to encounter with the course or 2) issues they think the course should address. Then assume the role of facilitator, recording student responses on the board or an overhead transparency. Check your un-

42 derstanding by restating the comments and requesting approval. Avoid appearing judgmental or dominating; such a display on the first day could be counterproductive to the later success of the course.

As the frequency of student suggestions begins to decline, suggest stopping. Make sure, however, that all students have had a chance to contribute, even if you have to coax the quiet ones. If some wish to speculate on how to address any of the points listed, keep a close rein on the discussion, not letting it stray too far afield. Tell students which of their questions will be addressed; this gives them something to look forward to. But also be honest about the ones your course will not cover.

Problem-posting is useful not only at the beginning of the course, but also later on when broaching a particularly difficult topic. The exercise accomplishes several purposes. First, it opens lines of communication between you and your students as well as among students. Second, it lends validity to their concerns and assures them they're not alone. Third, it reaffirms that you are approachable and as capable of listening as you are of talking. Finally, it encourages students to devise solutions to problems themselves, reducing their reliance on you for the definitive answers.

Common sense inventory. Another way to break students into the subject matter, as well as to help them grasp its relevance, is to have them respond to a brief inventory or pre-test (Nilson, 1981). Assemble five to 15 "common sense" statements directly related to the course material, some (or all) of which run counter to popular belief

or prejudice. (For example: "Suicide is more likely among women than men." "Over half of all marriages occur between persons who live within 20 blocks of each other.") Then have students individually mark each statement as true or false and share their answers in pairs or small groups.

Let students debate their differences among themselves, or thicken the plot by assigning each pair or group one or more statements, instructing members to reach consensus, and having a presenter from each group defend its position. After the presentations, you can give the "correct" answers-- which may spark even more debate--or take the cliff-hanger approach and let the class wait for them to unfold during the term.

Drawing Class to a Close

At the end of the class, you may want to ask students to write down their anonymous reactions (McKeachie et al., 1994). Pose general questions such as: What is the most important thing you learned during this first day? How did your expectations of this course change? What questions or concerns do you still have about the course or the subject matter? You can address remaining concerns as a warm-up activity to start the next class.

Finally--and it's worth repeating--do not dismiss the first class early. If you conduct some of the activities in this chapter, the time will be more than adequately filled and productively spent. Not only will your students enjoy an introduction to the course and its subject matter; they will also have a chance to get acquainted with you and their classmates.

Classroom Management

Classroom management is an acquired skill that is rarely discussed and often comes painfully through experience. This chapter will hopefully serve to make up for at least some experience. At the university level, classroom management pertains less to preventing and sanctioning disciplinary problems and more to maintaining a controlled, orderly environment that is conducive to learning.

Even minor disruptions can mar the atmosphere, break your concentration, and really get under your skin. Yet, no matter what, you are not allowed to lose your temper. This is why knowing some strategies for preventing and handling such situations can be very helpful.

Common Disruptive Behaviors

Ballantine and Risacher (1993) identified six common disruptive classroom behaviors from a Wright State University survey that asked students what behaviors *they* found annoying:
1) talking in class
2) packing up and/or rustling papers
3) arriving late and/or leaving early
4) cheating
5) wasting class time (e.g., being unprepared, asking repeated questions, asking for details on the last class meeting, etc.)
6) showing general disrespect and poor manners toward the instructor and other students.

You may want to add attending class irregularly, asking for extensions on assignments, and missing assignment deadlines.

The next few sections address strategies for minimizing disruptive behavior in general, followed by a section on specific tactics for preventing or responding to each of the behaviors listed.

Balancing Authority and Approachability

Usually students accept your authority without question, whether you are a faculty member or a TA. But a few students may be reluctant to accord the same respect to an instructor who violates the traditional "professorial stereotype" of the mature, white male with an imposing stance and a low, deep voice. Clearly, if you look young, are physically small, have a relatively high voice, are non-white, and/or are female, you *may* encounter some unspoken student resistance. A few of these simple strategies may help you look more authoritative (Nilson, 1981):
1) Stand up in front of your class instead of sitting, move around the room, and use broad gestures. The dramatic effect is to make you appear "larger than life." Interestingly, increasing one's apparent size is a common aggressive/defensive posture throughout the animal kingdom.
2) Try to deepen your voice slightly and to project it further by

44

speaking from your diaphragm.
Also try to avoid ending a
declarative sentence with a
questioning rise in pitch.

3) Favor more formal dress to convey that you are serious and
business-minded.

4) Add an air of formality and dig-
nity to your classroom. For instance, address students by
their last names, and ask that
they address you the same way.

5) Refer in class to your own research, where appropriate. This
establishes you as an authority
on the subject and elevates you
in your students' eyes.

Other instructors face the opposite problem of intimidating students. They can do so either by too
perfectly matching the somewhat
chilly professorial stereotype or by
violating it in the other, more imposing direction. From your students' viewpoint, you may fall in
this category if you are male and
are some combination of very tall,
physically large, deep-voiced,
rugged-looking, serious and reserved, or have an aggressive or
curt social style. A few behaviors
can make you seem more approachable (Nilson, 1981):

1) Assume a relaxed posture in the
classroom. Sit down or perch
casually on the corner of a desk.

2) Speak more softly in class, as
long as everyone can still hear
you. Also toss out more questions for students to address.

3) Dress down slightly (e.g., a loos-
ened tie and a sports jacket or a
two-piece suit vs. a three-piece
suit).

4) Chat casually with students before and after class so they can
see you as friendly and person-
able. Address students by their
first names. (If you are a TA,

consider asking them to call you
by your first name.)

5) Smile whenever appropriate.

6) If you are a TA, mention that
you, too, are a student and that
you can identify with the academic demands they are facing.

Setting Ground Rules

All the literature on classroom
management considers setting
ground rules essential (Nilson,
1981; Brooks, 1987; Ballantine and
Risacher, 1993). So announce on
the first day, especially in a large
class, exactly what disruptive behaviors you cannot tolerate in this
course--and why. Perhaps your
most convincing as well as
research-based reason is that such
behaviors annoy the other students
in the class. (Reiterate this reason
when handling a disruption.) Some
rules also belong in your syllabus,
especially your expectations and
any grading issues regarding attendance, tardiness, class participation, extension requests, missed assignment deadlines, and make-up
exams.

You may prefer to emphasize
appropriate behaviors rather than
disruptive ones. If so, express your
rules in a positive way--for example, "Students are expected to hand
in assignments on time" rather
than "Students will be penalized for
late assignments."

In Wright State University
courses where classroom management was a serious problem, a few
faculty members solved it by trying
a "contract" approach. On the first
day of class, they led a discussion
on the student behaviors that genuinely bothered the members of the
class. From the notes they took,
the instructors wrote up a contract
for students to sign at the next

class meeting, promising not to engage in the disruptive behaviors listed. After that, students pretty much policed themselves, keeping even minor violations to a minimum (Ballantine and Risacher, 1993).

Modeling Correct Behavior

Your efforts to model good manners do not guarantee that students will *always* imitate you. But they will consider your standards and requirements more fair if *your* behavior reflects them, and no doubt more students will honor them.

For instance, if you don't want students to interrupt one another during discussions, judiciously try not to interrupt students yourself. If you value punctuality, arrive in class ahead of the bell and complete your board work before class begins. If you want assignments turned in on time, return papers promptly. If you expect students to come to office hours, keep to your schedule faithfully.

Commanding Class Attention

Sometimes students become restless and potentially disruptive simply because their attention is wandering or they're bored. Your practicing good platform skills enables you to command their attention and interest for longer periods of time.

These skills come up briefly again in Chapter 14 because they strongly influence the motivational and teaching effectiveness of a lecture. They also affect how easily you can keep students awake, quiet, orderly, and on task for all or part of a class period. Aristotle had good reason then for evaluating

rhetorical oratory on not only invention (content) and arrangement (organization) but also style (sentence structure and word usage), delivery (vocal and physical performance), and memory (freedom from notes).

Excellence in public speaking involves many different behaviors. As Chapter 14 addresses invention and arrangement, and since you are probably gifted with respect to style, let us proceed directly to delivery. It, too, is comprised of many different behaviors, most of them "small," so to speak. But they add up to a tremendous difference in the way the speaker and the message are received and regarded.

Below is a simple listing of major platform skills (adapted from Toastmasters International speech manuals and other materials):

Effective use of voice: volume adjusted to be audible for the room and audience; words enunciated clearly; rich, resonant quality, projected from chest and diaphragm; vocal variety (changes in intonation to complement content and for emphasis); volume variety (either extreme for emphasis); varied and appropriate speaking pace (never hurried and dramatically slower for most important content); "pregnant" pauses (for emphasis before and after major points); imagery plays on words (e.g., drawing out "slow" and "long," saying "icy" in an icy tone, saying "soft" softly, saying "strong" with especially deep resonance).

Effective use of body: solid, natural stance (unless moving, legs comfortably apart, knees slightly bent, arms hanging at sides, shoulders relaxed, and back straight); natural movement around lectern/stage and out towards audience (for emphasis and to complement content); abundant gestures to complement content (especially broad ones before large audiences); word dramatization (e.g., momentarily acting out "timid," "angry," "anxious," "huge," etc.); varied facial expressions (more dramatic in a large room), including smiles where appropriate; only occasional glances, if any, at notes; steady eye contact with the audience (at least three seconds per audience sector or quadrant recommended).

Effective use of visual aids and props: In addition to rehearsing their use to avoid awkwardness, see Chapter 21 for pointers.

Emotions to project: relaxed confidence, conviction; enthusiasm, excitement, passion, dramatic interest; sincerity, concern, honesty, openness, warmth; a sense of humor, curiosity, suspense, surprise.

Minimization/elimination of distracting behaviors: um, uh, you know, sort of, kind of, and-and, that-that, etc.; mispronunciations; false sentence starts; mid-sentence switches to start of a new sentence; volume fade-outs at end of sentences; pacing, swaying, or other repetitive movements; leaning on lectern, against wall, against chalkboard, etc.; lengthy checks of notes; ritual apologies to audience (e.g., "I had hoped to have prepared this lecture more carefully").

Of course, all these skills assembled together seem impossibly numerous and precise to master. But you probably have inadvertently learned most of them already and may only need to polish a few. If your institution has a teaching center, it probably will videotape you

teaching a class and offer you the chance to view your tape with a trained specialist. This service can help you assess your current platform skills and identify ways to enhance your public speaking effectiveness.

For now, the most important skill you should check is your eye contact with your students. In large classes, it is easy to forget the far half of the class, but that is exactly the half you usually need to control the most. Your eye contact is a powerful control tool. Eye contact also personalizes your comments, encourages students to return your attentiveness to them in kind, and enables you to "read their faces" to gauge their interest and understanding.

Another skill to monitor is your vocal variety. Accurately or inaccurately, it reflects your level of engagement in the material and enjoyment of teaching. If you find yourself droning in a monotone through a dry section of your lecture, try consciously to modulate your voice to keep student interest.

If you ever see a sizable number of bored expressions and glazed eyes while you are lecturing, pause and change pace. Pose a question, open the floor for questions, or use any of the student-active breaks suggested in Chapter 14.

Handling Specific Disruptive Behaviors

If you encounter a discipline problem in your classroom, the first thing to do is to *stay calm*. Count to ten, breathe deeply, visualize a peaceful scene--anything to keep you from losing your temper. No matter how much an offensive student tries to bait you, you lose credibility if you lower yourself to his level. If you keep your composure, you win the sympathy and support of other students. They may even start using social pressure to discipline the offenders themselves.

Keeping your composure, however, does not mean just accepting and tolerating the abuse. There are some specific, appropriate measures you can take in response to disruptive behaviors (Nilson, 1981; Ballantine and Risacher, 1993).

Talking in class. Occasional comments or questions from one student to another are to be expected. However, chronic talkers bother other students and interfere with your train of thought. To stop them, try a long, dramatic pause. Then, if necessary, accompany your pause with an equally dramatic stare at the offenders. If still necessary, say something general like "I really think you should pay attention to this; it will be on the test" or "You are disturbing your classmates." If the problem persists, get stern with the offenders outside of class. Direct intervention and public embarrassment are strictly last resorts.

Packing up early. Routinely reserve some important points or classroom activities (e.g., quizzes, writing exercises, clarification of the upcoming readings, study guide distribution) until the end of class. Or have students turn in assignments at the end of class. Paper-rustling and other disruptive noise-making during class can be stopped the same way as is talking in class.

Arriving late and/or leaving early. State your policies clearly on these offenses in your syllabus and on the first day of class. You can insist that students inform you, preferably in advance, of any special circumstances that will require them to be late to class. You can even subtract course points for coming late and leaving early, as long as you set this policy at the start. You might draw attention to offenders by pausing as they walk in and out. Alternatively, you can set aside an area near the door for latecomers and early leavers. Finally, as you can do to discourage packing up early, you can routinely conduct important class activities for the beginning and the end of class.

Cheating. Academic dishonesty is such a serious and widespread problem in higher education today that the entire next chapter is devoted to preventing it.

Wasting time. If students habitually try to monopolize class time, encourage them to speak with you after class to clarify their questions. You can broaden the discussion and call attention away from the disruptive student by asking the rest of the class for the answers.

Another strategy is to put out a question box. You can read the questions after class and briefly address some of them at the next meeting. You can also encourage students to e-mail their questions to you or to put them on the course listserv or newsgroup. While less personal, these options offer a less confrontational format.

Asking Problematic Questions. These include a wide variety of questions: those that you've already answered, those that try to wheedle answers out of you that you want the students to arrive at on their own, those that ramble on

48

and on, those that you regard as argumentative, loaded, or hostile, and those you don't have the information to answer. Constructive ways to respond to such questions, whether or not they are ill intended, are covered in Chapter 16.

Showing disrespect. Once again, make your expectations for appropriate classroom manners clear from the start, and reinforce them continually by your exemplary behavior. Enlist the aid of other students to monitor and report disruptive incidents. Talk to offenders privately and explain that their behavior is affecting their fellow students' ability to learn.

Sometimes students show disrespect to get the attention they believe they cannot get through any other means, to vent their anger towards authority in general, or to express some other deep-seated emotional problem. Leave such cases to the professionals and refer such students to your institution's psychological or counseling center.

Attending class irregularly. In general, attendance drops off as class size increases. It is also lower in more lecture-oriented classes. So one obvious way to increase attendance is to build in more opportunities for student participation. Taking some of the following measures in combination should also help: basing part of the course grade on attendance; taking attendance regularly (even if you don't calculate it in the grade); basing part of the course grade on participation in discussion (see Chapter 15); giving frequent, graded quizzes; covering different material in class from that in the readings; not allowing commercial production of

your lecture notes; conducting cooperative learning group activities in class and grading students in part on peer performance evaluations (see Chapter 18); and conducting other frequent, graded in-class activities (see, for example, Chapters 17, 19, and 20).

Asking for extensions and missing assignment deadlines. In your syllabus, specify penalties for late work, with or without an "approved" extension (e.g., docking a portion of the grade). Some instructors feel comfortable strictly enforcing this policy. But if you prefer to be flexible, you probably realize that students occasionally have good reasons for not meeting deadlines. But they also occasionally lie. You must assess each extension request and excuse on a case-by-case, student-by-student basis, perhaps allowing a single, documented incident but drawing the line at the second.

A student with a habitual problem deserves a private talk along with the full penalties as described. You might ask your colleagues about any chronic cases among the majors in your department.

Your best strategy against all forms of disruptive behavior is prevention. Be aware of potential problems, and plan carefully to keep them from developing and to nip any stray weeds in the bud.

PRESERVING ACADEMIC HONESTY

The term "cheating" refers to a variety of behaviors generally considered unethical (Barnett and Dalton, 1981). In its basic form, it is theft of intellectual property. Whether a student plagiarizes a report, copies an answer on a test, or pays another student to write a term paper, he has dishonestly attained information and lied in passing off the work as original and his own.

Cheating has become a way of life for students at colleges and universities across North America, and studies suggest the trend is on the increase. According to a 1990 study by Rutgers anthropologist Michael Moffatt, 45 percent of the students questioned reported having cheated at some time in their careers, while an additional 33 percent admitted to being habitual or "hard-core" cheaters--i.e., cheating in eight or more classes over their four undergraduate years (Collison, 1990a). Only 20 percent claimed to have never cheated. Donald McCabe, associate professor of management at Rutgers, reported that 67 percent of the students surveyed at 31 highly selective American universities admitted to cheating in college (Kibler, 1992).

Who Cheats and Why

According to many college administrators, student cheating only reflects the ethics and behavior of the broader society (Collison, 1990a). Media depictions of "the good life" whet students' appetites for something that they are not sure they will be able to afford. Moreover, the now commonplace, scandalous antics of business and political leaders make amoral and immoral behavior seem "normal," and the small price these leaders pay makes it look profitable. As one student put it, "Cheating is a very common practice in our country. Everyone wants to make a lot of money, and cheating is a way to beat out other people" (Collison, 1990b).

Moffatt's findings lend credence to this view. Students gave motivations for cheating such as a desire for good grades, grade competition, and peer pressure from fellow fraternity and sorority members. These results led Moffatt, too, to blame the overall "decline of public morality" that the nation experienced during the self-centered era of the 1970s and 1980s. But he also cited the increasingly mass approach to higher education (Collison, 1990b).

Moffatt also examined the likelihood of cheating by majors and disciplines. He found economics majors most likely to cheat, with 50 percent reporting hard-core cheating behavior, followed by communications and psychology majors, with 42 percent qualifying as hard-core. English and history majors ranked third, with 18 percent hard-core. Interestingly, among science majors only 5 percent engaged in hard-core cheating.

According to student experts, cheating is easier in larger class-

50 rooms. It is quite easy to conceal wandering eyes beneath the bill of a baseball cap. In fact, looking on a classmate's paper during a test was the most common strategy in Moffatt's study, practiced by a third of all cheaters, while 18 percent reported using crib sheets. Five percent had relied on a stolen test paper, the same proportion had paid someone to write a paper, and ten percent had plagiarized (Collison, 1990b).

Barnett and Dalton (1981) researched the impact of several variables on the cheating behavior of college students. Some proved to have significant effects, while others surprisingly enough did not.

1) *Stress.* Test anxiety, grade pressures, the juggling act that taking several demanding courses requires may drive students to cheat. Instructors invariably underestimate the level of student stress and, therefore, may amplify that stress while failing to take precautions that reduce the temptation to cheat.

2) *Environment.* Cheating is quite common in large classrooms where multiple-choice tests are standard. Additionally, an emphasis on grades, an attitude that "everyone does it," and a low likelihood of getting caught and punished also promote cheating.

3) *Intelligence.* Some evidence suggests that cheaters score lower on I.Q. tests than non-cheaters. When the risk of detection is low, however, the intelligence difference between cheaters and non-cheaters narrows.

4) *Personality characteristics.* Students with a high need for approval may cheat more to garner positive evaluations. Some

studies also indicate that males are more likely to cheat than females, but other studies suggest that females are more likely to lie about cheating.

5) *Definitions of cheating behavior.* Instructors and students often differ on what they consider cheating. In one survey, for example, only 48 percent of the students considered unsanctioned group collaboration on a homework assignment cheating, while 84 percent of the faculty did. In addition, the more frequently an act occurs, the less likely students perceive it as cheating.

6) *Moral judgment and will.* Students who operate at the higher levels of moral reasoning (e.g., on Kohlberg's scale) *should* be less prone to cheat. But research finds that students at all levels behave similarly. While little cheating occurs under high-threat, high-supervision conditions, the cheating rate jumps among students at all levels of moral reasoning under low-threat, low-supervision conditions.

Barnett and Dalton's bottom line was this: The greater the students' chances of getting caught cheating (high supervision) and the greater the chances that getting caught will result in meaningful punishment (high threat), the less prevalent the cheating behavior.

One other factor may affect the incidence of cheating on the institutional level: the existence and enforcement of an honor code. As the cheating epidemic has spread, more and more institutions have been exploring the efficacy of honor codes. College and universities that have them report less cheating than at those that don't (Collison, 1990a; Gordon, 1990), but the reasons are not clear and the transferability of the effect across institutions is unknown. We don't know, for example, if the effect derives from the honor code requirement that students pledge their academic honesty in writing or from an institution's long-standing ethical traditions. Besides, the prevalence of cheating on honor-code campuses varies widely from very low to just not quite as high as on other campuses.

Cheating Prevention: The Best Cure

As with so many kinds of problems, the easiest way to deal with cheating is to prevent it from happening in the first place. Here are some ideas to help protect your students from the temptation of cheating (Barnett and Dalton, 1981; Office of Educational Development, UC Berkeley, 1985).

1) Be sensitive to the debilitating effects of stress and seek ways to reduce it. Start by fostering an environment in which students feel they can succeed without cheating and can feel welcomed seeking your help outside of class (see Chapter 10).

2) Communicate your and your institution's exact definitions of cheating to your students, along with examples of all forms of academic dishonesty. Be aware that collaboration and plagiarism are the most misunderstood forms of cheating among students.

3) State verbally and in writing your and your institution's policies on academic dishonesty and their applications to each assignments and exam you give.

Assure students that you will strictly enforce them and that you take academic integrity very seriously. Also include statements in your syllabus (see Chapter 4).

4) If you're a TA, be especially assertive. Some students may think they can get away with more in your class since they consider you less experienced and self-assured than faculty members.

5) Encourage your students to combat academic dishonesty actively wherever they see it. Since students don't want to be "squealers," you might appeal to social ethics and to their desire to protect their own intellectual property.

6) Make your exams as original as possible to reduce student reliance on old tests for study. You can solicit potential test questions from TAs and students to increase your pool of items.

7) Ensure equal access to study aids. Fraternities and sororities often have test files that members use to study. You might consider placing a file of old tests and assignments on reserve in the library for all students to use.

8) Assign paper topics that require original critical thinking. Topics that are too challenging as well as those that are trivial and boring may invite cheating.

9) Change your assignments as often as possible. If everyone knows you assign a paper on Shakespeare's use of floral imagery every semester, you may see reruns of last term's papers.

10) Guide students through the process of researching and writing a paper or essay for your

class. Students feel more confident when they know what is expected of them.

11) Take class time to discuss difficulties in the assignment and how to overcome them. Students may otherwise feel that they are the only one having trouble with an assignment.

12) Meet with students as early and as often as possible to monitor their progress on a major assignment and to gauge the development of their ideas.

13) Require students to submit first drafts. This ensures you see a work in progress. By providing early feedback, you can also help students improve their writing and thinking skills (see Chapter 29).

14) Give specific guidelines for the format of papers and assignments, and grade in part on adherence to them. This is an excellent deterrent to purchasing papers.

15) Ask students to turn in the original of their paper along with one copy for your files. You can refer to the copy file if you suspect piracy later.

16) Proctor tests judiciously, and enlist the aid of your TAs and colleagues, if possible. Do not permit yourself or your assistants to work on any other project while proctoring. Charge only one proctor (perhaps yourself) with answering any student questions during the test.

17) Alternate forms of multiple choice tests. Scramble questions and color-code the forms.

18) During tests, if the room permits, seat students with space between them and with personal belongings as far away from them as possible (e.g., at the front of the room).

19) In large lecture halls, have assigned test seats and keep a chart of students' names.

20) Supply scratch paper if it will be needed.

21) If bluebooks are used, have students turn them in early and redistribute them randomly.

22) Be aware that cheat notes have turned up in nearby restrooms, on the underside of baseball cap bills, on students' skin (perhaps visible only through a hole in their jeans), and in other highly imaginative places. Check such possibilities as far as your sense of discretion allows.

23) Collect tests from students individually to avoid a chaotic rush at the end of class.

24) When grading tests, clearly mark incorrect answers with an "x" or a slash. Also place a mark at the end of each answer to discourage additions after you return the tests.

25) Return exams, papers, and assignments to students in person, if possible.

Take swift, decisive action when you suspect academic dishonesty. Know precisely what institutional policies allow and forbid you as an instructor to do regarding a possible case. (You may not be able to do anything except to report the incident to an office for investigation.) Procedural information should be available from your Dean's office and your chair, as well as in your institution's instructor/faculty handbook, student handbook, and course catalog.

Making the Most of
Office Hours

When you think of your role as an instructor, you normally picture yourself lecturing, facilitating discussion, answering questions, and the like in front of a classroom or laboratory--in any case, interacting with a *group* of students. During office hours, however, you interact with and tutor individual students as well. Yet we rarely discuss or conduct research on holding effective office hours.

Face-to-face in private, students share their confusions, misunderstandings, and questions more candidly and completely than they do in class, and you are in the best position to give them the individual attention they need. The problem is getting them in your office.

Find out the number of office hours per week that your institution or department requires or expects of instructors. You may want to add another hour when you have a relatively large class or an intensive writing course, or if you are a professor without a TA.

Getting Students to See You

Students see TAs during their office hours with little hesitation. But most of them, freshmen in particular, are intimidated by the prospect of visiting even the kindest, most hospitable faculty member. If you're TA who teaches your own course, you may be mistaken for faculty and face the same problem. Spending your office hours alone with your own research and writing may seem attractive at first, but it won't after you see those disappointing first papers, lab reports, or quizzes. So it is best to make efforts to induce the students to see you. These efforts include finding the right place, setting the right times, and giving a lot of encouragement.

The right place. Office hours need not always be in your office. Professor Howard Gogel (1985) of the University of New Mexico School of Medicine conducted an informal experiment that broadens the location possibilities. During a three-year observation period, he scheduled his office hours in a remote office building for the first and third years and in a common study area in the medical library the second year. In the first and third years, only one student showed up each year, predictably just prior to an exam. In the second year, however, a full 20% of his students paid him visits at various times during the semester to discuss the material and to ask questions.

Could it be that students are more intimidated by your office than by you? Or perhaps the issue is the convenience of your office location. Does this mean you should move your office hours out of your office? If your office is out of the way for your students, the idea is worth considering, especially before exams and paper deadlines. You might even split your office hours between two locations-- some in your office and some in the

54 student union or an appropriate library.

The right times. Be careful and considerate in scheduling your office hours. If you are available only briefly during prime class time--that is, when students are attending their other classes--then you immediately reduce your students' ability to see you. If you teach a discussion, recitation, or laboratory section, make sure that your office hours do not overlap with the lecture portion of the course. If there aren't enough hours in the day, consider scheduling an early evening office hour, perhaps in the student union, the most appropriate library, or another student-friendly location.

During the term, remind your classes periodically that you also meet by appointment.

The right encouragement. Start out by publicizing your office hours, first in your syllabus, then on the board during the first day of class, and intermittently during the term before "high traffic" weeks (e.g., before exams and paper deadlines). You might even have your students write your office hours and location(s) on the front of their course notebooks. In addition, post your hours prominently outside your office door.

It also helps to establish a friendly classroom atmosphere on the first day of class by having students fill out index cards on themselves, by conducting ice breaker activities, and by sharing highlights of your own background (see Chapter 7). On that day and throughout the term, warmly invite students to stop by your office to talk about the course as well as the material.

But even the warmest series of invitations may not provide enough encouragement. You may have to "require" the pleasure of their company. Here are several acceptable ways:

- Make it a regular course requirement for each student to schedule a time to meet with you as early in the term as possible. The first meeting will pave the way for future voluntary visits.
- Have students schedule individual meetings with you as part of their writing the first paper. You can use this opportunity to review their first draft and to clarify your expectations for the paper.
- Have students turn in papers, problem sets, lab reports, extra credit work, etc. *not* in class but in your office during certain hours of a non-class day.
- Have students schedule meetings with you to get their grades on their papers or written assignments. You can return their marked papers or assignments in class for them to review before their meetings with you, but hold the grades "hostage."
- If you divide your class into cooperative learning groups or assign group projects, you might have each group schedule at least one appointment with you to give a progress report.

When students arrive, especially the first time, try to make them feel welcome. It is helpful to spend the first minute or two finding out how they are, how they find the course, and what they think of their college experience. A few moments of personal small talk can make them feel more at ease. After all, they're on *your* turf, and it takes courage for them to be there.

In this day and age, however, too warm an approach can be misunderstood. If you are meeting in your office, close the door for privacy but leave it slightly ajar. Also maintain a respectable seating distance.

Should an emergency or illness prevent you from making your office hours, it is best to leave a note, or ask your department staff to leave a note, apologizing for your unavoidable absence.

Making the Time Productive

Most students who come to your office hours do so with a definite purpose in mind, often one that you have defined in class. So it is worth a little class time, if not a section in your syllabus, to advise students on how to prepare for meetings with you. You cannot be expected to read their minds.

For instance, you might instruct them to come with appropriate materials: their journals and/or lecture notes, their lab books, their homework problems, the drafts of their papers, and/or the readings with troublesome passages marked. You might even tell them to write out their questions or points of confusion as clearly as they can. If the issue is a homework problem, insist that they work it out as far as they can, even if they know their approach is faulty. If it is a grade, tell them to come prepared to argue ideas, not points. Before you even agree to see them, you might require them to write out their arguments with citations to the lectures, discussions, labs, and/or readings (see Chapter 29).

Reserve the right to terminate and reschedule a meeting if a stu-

dent is not adequately prepared. Why waste both your time? In addition, you might inform students that they are not to use your office hours to get a condensed version of the classes they've missed nor to get you to write their papers or do their homework problems for them. See the last section of Chapter 16 for suggestions on handling problematic student demands and questions.

When a student does come properly prepared, try to give him your undivided attention. If you cannot prevent intrusive phone calls, do keep them brief. If other students are waiting outside your door, work quickly without letting their presence distract you.

To maximize the value of your consultation, make it as student-active as possible. You might refer to Chapter 13 on the discovery method, especially the section on the Socratic method, and Chapter 16 on questioning techniques for recommendations on how to help students work through their confusions as much on their own as possible. It may be helpful to respond to their questions with other questions that will lead them to answers. After all, they won't really learn what *you* tell them, only what they themselves realize (Bonwell and Eison, 1991).

Sometimes students want to see you to give them a sense of security. For instance, they have revised their paper according to your or their peer group's specifications, but they lack confidence in their writing. Or they have done their homework problems, but they want you to check them over. Rather than giving just perfunctory affirmations, you can help them acquire their own sense of security by having them explain and justify to you

Making the Most of Office Hours

their revisions or problem solutions. If they can "teach" their rationales, they've earned the right to feel confident.

Identifying student errors calls for extra gentleness. Students who come to you for extra help are probably feeling somewhat insecure and self-conscious. So it is a good idea to praise their smallest breakthroughs generously, and let them know you appreciate their coming to see you. You want them to feel welcome to come back.

If a student fails to show up on time for an appointment, call to remind her and if necessary reschedule. If she simply forgot, counsel her that your time is too valuable a commodity to be forgotten.

Students in Academic or Emotional Trouble

Dealing with students in serious trouble is beyond the scope of an instructor's responsibility. Students who seem overwhelmed by the material or who lack basic writing, reasoning, and mathematical skills should be referred the learning skills or academic assistance center on your campus. As described in Chapter 1, a unit of this type usually offers individual tutoring and workshops on a range of academic skills--such as, textbook reading, writing, studying, problem solving, note-taking, critical thinking, test preparation, and general learning.

Emotionally distressed students usually need professional help. For your own peace of mind, it is important to remember that you are neither the cause of nor the solution to their problems, even if they try to attribute them to a grade you've assigned. You can be most helpful by knowing how to identify such students, promptly referring them to your institution's psychological or counseling center, and informing the center about the encounter. Here are some warning signs:

- angry challenges to your authority
- physical aggression, either real or threatened
- complaints of rejection or persecution
- distorted perceptions of reality
- unjustified demands on your time
- expressions of hopelessness or extreme isolation
- apparent drug or alcohol abuse
- dramatic mood swings or erratic behavioral changes
- continual depression or listlessness

The most immediate proper responses to aggressive behaviors are simple and easy to remember: When dealing with verbal aggression, make arrangements to meet with the student later in a private place to allow the emotions to defuse (verbal, private). If you sense the situation may elevate to physical abuse, move yourself and the student into a public area (physical, public).

It is impossible to anticipate all the different kinds of help that your students may need. To refer them to the right office, keep in mind the campus service units described in Chapter 1.

Motivating Your Students

In the academy, the term "motivating" means stimulating interest in a subject and, therefore, the desire to learn it. Let us begin with some basic principles about motivation (Frymier, 1970). First, the motivation to learn is neither fixed nor easily modified in the short term. Second, motivational incentives work most effectively in optimal rather than maximum doses. In other words, they reach a point of diminishing returns, as do many other investments. Third, highly motivated students have better self images than the less motivated. Fourth, these students also make better, more informed judgments about careers, courses of study, and their futures in general. They take the past, present, and future into account, while less motivated students tend to avoid decision-making altogether. This last principle suggests that instructors must use a variety of motivational strategies to reach different segments of the student population.

Extrinsic and Intrinsic Motivators

Motivation may derive from either extrinsic or intrinsic factors. Among the most powerful extrinsic forces are the expectations of significant others, such as parents, spouses, and employers. Teachers, other relatives, and family associates can also shape a student's aspirations.

Other extrinsic motivators are more material in nature. Returning students often have their eye on a promotion or a favorable career change. Many younger students, especially these days, are interested in a field because of its earning potential. For them, high achievement in the form of top grades may mean entrance into a professional school and ultimately a high-paying occupation. Other students may care about grades just so they can stay in school or have someone else pay for it. In the 1960s, some male students were motivated to excel in part to stay out of the Vietnam War. To them, their lives depended on decent grades.

Intrinsic factors are of the purer sort and pertain more to the subject matter itself. These include a genuine fascination with the subject, a sense of its relevance and applicability to life and the world, a sense of accomplishment (for its own sake) in mastering it, and a sense of calling to it. While instructors can't always affect extrinsic forces, they *can* enhance their subject matter's intrinsic appeal to students.

Strategies for Motivating Students

Happily, effective motivational techniques and effective teaching techniques greatly overlap. Of course, by definition, more motivated students want to learn more, so they achieve more. But it is also true that better teaching generates

58 more rewarding learning experiences, which beget more motivation to learn. It is not surprising, then, that you motivate students using the same methods and formats that you do to teach them effectively. To reach as many students as possible, consider using as many of the following strategies as you can (Owens, 1972; Ericksen, 1974; Gigliotti and Fitzpatrick, 1977; Cashin, 1979; Marsh, 1984; Watson and Stockert, 1987):

1) Deliver your presentations with enthusiasm and energy. Strive for vocal variety changes and constant eye contact. Change your speaking pace frequently and add dramatic pauses. Gesture and move around the class. Be expressive. To your students, right or wrong, your dynamism conveys your passion for the material and for teaching it. As a display of *your* motivation, it motivates *them* (see also Chapters 8 and 14).

2) Make the course personal. Give reasons why you are so interested in the material, and make it relevant to your students' concerns. Show how your field fits into the big picture and how its contributions are important to society. In so doing, you also become a role model for student interest and involvement.

3) Get to know your students. Find out their majors, interests, and backgrounds (see Chapter 7). This information will help you better tailor the material to your students' concerns, and your personal interest in them will inspire their personal loyalty to you.

4) Give students some voice in determining what the course will cover. If they have input, they will feel more invested and more responsible for their learning.

5) Use examples and case studies freely. Many students belong to the "Don't just tell me, show me" school of thought.

6) Use a variety of presentation methods to accommodate various learning styles (see Chapter 12).

7) Teach by discovery whenever possible. Students find nothing so satisfying and intrinsically motivating as reasoning through a problem and discovering the underlying principle on their own (see Chapter 13).

8) Use various student-active teaching formats and methods, such as discussion, debates, press conferences, symposia, role playing, simulations, problem-based learning, the case method, problem solving, writing exercises, etc.--all covered in later chapters. These activities directly engage students in the material and give them opportunities to achieve a level of mastery for achievement's sake.

9) Use cooperative learning formats. Not only are they student-active, they add the motivational factor of positive social pressure (see Chapter 18).

10) Make the material accessible. Explain it in common language, avoiding jargon where possible. Perhaps John Kenneth Galbraith (1987) said it best: "There is no idea...that cannot be expressed in clear English. When one resorts to jargon,...one is engaged in an old habit by which people...seek to establish a priestly difference from the rod of mankind. It is unnecessary."

11) While students must acquire some facts to master the basics of any discipline, stress conceptual understanding above rote

memorization. Facts are only tools with which to construct broader concepts, thus means to a goal, not goals in themselves.

12) Set realistic performance goals and help students achieve them by encouraging them to set their own reasonable goals. Striving to exceed one's personal best is a mighty motivator.

13) Design assignments that are appropriately challenging in view of the experience and aptitude of the class. Assignments that are either too easy or stressfully difficult are counterproductive.

14) Place appropriate emphasis on testing and grading. Make tests fair, which means consonant with your course goals, your topical emphases, and your previous quizzes and assignments. Tests should be a means of showing students what they have mastered, not what they haven't.

15) Accentuate the positive, especially in grading. Be free with praise and constructive in criticism. Acknowledge improvement. Negative comments should pertain to particular performances, not the performer (see Chapter 29).

16) Use humor where appropriate. A joke or humorous anecdote lightens the mood and can enhance learning. In fact, according to Norden (1994), the cerebrum's learning center is adjacent to the emotional center. Given this proximity, positive emotions, such as humor, indirectly stimulate learning. Just be sensitive to the context, setting, and audience.

17) Foster good lines of communication in both directions. Convey *your* expectations and assessments, but also invite your students' feedback in the form of classroom assessment exercises (see Chapter 25) and some form of midterm evaluation (e.g., your own questionnaire or a small group instructional diagnosis conducted by your institution's teaching center).

18) Appeal to extrinsic motivators as well. Inform students about what jobs and careers are available in your discipline, what attractions they hold, and how your course prepares students for these opportunities. Whenever possible, link new knowledge to its usefulness in some occupation.

"Liberating the Imagination"

UCLA history professor E. Bradford Burns (1993) practices an effective motivational/instructional technique that he calls "Liberating the Imagination." Using his Latin American history course as an example, he demonstrates how to elucidate the potentially dry facts of Central and South American politics through regional art and literature. The class learns, for example, about the changing role and power of the Church and the estate patron by tracing their portrayal in paintings over the years. Students across learning styles find this interdisciplinary approach refreshing and instructive, and it gives them a true feel for the times and places.

The idea of liberating the imagination seems natural in some disciplines, especially the humanities. But it is amenable to even the sciences. One biology instructor prefaces his lectures with brief, relevant selections of classical music, poetry, and prose to pique students' appreciation for the day's subject

60   matter. Mussorgsky's "Ballet of the Unhatched Chicks" from *Pictures at an Exhibition* seed the discussion on observing animals in nature. Pastoral sonnets by the Kentucky poet Jesse Stuart help students visualize an ecosystem. African and Far Eastern myths and legends inspire students to reflect on the reverence held for nature in agrarian societies. By stirring emotions through esthetics, these preludes effectively motivate students to care about the material, thus readying them to learn.

Equity in the Classroom

Equity is not just an abstract, ethical issue. Its opposite negatively impacts the motivation, thus the achievement of the disadvantaged students. Not that instructors purposely show favoritism, but research documents that many do so inadvertently or unconsciously.

Studies have uncovered gender inequity in classrooms from primary school through college, with males being favored over females (e.g., Hall and Sandler, 1982; Krupnick, 1985). Teachers often praise (or at least fail to punish) boys for being aggressive in the classroom but discourage girls from acting similarly. In college, many instructors express this same bias by allowing males more time to respond to discussion questions and giving disproportionate approval to males' marginal answers. Females, as well as minority and disabled students, are more likely to be ignored or interrupted, and their correct answers, merely accepted.

Equity in the classroom begins with instructor awareness of these unconscious dynamics. The following guidelines translate this awareness into behavior:

1) Give attention to all students as equally as possible. If a white male in the front row tries to answer every question, wait until other students raise their hands and spread the participation around.
2) Praise students equally for equal quality responses.
3) Use non-stereotypical examples in presentations. If you use a female in an example, make her a scientist, an accountant, or a surgeon rather than a nurse, a teacher, or a secretary.
4) Use gender-neutral language. Try to avoid using the pronouns "he" and "him" exclusively when discussing people in general.
5) Resist falling into reverse discrimination. Do not give inordinate attention to minority and disabled students, as this may appear to reflect your expectation of their failure.
6) Be sensitive to any difficulties your students may have in understanding you. International, ESL, and hearing-impaired students may have trouble with your idiomatic expressions or accent. Ask such students privately if they do, and encourage them to ask for clarification.

These are just a few suggestions for ensuring classroom equity. Chapter 15 on discussion contains many more, especially in the section, "Increasing Participation Through Skillful Discussion Management." Equity is really about increasing and broadening student participation, not only in discussion, but in higher education and beyond.

PART III.

VARIETIES OF LEARNING

AND TEACHING STRATEGIES

LEARNING STYLES

People learn, or more precisely, *prefer* to learn in different ways. Many favor learning by doing hands-on activities, some by reading and writing about a topic, others by watching demonstrations and videos, and still others by listening to a lecture. All of these preferences key into the different ways people learn, commonly known as learning or processing styles.

Should instructors then teach their material in different ways to "cater" to these different styles? Maybe they should prepare students for life in the real world by not giving them special treatment. On the other hand, it also prepares students for the real world to teach them to identify and take advantage of their own styles of learning, as well as to recognize their learning weaknesses. Particularly now when our society is concerned with fairness and equality for persons of different genders, races, ethnicities, and abilities, teaching to different learning styles is a major facet of equity.

Of the many models of learning styles, two are particularly popular, accessible, and relevant to college students: David Kolb's model of the learning cycle and learning styles (1984) and the sensory-based learning styles typology advanced by Fleming and Mills (1992). Both frameworks propose ways to categorize and identify the preferred learning styles of students.

Kolb's Cycle of Learning Modes

Kolb portrays the process of meaningful learning as a series of events that integrates the functions of feeling, perceiving, thinking, and acting. The learner moves through a cycle comprised of four different phases: concrete experience (CE), reflective observation (RO), abstract conceptualization (AC), and active experimentation (AE).

Let us take experiential learners as an illustration. By directly involving themselves in new experiences, these learners enter the first phase of the cycle, designated concrete experience (CE). As they observe others and reflect on their own and others' experiences, they proceed to the reflective observation (RO) phase. Next, they attempt to assimilate their observations and perceptions into logical theories, thus moving into the third phase of abstract conceptualization (AC). When they use concepts to make decisions and solve problems, learners exhibit the final phase of the learning cycle, that of active experimentation (AE).

Individual learners enter the cycle at different points, typically because they prefer the activities associated with a particular part of the cycle. Thus, the various phases of the learning cycle form the basis for categories of learning modes.

The *concrete experience* mode is characterized by a reliance more on feeling than on thinking to solve

64 problems. In this mode, people interpret human situations in a very personal way and focus on the tangible here and now. Intuitive, open-minded, social, and artistic in their information processing, these learners center on knowledge that demonstrates the complex and the unique vs. systematic, scientifically derived theories and generalizations.

The *reflective observation* mode is similarly marked by intuitive thinking, but as applied to observing and understanding situations, not solving and manipulating them. Using this mode, a learner is quick to grasp the meanings and implications of ideas and situations and can examine situations and phenomena "empathetically" from different points of view. Patience, objectivity, and good judgment flourish in this mode.

Reliance on logical thinking and conceptual reasoning characterizes the *abstract conceptualization* mode. It focuses on theory building, systematic planning, manipulation of abstract symbols, and quantitative analysis. This mode can generate personality traits such as precision, discipline, rigor, and an appreciation for elegant, parsimonious models.

Finally, the *active experimentation* mode is directed towards the practical and concrete (like the CE) and rational thinking (like the AC). But its orientation is towards results: influencing people's opinions, changing situations, and getting things accomplished--purely pragmatic applications. This mode fosters strong organizational skills, goal-direction, and considerable tolerance for risk.

Now visualize a graph with two axes: the x-axis from active (on left) to reflective (on right), and the y-axis from abstract (at bottom) to concrete (at top). This arrangement places the concrete experience mode at 12 o'clock, the reflective observation at 3 o'clock, abstract conceptualization at 6 o'clock, and active experimentation at 9 o'clock. Connecting the modes by arrows going clockwise, you can see Kolb's theoretical learning cycle.

Kolb's Derived Learning Styles

Kolb went a step further to define a "learning style" and a "learning type" in each quadrant. *Accommodators* rely heavily on concrete experience and active experimentation. They enjoy engaging in new and challenging experiences, particularly those requiring hands-on involvement. They attack problems intuitively with a trial-and-error methodology and tend to gravitate toward action-oriented careers, such as marketing and sales.

Divergers, on the other hand, utilize concrete experience as well as reflective observation. They examine situations from different angles and like to be personally involved with their work. They tend to move toward service fields, the arts, and the social sciences.

Convergers rely primarily on their skills of abstract conceptualization and active experimentation in their learning. They are often characterized as asocial and unemotional, preferring to work with things rather than people. They enjoy assignments that require practical applications and precise, concrete answers. In general, many engineers and computer scientists fall into this category.

Assimilators combine abstract conceptualization and reflective observation into a style that excels at organization. They may integrate large quantities of data into a concise, logical framework, from which they extrapolate theories and generalizations. These individuals focus on abstract ideas and concepts rather than people or practical applications. Many scientists and academicians are assimilators.

In reality, people's learning styles may shift from situation to situation, encompassing an area that spans two and even three quadrants. So take care not to categorize yourself or others too rigidly. Still, when designing a course, try to build in various opportunities for students to board the learning cycle: some lessons that are experiential and tangible, some reflective and intuitive, some logical and conceptual, and others applied and practical.

Fleming and Mills' Sensory-Based Learning Style Typology

Fleming and Mills (1992) advanced another framework of learning styles that uses a more descriptive classification nomenclature. Here, the terminology reflects the preferred physical sense involved in learning, as reflected in the four categories of auditory, visual, digital, and kinesthetic. The model allows room for individuals to rely on more than one style.

Digital. Students with a digital learning style excel when asked to read and write about a topic. They rely heavily on recognizing logical, deductive relationships, such as the classic outline form, and can easily find pattern and flow in a well constructed lecture or textbook. Their memory structure is more abstract than that of any other style. They

store information as organized sets of symbols, such as outlines, equations, diagrams, and typologies. As you can imagine, digital learners do well in the traditional educational setting; the reading and lecture format so common in classrooms is tailor-made for them. They need no special instructional considerations.

Auditory. Students with an auditory learning style perform well when they are given information in a form they can hear, such as a discussion, a lecture, a debate, or another type of verbal presentation. In fact, they learn best when they can hear themselves express an idea. Consequently, they benefit from most standard teaching methods, especially those that require student participation. As they process and store information in chronological relationships, they thrive in fields that base data and analysis on stories, cases, and events, such as history, political science, law, business administration, and literature. Many also have musical talent. Strong auditory learners can retrieve knowledge in "memory tapes" and are aided by mnemonic devices.

Students who rely more on the next two styles face difficulties in the typical college classroom. Unless they also have digital or auditory processing on which to rely, visual and kinesthetic learners are often left behind in lecture situations, through no fault of their own. So additional forms of stimuli may be necessary in order to optimize their learning experience.

Visual. Individuals with a primarily visual learning style rely on their sight to take in information. They work well with maps and rarely forget a face, a scene, or a place. Some gravitate to artistic fields where they can express their flair for design and color. Consistent with their visual nature, these individuals organize knowledge in terms of spatial interrelationships among ideas and store it graphically as static or moving snapshots, pictures, or diagrams. Some even have photographic memories.

With little additional preparation, you can easily supplement your teaching presentations with aids for visual learners. The object is to portray knowledge in two-dimensional spatial relationships that reflect the logical, chronological, or mechanical links among concepts, processes, and events. The less "space" and more connections between two ideas, the more closely related the visual learner will comprehend and remember them. The means to this goal include illustrations, pictures, diagrams, flow charts, graphs, graphic models, graphic organizers (conceptual "tree" and "bubble" diagrams), and graphic metaphors. This last type of graphic is a drawing of an analogical relationship, such as a sketch of a building to represent a Marxian view of society, with the basement as the "substructure" and the floors above as the "superstructure."

The teaching tools are readily available: the chalkboard, overhead transparencies, slides, and handouts. Some instructional computer software and videotapes also feature outstanding visual depictions of mathematical, physical, and biological relationships (see Chapter 21).

Using only the least expensive options, you can diagram the relationships among major points in your lectures and the readings. You can add visual components like graphs and histograms to the day's lesson. You can chart complex, logical relationships among overlapping concepts with Venn diagrams. You can draw flow charts of multistage assignments, such as the essay writing process, problem solving strategies, and laboratory procedures. You can even flow-chart your syllabus to make your course organization crystal clear. Since students have such trouble taking notes on class discussions, you might "spider map" them as they proceed--that is, diagram a discussion with the central theme as the hub and web lines to the related arguments or points the students make. Then "web off" the evidence presented to support each point.

Kinesthetic. This final learning style uses active involvement as the primary learning mode. Those strong in this style demonstrate superb eye-hand-mind coordination and natural-born mechanical ability. In the traditional educational regime, however, these learners are often maligned and are rarely taught "their way" except in shop or home economics courses. While mechanical skills may seem narrow and unintellectual, kinesthetic individuals make excellent surgeons, dentists, health care professionals, musicians, technicians, engineers, and architects. In processing information, they easily grasp physical interrelationships and store knowledge as experiences with both physical and emotional components.

You can reach strongly kinesthetic students using the same techniques as you do for strongly visually oriented students, as both types relate well to graphic representations of themes and concepts. But since kinesthetic processors rely heavily on inductive reasoning, they especially benefit from abundant examples and hands-on experiences from which they can formulate general hypotheses and principles. Thus they learn best from student-active, experiential teaching formats like simulations, case studies, role plays, field trips, independent (but instructor-guided) research projects, laboratories, problem-based learning, service learning, and discovery methods, all of which are explained in later chapters.

Physical models and analogies are also important learning tools to these students. For instance, an English instructor faced a kinesthetic student with little concept of how to organize the assigned literature review, even after hearing several instructional lectures. So the instructor decided to use a mechanical illustration. With paper and pencil in hand, she compared the introduction, which contains the thesis, to the motor that drives the paper. The next paragraph contains the points supporting one view, like a series of pulleys all turning in the same direction. The direction of the paper then shifts to the opposing arguments and evidence, much as a mechanical system changes direction if the drive belts are twisted. Finally, in the conclusion, the writer chooses to endorse one direction or the other.

Multi-Sensory Teaching: Most Effective for Everyone

In this sensory-based learning style framework, as in Kolb's, it is important to remember that learners prefer one or two learning styles, but they may also use the other modes to a lesser extent. In fact, *all* students learn more and better from multiple-sense presentations.

Perhaps because of the passive way most people read, they remember only ten percent of what they read. With only 50,000 neurons connecting the ear to the brain, they retain only ten percent to 20 percent of what they hear. By contrast, the eye has 1.2 million neural links to the brain, which is why most students can recall 30 percent of what they see in pictures and graphics--roughly twice as much as what they hear (Woods, 1989; Clute, 1994).

The major benefits derive from "multi-sensory teaching." Students remember half of what they hear *and* see. Because speaking involves active cognition as well as hearing, they retain 70 percent of what they say. Couple speaking with doing and the recall rate soars to 90 percent (Woods, 1989). But teach in three sensory modes--the auditory, the visual, and the experiential--and students remember 97 percent of the material (Clute, 1994).

Teaching to different learning styles and multiple senses can also help revitalize classroom presentations that have become routine through repetition. Adding visual and kinesthetic components may take some time and effort, but the change can avert burn-out.

Therefore, to maximize all students' learning and your own professional fulfillment, try to use a rich variety of teaching techniques and learning media in your courses. In addition, acquaint your students with the broad range of learning and studying strategies. The three tables that follow suggest different strategies of knowledge intake, study, and recall for each learning style. Feel free to share the recommendations with your students.

Table I
Intake and Mastery of New Knowledge

Digital	Auditory	Visual	Kinesthetic
list outline	attend lectures	underline, highlight	use all senses
study headings	attend study sessions	books, notes	take advantage of
refer to dictionaries,	discuss topics with	make symbols, flow	laboratories, field
glossaries	students, instructors	charts, graphs,	trips, exhibits, tours
read handouts,	explain new concepts	pictures, videos	films, simulations,
manuals, textbooks,	to others	spatially arrange	role plays, cases,
books	use tape recorder	concepts on page	problem-based
take lecture notes	recall stories, jokes,	study textbook	learning
write essays	case studies,	diagrams	study examples,
	mnemonic devices	recall instructor's	applications
		gestures,	do trial-and-error
		mannerisms	experiments
			collect specimens
			develop procedural
			recipes
			study previous exam
			papers

Table II
Study Suggestions

Digital	Auditory	Visual	Kinesthetic
outline text, notes	expand notes through	condense notes into	recall real things,
recopy notes	discussion	spider map, pictures	examples
reread notes	summarize notes on	make tables, charts,	use examples in
rephrase key ideas,	tape	graphs, diagrams	summaries
concepts	explain topics to	rearrange images	discuss notes with
organize visuals into	others	redraw pages from	others
statements	read notes aloud	memory	use pictures to
turn actions, reactions	make up mnemonic	replace words with	illustrate ideas
into words	devices to remember	symbols	return to lab or lab
imagine lists as	lists, principles		manual
multiple choice			recall laboratories, field
questions			trips, exhibits, tours,
			films, simulations,
			role plays, cases,
			problem-based
			learning
			record and recall
			reactions to material

Table III
Output and Applications for Teaching and Evaluation

Digital	Auditory	Visual	Kinesthetic
write exam answers	talk with instructor	recall page layouts	write practice answers
practice multiple	practice writing	make diagrams from	role-play exam
choice questions	answers	memory	situations alone
write essays	read, practice answers	turn visuals back into	
arrange words in	aloud	words	
hierarchies	request oral exam		

Teaching at Its Best

An Introduction to Student-Active Teaching: The Discovery Method

Bonwell and Eison (1991) present a book's worth of research findings documenting that, at the college level, student-active teaching methods ensure more effective, more enjoyable, and more memorable learning than do passive teaching methods--the most passive being the lecture. Most people neither absorb nor retain material very well simply by reading or hearing it. The best methods permit learning by *doing*, by *acting out*, by *experiencing first-hand*, or by *thinking through to realization*.

Student-active teaching methods also build in motivation. As they don't allow for wallflowers, they engage even the most reluctant students in the material, giving it a chance to capture their interest. In addition, they pique natural human curiosity, set up doable, short-term challenges, and leave students with satisfying senses of accomplishment and ownership of the material they learn. Finally, as student-active methods often involve application of knowledge, they may demonstrate to students the practical utility of the material. All of these features motivate learning (Gigliotti and Fitzpatrick, 1977; Bandura, 1977; Cashin, 1979; Nosich, 1993).

This chapter focuses on a subset of student-active teaching techniques that fall under a loose classi-fication called "the discovery method." These include four activities for in-class discussion or home-work assignments forwarded by Nosich (1993) and the Socratic method of teaching by questioning. The chapter concludes with a summary of other student-active formats, to be covered in greater detail later, that allow discovery through the processes of identification and direct experience.

Recreating Historical Discoveries

Nosich (1993) offers a number of examples that may inspire you to set up historical recreations for your particular courses.

In a physics course, ask students how they could tell whether two flashes of lightning occurred at the same time. They can tackle the problem in small groups or in a general class discussion, if the class is not too large. With a little background, they should be able to restructure Einstein's experiment on simultaneity and rediscover aspects of his theory of relativity.

In chemistry, ask students how an early scientist like Lavoisier could have devised an experiment to discover something as counter-intuitive as the weight of oxygen.

In biology, students can rediscover pecking orders in various species of animals by making observations at a zoo, a wildlife park, or a farm. You can make this an outside assignment or a class field trip.

In nursing, allow students to discover the nursing process on their own by making observations in a medical facility--again as an assignment or a field trip.

In art or art history, set up an arrangement of cubical blocks that lets students discover the principle of perspective and the vanishing point on their own.

In music, rather than telling students about the concept of resolution and how Wagner avoided it in *Tristan and Isolde*, give them the first four chords of the piece, without identifying them as such, and assign them the task of writing 12 more bars of chords that do not reach resolution. Students will discover first-hand how difficult it is to avoid resolution and will then appreciate why Wagner made the chord choices he did.

Discovering Naive Misconceptions

Here the challenge is to induce students to realize that their current thinking on a subject is naive--and, therefore, that the knowledge your course offers has relevance--*without your telling them.* Your task is to explicitly or implicitly present their misconception as a proposition and to elicit discussion by offering a key counter-example. After the discussion, ask students to reconsider the original proposition (Nosich, 1993).

In physics, students invariably enter an introductory course with an Aristotelian working concept of the world. The problem is, they often leave it the same way. Present a demonstration or devise a labora-tory experiment that yields results that run completely counter to their Aristotelian world view. They will then be more open to and appreciative of Newtonian, then Einsteinian concepts.

In chemistry, raise the proposition that putting chemicals in things is bad, and either toss out a counter-example or ask the students if they can think of any.

In biology or paleontology, have students consider the popular evolutionary belief that *Homo sapiens* "progressed" from the "lower" forms of life, or from the dinosaurs, or insects, or chimpanzees. You can direct the discussion to examine the notion of "evolutionary progress" and "lower" forms of life, as well as to introduce cladistics.

In history or political science, invite students to examine the premise that the majority rules in the United States.

In sociology, have them take another look at their private belief that social taboos and restraints don't influence them personally.

Discovering Our Ignorance

One of the most thought-provoking discoveries that people can make is realizing what they *don't know.* We may not fully appreciate the value of our ignorance because we are constantly on the lookout for unknowns in our own field so we can intelligently direct our research agenda. Students, however, tend to think they "know" African history or physical chemistry or nineteenth-century French literature or anthropological linguistics after completing a course by that name. They may never know what they *didn't* learn, let alone what *we* know we don't know.

One way to evoke such discoveries is to ask the class after a reading assignment, "What did the article (or book) *not* tell you?" Nosich (1993) gives an extended example of what a typical book on the revolutionary war doesn't tell students, and what they can discover by an instructor's asking what they didn't learn--for instance: What were children doing during the war? What was it like to be gay or lesbian at the time? What did the troops eat? Or people in general? Suddenly, students become curious about issues that never crossed their minds before.

Another method is to let your entire class or small groups chew on a question the reading and lectures never actually address, such as, "Why doesn't an atom fall together?"

A final thought-provoker: Human beings discovered fire. Let us consider, what have we missed?

Discovering Alternative Explanations

This technique works especially well in the social sciences, history, literary criticism, and psychology, in which a book or article, however scientifically respectable, may reflect a particular theoretical or ideological point of view among several that exist. They also work in the physical and biological sciences but at somewhat advanced levels of study, where such debates tend to emerge.

First, have your students demonstrate that they understand the explanation, hypothesis, interpretation, or argument in the assigned reading. Second, invite them to develop an alternative explanation, then either to defend it with evidence or to design a re-

search project that would adequately test it against the one in the reading (Browne and Keeley, 1986; Nosich, 1993).

You can simply have your class brainstorm and discuss alternative explanations and the type of evidence or research needed to examine them. Or you can make it an assignment in which students work either individually or in small groups. It can be done in class, as homework, or as an essay question on an exam.

Discovery by the Socratic Method

Socrates himself never wrote a word. But Plato, one of his admiring students, recorded Socrates' teaching strategies in *Dialogues*, particularly in "Meno," "Symposium," and "The Apology," Socrates' defiant, unsuccessful defense at his trial.

Perhaps the purist proponent of the discovery method, Socrates started with the rather radical learning theory that the human mind contains *all* knowledge within it--quite the opposite of the "clean slate" portrayal. The mind cannot actually "learn" anything in the sense of taking in new knowledge. Rather the challenge is to access the knowledge that is already there. The role of teaching then-- and the only thing it can hope to accomplish--is to bring this knowledge to consciousness--as Socrates put it, to help the student "remember." How? By asking a series of questions that taps into the knowledge.

"Meno" contains a demonstration of Socratic learning and questioning techniques. By drawing a simple diagram and asking a series of questions, Socrates coaches an uneducated slave boy to reason through and discover some basic geometric principles (the relationship between the lengths of the sides of a square and its area). When the boy makes an error in reasoning and reaches an impasse, Socrates comments to his friend Menon, "Just notice how after this difficulty he will find out by seeking along with me, while I do nothing but ask questions and give no instruction" (Rouse, 1984, p. 48).

Socrates also took on adults and their conceptions of abstract notions such as love and virtue. Here is a sample of his style from "Symposium." In this section he is responding to an informal speech given by an associate, Agathon (Rouse, 1984, pp. 96-97; only dialogue extracted):

S: Come now, let us run over again what has been agreed. Love is . . . of those things which one lacks?

A: Yes.

S: This being granted, then, remember what things you said in your speech were the objects of Love . . . [that] there could not be a love of ugly things. Didn't you say something like that?

A: Yes, I did.

S: And . . . if this is so, would not Love be love of beauty, not of ugliness? . . . Then Love lacks and has not beauty?

A: That must be.

S: Very well: do you say that what lacks beauty and in no wise has beauty is beautiful?

A: Certainly not.

S: Then if that is so, do you still agree that love is beautiful?

A: I fear, Socrates, I knew nothing of what I said!

Couched in conversation, Socrates' questions appear to be spontaneous responses to the answers he receives. But they are also carefully crafted to lead the usually unwitting student down the blind alley of his or her position to an internal contradiction or absurd conclusion.

Being shown in public to have erred in reasoning didn't bother the slave boy nor apparently Agathon. But the affluent and powerful of Athens, many of whom Socrates also challenged, had much less gracious reactions. It took them decades, however, to bring him to trial on the charges of introducing new gods and corrupting the youth. In "The Apology," he argued that all he ever did was to ask people questions, and if their ill-reasoned answers made them look foolish, they could choose to learn. Those who instead were prosecuting him for their being wrong were only proving him to be right all along, he contended. This thoughtful but hardly conciliatory defense did nothing to soften the judges. But Socrates reached the ripe old age of 70 before being condemned to death in 399 B.C.

Socrates' learning theory and version of the discovery method may indeed seem extreme today. It is one thing to reason through basic mathematics and philosophical issues via a series of questions; both fields are reason-based. But questions alone could hardly impart foreign languages, literature, the arts, or data-based fields like history and the sciences.

Still, these fields wouldn't progress far without questions *about* that knowledge. Moreover, at least some of them do have data-independent, reason-based subfields, such as literary analysis, historical methods, statistical analysis, and the scientific method in general. Guided by the right questions, students no doubt can "reinvent" many of the principles in these areas.

A psychology professor who relies on the Socratic approach, Overholser (1992) gives numerous examples of his students' "rediscovering" or "reinventing" basic research and clinical principles in response to a series of questions. His Case Western Reserve University students reason through the need for a control group and double blind research controls, successively narrow down clinical diagnoses, progressively refine definitions, generate hypotheses from theories, and come to understand the effects of experimenter's expectancies and self-fulfilling prophecies.

The questioning style that Socrates employed also contained a fatal (as it turned out) flaw: It alienated people, all but the most humble, eager, and open-minded. The modern university ethos eschews trying to teach students by verbally "backing them up against a wall," cross-examining them for crimes of ignorance, or otherwise publicly humiliating them. (Some of us might admit though to taking vicarious glee in the Professor Kingsfield character in "The Paper Chase.")

However, we can use the Socratic method with tact and gentleness. When a student ventures a wrong answer to a reasoning question, we can take the focus off that particular student and warn him or her and the entire class where your next question will lead. For instance, you can say, "I imagine that some of you agree with Bob, but I doubt that many of you agree with the implications of his statement. If you have only one group in your design, and you give it the treat-

ment and measure the change, how will you know that the change is due to the treatment?" If Bob still looks blank after a patient wait and extra encouragement, call on another student for an answer.

Chapter 15 offers guidelines and suggestions for managing classroom discussions, including those that incorporate Socratic questioning. Chapter 16 provides an overview of other questioning schema, as well as tips on constructing thought-provoking questions. For a more extensive, cross-disciplinary treatment on framing questions that generate "reinventive" and critical thinking, see Browne and Keeley (2nd ed., 1986), aptly entitled *Asking the Right Questions*.

Discovery in Other Student-Active Formats

The next several chapters cover a wide variety of other student-active techniques, many of which contain elements of discovery. Some are brief enough to sandwich between sections of your lecture. Structured around well-crafted questions, discussion can direct students to discover subtle facets of the material.

Experiential formats, both simulated and real, provide discovery learning opportunities as well. In role playing and simulations, for instance, students discover, by identification, how it "feels" to be in certain positions in lifelike situations. The case method also relies on identification and empathy as students discover how to use what they've learned to solve realistic problems. Discovery also grows out of direct experiences, for example: field trips, "real-world" guest speakers, videotapes and films, labora-

74 tory experiments (not, however, the cookbook variety), outside research projects, and service learning experiences.

The key to making these experiential formats successful is to refrain from instructing students what to find and what to infer. Discovery learning depends on students' inductively arriving at *their own* conclusions. If this process strikes you as hit-or-miss, you can significantly reduce students' mindless "hacking" by having them analyze an experience cooperatively in small groups.

MAKING THE
LECTURE
A LEARNING
EXPERIENCE

The bell rings; class begins. The instructor takes his place at the lectern at the front of the room and begins his lecture. He has prepared a full 50 minutes worth of material that he must deliver non-stop. After all, the material must be covered.

It has bothered him for some time that students don't seem to pay much attention to his lecture, at least not after the first several minutes. He sees some of them glancing through the student newspaper, others whispering to their neighbors, and a few just staring into space. Even those looking at him are doing so through glazed eyes. Don't they understand this course is required for graduation? That they must pass it for the major?

This is all too familiar a scene on university campuses across the country, probably around the world. But it is no mystery. Extensive research on the learning experiences of college students whose instructors depend heavily on the lecture format explains why this rather grim educational scenario is so common.

The Effectiveness of Lecture: Learning, Motivation, and the Lecturer

McKeachie et al. (1994) cites a long list of studies that show that the lecture is as effective as any other method in conveying factual knowledge. But on other criteria-- attitude change, development of thinking and problem solving skills, transfer of knowledge to new situations, student satisfaction with the course, motivation for further learning, and post-course retention of knowledge--the lecture falls short of more student-active methods such as discussion.

Actually the lecture *can* be highly motivational, but its success depends on the *lecturer*. A very expressive, enthusiastic instructor can ignite students' interest in the material, while a reserved, reticent one can douse it.

To some extent, the platform skills that convey energy and dynamism can be learned. Public speaking courses and clubs help people develop and practice effective verbal pacing and pausing, gestures and movements, facial expressions, eye contact, vocal quality and variety, lectern and microphone use, visual aid display, etc.

(see Chapter 8). Those who start out weak in these skills but who work diligently on them can achieve impressive results within a year.

Some scholars may dismiss such presentation techniques as mere acting. In fact, some people seem to have a knack for them, while others indeed acquire them only with concentration and practice. Acting or not, like it or not, these public speaking techniques have a powerful impact on students' motivation and learning, as well as on their course and instructor evaluations (see Chapter 30) *to the extent that an instructor relies on the lecture format.* But with the variety of teaching methods available, no instructor *need* rely on it much at all.

Therefore, instructors have a choice: Those who happen to have an expressive, dynamic public personality, or are willing to acquire the trappings of one, can afford to use the lecture more in their teaching. (For the sake of student learning, however, even the most charismatic instructor should not depend on it exclusively.) Those who do not have such a persona and are not inclined to learn how to "act" it can avoid lecturing whenever possible and appropriate and employ other, more student-active methods. In brief, instructors can play to their natural and acquired strengths. Let these alternatives put to rest the notion that good teachers are born and not made.

The Effectiveness of Lecture: Time and Attention Spans

According to studies cited in Bonwell and Eison (1991), a lecture begins with a five-minute settling-in period during which students are fairly attentive. This attentiveness extends another five to ten minutes, after which time students become increasingly bored, restless, and confused. Focus and note-taking continue to drop--some students effectively fall asleep--until the last several minutes of the period when they revive in anticipation of the end of class. Even medical students display similar patterns of concentration levels: an increase over about 15 minutes, followed by a sharp decrease.

This should come as unsettling, sobering news to the higher education community. After all, if highly motivated learners like medical students demonstrate such a brief attention span, what can we expect of our undergraduates? If we are realistic, we should expect the scenario described at the beginning of the chapter.

No doubt the enthusiastic, engaging lecturer can modestly extend that narrow time horizon. But students are programmed from far too young an age to override the pattern entirely. So when we must lecture, what can we as instructors do?

In a word, pause. One study supports the practice of pausing at least three times each lecture to allow pairs or small groups of students to discuss and clarify the material (Rowe, 1980). Another recommends pausing for two minutes every 15 to 18 minutes to permit student pairs to compare and rework their notes (Ruhl, Hughes, and Schloss, 1987).

This latter study was designed experimentally with a control group receiving a series of traditional non-stop lectures and a treatment group hearing the same lectures with periodic pauses. Both groups took 1) free-recall quizzes during the last three minutes of each lecture (that is, students individually wrote down everything they could remember from the lecture) and 2) the same 65-item multiple choice test 12 days after the last lecture. In two different courses repeated over two semesters, the treatment group performed much better than the control group on both the quizzes and the test, better enough to make a mean difference of up to two letter grades, depending upon the cut-off points (Ruhl, Hughes, and Schloss, 1987).

Translated into learning terms, sacrificing the least important 12 percent of your lecture content for periodic two-minute pauses can increase the learning of your current "C" students to that of your current "B" and even "A" students.

Graded or not, quizzes at the end of a lecture drastically enhance students' retention of the material. From research dating back to the 1920s, lectures have the infamous reputation for being utterly forgettable. Their much-replicated "forgetting curve" for the average student is 62 percent immediate recall of the material presented, 45 percent three to four days later, and only 24 percent eight weeks later. Giving some kind of test right after a lecture doubles both factual and conceptual recall after eight weeks (Menges, 1988).

To Lecture or Not to Lecture?

The eminent psychologist Abraham Maslow once said, "If your only tool is a hammer, you're apt to go around treating everything as if it were a nail." For centuries, the lecture has been the primary teaching tool in higher education, and indeed almost all knowledge and students have been hammered like nails.

Since college-level teaching research came into its own in the early 1970s, we have been learning that the lecture is only one of dozens of devices in a well-stocked instructional tool box. Sometimes a hammer is just the thing, and at other times it isn't.

The lecture is probably your most effective and efficient option, at least for part of a class period, when your objective is one of the following (most from McKeachie, et al., 1994):

- To pique student curiosity and motivation to learn *if your style is very expressive*
- To model an approach to problem solving or a style of thinking
- To give a background knowledge summary that is not otherwise available
- To adapt very sophisticated or theoretical knowledge to your students' level and needs in a way that no other available source does
- To present a particular organization of the material, one that clarifies the structure of the textbook or the course or that helps students organize the readings
- To add your personal viewpoint on the material, including your own related research
- To present up-to-date material that is not yet available in printed form.

Under other conditions, however, the lecture only wastes precious class time. This book suggests many student-active teaching formats and techniques that will convey the material and meet your objectives much more effectively. Demonstrations, films, and videos may also better serve the purpose. Alternatives to the lecture are most appropriate when you want your students to accomplish the following (most from literature summaries in Bonwell and Eison, 1991 and McKeachie et al., 1994):

- To become interested in a topic in which they are not already interested *if your style is not very expressive*
- To examine and possibly change their attitudes
- To explore controversial or ambiguous material with open minds
- To be able to transfer knowledge to new situations
- To develop problem solving skills (broadly defined)
- To develop higher-order or critical thinking skills
- To learn a performance technique or technical procedure
- To improve their writing
- To continue to pursue the subject beyond the particular course
- To remember particular knowledge for months or years to come.

Two other circumstances call for restraining from lecturing. First, if you are uncertain of your students' level of expertise, preparation, and interest, have them do a classroom assessment exercise (see Chapter 26) before planning your presentation. Otherwise, you risk going over the students' heads or boring them with basics.

Second, it is best not to lecture if the material you plan to cover simply duplicates what is already in assigned readings or other course materials. Not that duplication is necessarily a problem in itself, but student-active exercises can dupli-

cate the material at a higher cognitive level, such as application, analysis, synthesis, and evaluation. Deleting a redundant lecture frees plenty of class time for other activities. Besides, if a lecture primarily repeats the readings, any rational student will decide *either* to do the readings *or* to attend lecture. No doubt this is *not* what you intend.

Preparing an Effective Lecture

Class objectives. First, determine your objectives for the class period. What precisely do you want your students to learn that day? Perhaps the lecture will serve only one or two of three goals you have for the class. Then the lecture should fill only part of the period.

Overview. Whenever possible, limit one class's lecture to *one major topic*. Some students find it difficult to pick up a lecture from one period to the next. Then you can lay out a time-content schedule, bearing in mind the two most common lecturing errors: trying to include too much material and delivering the material too fast. While you're lecturing, you will have to proceed slowly enough--including pausing after major points--for students to take notes. So if anything, *under-budget content.*

To start planning your lecture, you might begin by *subdividing the major topic into ten to 15 minute chunks.* Then plan *student-active breaks of two to 15 minutes* between these chunks. The next section suggests a wide variety of timed break activities of different lengths that you can use, but feel free to devise your own. Most of these activities can be (and have been) conducted in large lectures of hundreds of students, as well as smaller classes. So class size need not deter you. Finally, allow *two to five minutes* for some kind of *recap activity* at the end.

Then turn to *internal organization*. The skeleton for any lecture is the introduction, the body, and the conclusion.

Introduction. The ideal introduction has three parts, the order of which is really an aesthetic decision: a statement that frames the lecture in the context of the course objectives; a statement reviewing and transitioning from the material covered in the last class period; and an attention-grabber for the new material. Effective attention-grabbers include an intriguing question the lecture will answer, a story or parable that illustrates the new subject matter of the day, a demonstration of a non-obvious phenomenon, a reference to a current event or movie, a case or a problem that requires the lecture's information to solve, or a strong generalization that contradicts common thought. The idea is to draw in the class with surprise, familiarity, curiosity, or suspense.

Body. The body is your presentation and explication of new material. It is within this section that you subdivide the major topic into *"mini-lectures,"* each of which should revolve around *one and only one major point*. There is no best logic to follow in organizing a mini-lecture, except to keep it simple. You can choose from an array of options: deduction (theory to phenomena/examples); induction (phenomena/examples to theory); hypothesis testing (theory to hypothesis to evidence); problem to solution(s); cause to effect; concept to application; familiar to unfamil-

iar; debate to resolution; a chronology of events (a story or process)--to name just some common possibilities. To appeal to different learning styles, try to vary your organization from one mini-lecture to another (see Chapter 12).

Organizational outline. It is an excellent idea to make whatever organization you select explicit to students. For instance, tell the class, "I am going to describe some common manifestations of dysfunctional family behavior, then give you a definition and general principles that apply to the phenomenon." In fact, it is best to provide an outline of the body of your lecture on the board, on an overhead, or in a handout. An outline will ensure that students are following your logical flow, especially if you occasionally refer to it to point out your location in the lecture. It should also highlight new terms you are introducing.

In addition, try to integrate as many of these learning aids as you can:

Visuals. As you plan the material, think about how you can convey or repackage it visually--in pictures, photographs, slides, graphic metaphors, diagrams, graphs, and spatial arrangements of concepts or stages linked by arrows. Prepare them for presentation to the class. While such visual aids facilitate almost everyone's learning, they can be critical for students with a visual learning style.

Examples. Also think about illustrating abstract concepts and relationships with examples. Ideally these examples should be striking, vivid, current, common in everyday life, and related to students' experiences (past, present, or future). Making them humorous also helps students remember them.

80 Students who favor a kinesthetic learning style rely on examples to process and retain new material.

Restatements. Consider, too, how you can restate each important point in two or three different ways--in scholarly terms, in layperson's formal language, and in informal language. Restatements not only demystify the material, making it more comprehensible; they also build students' vocabulary and encourage their own paraphrasing of the material.

Conclusion. For learning purposes, the conclusion should be a two-to-five-minute recap of the most important points in your lecture. It is too important to be rushed after the bell. You should plan and direct the recap activity, but the *students* should do it. The prospect of having to summarize the material helps keep all students on their toes. The recap activity may take the form of a oral summary presented by one or more students, a free-recall writing exercise (see Chapter 20), or a classroom assessment technique, such as a one-minute paper (see Chapter 26).

Lecture Notes. Your lecture notes should be easy to read at a glance and as sketchy as you can handle. After all, you know the material; you will even in front of a group. So all you need is a map showing your next conceptual destination. Therefore, consider laying out the lecture *graphically* in flow charts, tree diagrams, Venn diagrams, network models, bubbles and arrows, etc., including any visual aids you plan to put on the board. Some instructors like to color code their notes for quick visual reference. If a graphic organization does not appeal to you, make a sketchy outline of your lecture. But be sure it's very sketchy. In any case, write big and leave a lot of white space.

The habit to avoid is writing out sentences (except direct quotes). Doing so may tempt you to read them in class. Then you'll lose spontaneity, expressiveness, flexibility, eye contact, and most importantly psychological contact with the class, lulling students into a passive, even inattentive state of mind (Day, 1980). Confine the words in your notes to key concepts and phrases, transitions to make explicit to the class, and directions to yourself (e.g., "board," "pause," "overhead," "survey class," "ask class question," "break activity #2 - voltage problem").

Options for Student-Active Breaks

Once you incorporate student-active breaks into your lecture, you are giving an "interactive" lecture, during which your students are in some way interacting with the material for brief, controlled periods of time. The focus is on "controlled." You must carefully time-control the student-active breaks by informing your students that they will have exactly X number of minutes to complete the activity you assign them. Strictly enforced time limits keep students focused on the task. To make managing easier, bring a timer or stopwatch to class.

These breaks work well in any size class. In larger classes, however, having students work with their neighbor(s) (in *ad hoc* pairs or triads) is quicker and easier than having them get into pre-organized small groups.

During any pair or small group activity, you might circulate around the classroom to let students know you are listening to them and are willing to answer any procedural questions.

Ask students to work and talk as quietly as they can, but you can still expect the classroom to get noisy. After their activity time is up, you can bring even the largest class to silence within seconds by taking this tip from cooperative learning researchers: Set the rule that you will raise your hand when the time is up. Tell your students that, as soon as they see your hand up, they should immediately stop talking and raise their hands. The rest of the class will quickly follow suit.

Below are some commonly used break activities, along with the number of minutes each typically take. They come from Bonwell and Eison (1991), Cross and Angelo (1993), McKeachie et al. (1994), and informal collegial exchanges. Let them serve as your inspiration to conceive and experiment with your own innovations.

Pair and compare. Students pair off with their neighbor and compare lecture notes, filling in what they may have missed. This activity makes students review and mentally process your lecture content. Time: 2 minutes.

Pair, compare, and ask. Same as above but with the addition that students jot down questions on your lecture content. You then field questions that students cannot answer between themselves. Time: 3 minutes, plus time to answer students' questions.

Periodic free-recall, with pair-and-compare option. Students put away their lecture notes and write down the most important one, two, or three points of your lecture thus far, as well as any questions they have. The first two times you conduct this, use an overhead or the board to give instructions; then just telling them will do. Again, this activity makes students review and mentally process your lecture content. Students may work individually, but if they work in pairs or triads, they can answer some of each other's questions. Time: 2 minutes, plus time to answer students' questions.

Listen, recall, and ask; then pair, compare, and answer. Students only listen to your mini-lecture--no note-writing allowed--then open their notebooks and write down all the major points they can recall, as well as any questions they have. Instruct students to leave generous space between the major points they write down. Finally, they pair off with their neighbor and compare lecture notes, filling in what they may have missed and answering one another's questions. Again, this activity makes students review and mentally process your lecture content. Time: 3-4 minutes for individual note-writing, 2-4 minutes for pair fill-ins and question answering, plus time to answer any remaining questions.

Solve a problem. Students solve an equational or word problem based on your lecture content. (Chapter 24 describes a problem-solving strategy you can teach them.) They can work individually or, better yet, in *ad hoc* pairs or triads. Put the problem on the board or an overhead and, to make class debriefing easier, give four multiple choice options. Ask for a show of hands for each option. Eric Mazur, Professor of Physics at Harvard, also asks student pairs to rate their confidence level in their answer. This activity makes students apply your lecture content and informs you immediately how well they have understood your lecture material. You can then clarify misconceptions before proceeding to new material. Time: 1-3 minutes for problem solving, depending upon the problem's complexity, plus 1-3 minutes to debrief and answer questions.

Quick case study. Students debrief a short case study (one to four paragraphs) that has them apply your lecture content to a realistic, problematic situation. Chapter 19 addresses the case method, including tips on developing your own cases. Display a very brief case on an overhead; put longer ones in a handout. You may add specific questions for students to answer, or teach your class the standard debriefing formula: What is the problem(s)? What is the remedy(ies)? What is the prevention(s)? Instruct students to jot down their answers. They can work individually or, better yet, in *ad hoc* pairs or small groups. Time: 3-8 minutes, depending upon the case's length and complexity, plus 10-15 minutes for class exchange and discussion.

Pair/group and discuss. Students pair off with their neighbor or get into small groups to discuss an open-ended question that asks them to apply, analyze, or evaluate material in your lecture or to synthesize it with other course material. The question should have multiple possible correct answers. Refer to Chapter 16 for helpful

questioning schema and question framing techniques. Students should outline their answers in writing. This activity makes students examine and extend as well as process your lecture content and serves as a perfect prelude to a general class discussion. Time: 3-10 minutes, depending upon the question's complexity, plus 5-15 minutes for class exchange and discussion.

Pair/group and review. Same as above but with an essay question designed for pre-exam review. Student pairs/groups present their answers to the class, while you mock-grade them and explain your assessment criteria. You can also have the rest of the class mock-grade pair/group answers to help students learn how to assess their work. Time: 3-10 minutes, depending upon the question's complexity, plus 5-15 minutes for pair/group presentations.

You will find many other options for student-active breaks in Chapter 18 (cooperative learning), Chapter 20 (writing-to-learn activities), and Chapter 26 (classroom assessment techniques).

Helping Students Take Notes

Research conducted on lecture note-taking provides several useful insights for both instructors and students (Carrier, 1983; McKeachie, 1986; Johnstone and Su, 1994; McKeachie et al., 1994). Your classes may even be interested in hearing about them.

First of all, it is well worth recommending that your students take lecture notes, specifically *their own* lecture notes. Students who do take notes learn and remember more than those who just listen. Note-taking fosters deeper cognitive processing--that is, more thoughtful and active listening involving paraphrasing, interpreting, and questioning, as well as integrating new material into one's organized bank of prior knowledge. It also makes students process the knowledge for "far transfer," which means the ability to apply it in new and different situations. Put in terms of students' immediate interests, note-takers perform better on both objective and essay tests.

Second, advise your students to review their notes as well. Again, research shows that they will learn more, remember more, and perform better on all kinds of tests if they do. Of course, you can structure break activities during class periods to ensure students review their notes.

Third, instructors can facilitate note-taking by organizing their lectures clearly and simply, making this organization explicit to students, and highlighting the most important material. This chapter has already detailed these methods. Fourth, instructors can also present material in ways that compensate for students' most common note-taking weaknesses. For instance, students record 90% of information written on the board and overhead transparencies. But they rarely record detailed sequences of arguments, examples of applications, the meanings of technical terms and symbols, or information related to demonstrations. When such material is genuinely important, instructors should say so and should display or distribute it in written form. In addition, students tend to make errors in copying diagrams, equations, and numerical figures. Instructors can easily

overcome this problem by disseminating such material in handouts (Johnstone and Su, 1994).

Finally, students need to find their own best note-taking strategy, as no one strategy is effective for everyone. Some students benefit most from a formal outline structure, others from graphic diagrams, a few even from practically transcribing a lecture. Note-taking, however, can actually interfere with learning and retrieval for a small subset of students: those with relatively low ability, poor short-term memory, or little prior knowledge of the subject matter. These students are unable to assimilate new material as quickly as a lecture demands. They are dependent on instructional aids, such as lecture outlines you provide and published course notes, and on student-active breaks like "pair and compare" that allow them to draw on their neighbor's notes.

Whatever your students' note-taking styles, you can offer pointers that will help *most* of them. Share with your class the applicable tips in the box below, "29 Lecture Note-taking Tips for Students." They come from a wide variety of study skills manuals and handouts. Maybe you can add a few of your own, including some specific to your subject matter. Refer students who need more than pointers to your institution's learning skills/academic assistance center; it may offer a note-taking workshop.

29 LECTURE NOTE-TAKING TIPS FOR STUDENTS

1. You learn better by taking notes actively than by tape-recording a lecture passively. Besides, reviewing written notes takes less time than does listening to a taped lecture.

2. Keep a separate notebook for each course. Date, number, and label your notes from each class period. Also date and label handouts from each class, and attach them securely to your class notes with staples or tape.

3. Complete the reading assignment due the day of the lecture *before* you attend lecture. The material will probably make a lot more sense.

4. Come to the lecture well prepared with your favorite pen, a back-up pen, a pencil or two, your notebook, any applicable handouts, any study guides on the readings assigned for the day, and anything else you think you may need. Unlike when you travel, it's better to overpack for class than to underpack.

5. Sit near the front towards the center. You can see the board and screen better, hear the lecture better, and avoid distractions more easily. In addition, there's some evidence that students who sit front and center perform better on tests.

6. Arrive early to warm up your mind. Review your notes from the previous class and from the readings assigned for the day.

7. Take note of what you don't completely understand from the last class and the assigned readings, and plan to ask for clarification as early in the class period as possible.

8. Avoid cramming your notes or writing them too small. Strive for easy readability. Leave a generous left margin, as you may want to use it later to write in key words and abbreviations for important material.

9. Organize your lecture notes according to the instructor's introductory, transitional, and concluding words and phrases, such as "the following three factors," "the most important consideration," "in addition to," "on the other hand," and "in conclusion." These signal the structure of the lecture: cause and effect, relationships, comparisons and contrasts, exceptions, examples, shifts in topics, debates and controversies, and general conclusions.

10. Identify the most important points by watching for certain instructor cues: deliberate repetition, pausing, a slowdown in speaking pace, a rise in level of interest or intensity, movement toward the class, putting up an overhead transparaency, and writing on the board.

11. Pay close attention to the instructor's body language, gestures, and facial expressions, as well as changes in pace, tone, and intonation. The instructor's subtlest actions punctuate and add meaning to the substance of the lecture.

12. Record your lecture notes in outline or graphic form, whichever works best for you. (If you're not sure, experiment with both for a few weeks.) Outline form involves indenting less important

and supporting points below the more important, more general ones. This way, the more important material stands out. Points of equal importance or generality should start at the same distance from the left margin. (Some outlining enthusiasts also number and letter different points.) Graphic form involves clustering closely related concepts, steps, stages, etc. and linking them with arrows representing relationships between them. An arrow pointing to the right means "causes," "leads to," or "implies, while one pointing to the left signifies "is an effect of", "derives from," or "is implied by." When in doubt, label your arrows.

13. Whenever possible, draw a picture or a diagram to organize and abbreviate the relationships in the lecture material. It is easier for most people to recall a picture than it is a written description.

14. Avoid writing complete sentences unless the specific wording is crucial.

15. Develop and use your own shorthand, such as abbreviations and visual symbols for common and/or key words (e.g., btw for between, "+" for and, b/c for because, rel for relationship, df or "=" for definition, cnd for condition, nec for necessary or necessitates, hyp for hypothesis, T4 for therefore, "+" and "-" for more and less, up and down arrows for increasing and decreasing, two opposing arrows for conflicts with, a delta triangle for change).

16. Take notes sparingly. Drop all unnecessary words from your note-taking vocabulary. Write down only the words and symbols that are essential to make you recall the idea for which they stand.

17. Take notes fast and at opportune times. Use the instructor's pauses, extended examples, repetitions, and lighter moments to record notes. You can't afford to be writing one thing when you need to be listening to another.

18. If the instructor tends to speak or to move from point to point too quickly, politely ask the instructor to slow down. You are probably the most courageous student of many who cannot keep up either.

19. To help speed your note-taking, try different pens until you find an instrument that glides smoothly and rapidly for you.

20. Occasionally glance back over the last few lines of notes you've taken, and rewrite any illegible letters, words, or symbols.

21. Make key words, important relationships, and conclusions stand out in your notes. Underline, highlight, box, or circle them, and/or rewrite/abbreviate them in the left margin.

22. Practice keeping your mind on the lecture. Try to understand the value of the content.

23. If you lose focus or listening-writing coordination and miss part of a lecture, leave a space, and ask a classmate, the TA, or the professor to help you fill in the blank. Tell whoever is willing to help you exactly what happened. You may even get some sympathy; it happens to everyone.

24. If, on the other hand, you come into the lecture late, leave it early, or spend part of it in private conversation or any other activity,

you deserve no sympathy nor back-up assistance. The University community regards such behavior as extremely discourteous. It is distracting and disruptive to both the instructor and your fellow classmates.

25. Postpone debating the instructor. If you fight new material, you won't learn. Note your disagreement and, if it persists, debate the instructor in private.

26. Separate from your lecture notes your own comments and reactions to the material. Write your thoughts in the margin or a corner of the page, perhaps with a box around them, or on a self-stick removable note.

27. Try not to evaluate the worth or validity of the material on the basis of the instructor's lecture style. The two are totally unrelated.

28. Review, edit, clarify, and elaborate your notes within 24 hours of the lecture, again a week later, and again a month later--even if for just a few minutes. When you review your notes, recite, extract, and rewrite the key concepts and relationships. With enough review, the knowledge will become yours forever.

29. When your attention or motivation sags, remember that this course is designed to serve some goal related to your longer-term educational, career, and/or personal aspirations. Flow with it for your own sake. Try to think of ways the material you're learning may be useful, or ask your instructor for insight.

LEADING
EFFECTIVE
DISCUSSIONS

In the last chapter we considered some of the weaknesses of the lengthy lecture and suggested breaking it up with intermittent activities that allow students to work with and test their understanding of the material. In all but very large classes, one of the easiest to administer yet most effective student-active options is the well-directed discussion. In smaller classes and seminars, discussion may best serve your course goals and be your primary classroom activity. Certainly a "discussion section" should remain true to its name and rely heavily on this format.

When might discussion be your technique of choice? Early studies on the efficacy of discussion have been replicated over decades with similar results: While lecture and discussion are roughly equal in helping students acquire factual and conceptual knowledge, discussion is superior in developing their problem solving skills. (See McKeachie et al., 1994 and Bonwell and Eison, 1991 for complete literature summaries.)

These skills apply not only to solving math problems but to all kinds of solution-oriented tasks, whether they call for one correct answer, one best answer, or many possible correct answers. Such tasks include designing a research project, explaining deviations from expected results, writing a computer program, solving a case study, evaluating one's own and others' positions on an issue, analyzing a piece of literature, and developing approaches to tackling real-world social, political, and environmental problems.

Discussion also surpasses the lecture in changing students' attitudes, helping them transfer knowledge to new situations, and motivating them to further learning. In addition, students retain material acquired in discussion longer than they do the same material learned from a lecture.

One final benefit of discussion for you as well as your class: Across disciplines, student ratings of instructors vary positively with the amount of time and encouragement an instructor gives to discussion (Cohen, 1981; Cashin, 1988).

So what exactly is a discussion? It is a productive exchange of viewpoints, a collective exploration of issues. To be productive and not degenerate into a free-association, free-for-all bull session, you as the instructor must chart its course and steer it in the right direction. It is your responsiblity to plan and control the content and conduct, to keep hot air from blowing it off course. But it is also your responsibility to go with the breezes occasionally, to keep it flexible and fluid. Your challenge is to strike

88

that delicate balance between structure and openness. Finding that balance helps you broaden participation and keep all hands on deck.

A Discussion Primer: Starting Out

Explaining the role of discussion. If you plan to make discussion an integral class activity, even if not a primary one, it is best to inform your students at the beginning of the term. Making an announcement about its role in your course will encourage students to take discussion more seriously. So will telling them your reasons for using discussion (e.g., how the research supports its effectiveness in developing problem solving skills). Follow up by explaining how class discussions will relate to other assignments such as papers, readings, and tests. It is wise to build quizzes and exams around both reading assignments and the discussions around them.

Grading on participation. You may or may not wish to include the quality and quantity of class participation in your final grading scheme. Doing so, however, will increase the likelihood of students coming to class prepared. If you do, you should make this very clear in your syllabus and your first-day presentation. You might even explain your conception of adequate quality and quantity.

Consider, too, the class level and size in deciding the weight to give participation. Freshmen may feel comfortable with 20% in a class of 20-25 but may find it unreasonably stressful in one of 45-50. More advanced students should be able to handle a slightly higher percentage even in a large class. An alternative is to have students vote on the percentage (give them options) and follow the majority rule.

Setting ground rules for participation. To help ensure that all students get involved in discussions, set the ground rules on the first day that everyone's participation is expected; no backbenchers allowed. Describe how you foresee the conduct of class discussions, and explain how you will call on students. You have several options for calling on them: 1) by random selection (e.g., shuffling and drawing index cards or simply finding students who haven't spoken recently); 2) in some predetermined order (e.g., according to seating, alphabetically, or by index card order); and 3) by raised hands.

The first method obviously ensures broad participation and may encourage preparation. But it can engender a stressful class environment. The second method, too, ensures broad participation and preparation, but it creates a stiff, recitation type of atmosphere. In addition, it raises the stress of the student next in line while encouraging others to tune out. Used alone, the raised-hand method keeps the class relaxed but does little to motivate preparation. Most important, participation is bound to be uneven, with a few verbal individuals monopolizing the floor and most students becoming passive wallflowers.

Too often, if you rely on voluntary participation alone, you will inadvertently wind up reinforcing social inequities. According to numerous gender and ethnic bias studies, female and minority students are unconsciously discriminated against in the discussion dynamic because of the dominant posturing of white male classmates (see Chapter 11).

For many reasons, then, you may want to combine methods in your policy for calling on students. For example, when the hands-raised method fails to generate broad enough participation, you might plan to shift to a variant of random selection--perhaps calling on students who have been silent for a while.

If you intend to ever use the random selection or predetermined order methods, another good ground rule to set is the "escape hatch." In other words, you will permit a student to pass on answering a question. It is demoralizing to the class, as well as counterproductive to the discussion, to badger, belittle, or otherwise put a student on the spot for not having a comment when you demand it. A student with nothing to say may simply have nothing new to contribute. While it's possible he isn't prepared, he may simply agree with other recent remarks, or may have no questions at the time, or may be having a bad day and not feel like talking. To cover these instances, inform your class that you will occasionally accept responses such as "I don't want to talk right now" or "Will you please call on me later?"

A final rule to set is a reassurance: "The only stupid question is the one you don't ask." Students are downright terrified by the prospect of looking stupid or foolish to you or their peers. They appreciate being told that you will welcome *all* questions and ensure that they are answered. A similar but modified rule should apply to all *answers* as well: You will welcome all contributions given with good intentions. But this *doesn't* mean that you won't correct faulty answers or allow other students to correct them.

By the same token, you should make it clear that excessive attempts to divert the purpose of the discussion towards a comedy act or to instigate an inappropriate debate will not be tolerated. Being explicit on these issues will help you maintain classroom control.

Creating the social environment. As Chapter 7 recommends, try to create a discussion-friendly setting. If at all possible, start spatially with arranging the chairs so that students can see one another. It isn't easy to talk to the back of a classmate's head.

Secondly, try to learn your students' names as quickly as possible, and use them regularly in class. More than this, it is important to get to know your students. You might have them fill out index cards to familiarize you with their hobbies, hometown, academic and outside interests, current beliefs about your subject, reasons for their taking the course, etc. Make individual or small group appointments with them early in the semester, and include casual conversation on the agenda.

Your knowledge of your students will help you pitch the course at the right level, as well as to develop a solid rapport with your class quickly. If your students are comfortable with you as a person, and you feel comfortable with them as well, your discussions will flow more evenly and honestly.

Help your students get to know each other, too. They will find it easier to speak out among "friends." So conduct social or subject-oriented ice-breakers on the first day (see Chapter 7). Try to get every student to say something that day. You might draw students out by directing questions to them individually, such as, "Jane, what interested you in this seminar?" or "Matt, what topics would you like to see addressed in this course?" Alternatively, you might invite them to expand on information they offered on their index card.

Finally, establish good eye contact and physical proximity with all of your students as equally as possible. A good rule of thumb is to maintain eye contact with one student (or, in a large class, a cluster of students) for at least three seconds. Your very look makes a student feel included. If your class sits in a circle or around a table, varying where you sit can help you equalize your eye contact and physical proximity. If you do not normally sit down in class, move about the classroom as much as you can.

Breaking the class into discussion groups. A time-saving way to guarantee broad participation, especially in larger classes, is to break the class into discussion groups. If you intend to do so only on occasions and/or as a brief warm-up to a general discussion, you may simply want to break the class into informal, *ad hoc* "buzz groups" based on seating proximity.

But if you'd like students to work on a project together for at least a few weeks of the semester, then long-term, "formal" groups are recommended. Such arrangements allow group members to get to know one another well enough to develop a sense of loyalty, group identity, and mutual respect; these go a long way towards improving performance. Stable groups also provide a context for confidential "peer group evaluations"--that is,

your having students grade one another on the quality and quantity of their group contributions. If you give them guidance on what criteria to evaluate, you should get a valid and reliable picture of each student's relative leadership, preparation, participation, work share, and cooperative skills. Then you can incorporate these peer assessments into the course grade, as little as 10% or as much as 25%.

If you are considering or planning to use groups in your course, you might refer to Chapter 18. It covers cooperative and team learning in much greater detail.

Improving Participation Through Skillful Discussion Management

Having covered the mechanics of setting up a discussion format, let us consider how to keep it going with optimal student involvement.

Your roles as instructor. First and foremost, you are the discussion *facilitator*. This may seem a trendy and hackneyed term, but it is a fitting one nonetheless. To faciliate a discussion means to make it easy for students to participate. Doing so can begin even before class. By arriving a little early and casually chatting with students as they arrive, you can loosen them up for dialogue. Facilitating also entails starting off the discussion and adding to it when necessary. But once the discussion takes off, it largely involves directing traffic (see section by that name). Still, at all times, you serve as *manager-on-call* to control the focus and structure of the exchange.

Depending upon the circumstances, you may briefly assume a wide variety of roles: *coach, moder-*

ator, *host/hostess, listener, ob-server, information provider, pre-senter, counselor, recorder, moni-tor, instigator, navigator, transla-tor, peacemaker,* and *summarizer.* During particularly animated or agitated student exchanges, you may even find yourself playing *referee!*

Motivating preparation. You can motivate your students to pre-pare for discussion by including the reading assignments on the topical agenda of the day they are due. Reading-focused discussions can be enriched by having students take notes on the readings, draft an-swers to study guide questions you've prepared, bring in their own written questions on the readings, or make journal entries about their responses to them. Then allow stu-dents to use these notes and ques-tions in the discussion. They will feel more confident and more will-ing to participate with a written point of reference in front of them. (If you want your students to write notes, study guide answers, or jour-nals on the readings, be sure to col-lect these regularly or periodically to ensure their keeping up.)

Presenting a road map. Be-fore or at the beginning of class, put an outline on the board or an overhead of the day's activities, ob-jectives, topics, or the process through which you will guide them. (A list of discussion questions may justify a handout.) In other words, lay out the territory for the class to cover. Not only will you *look* more organized, you will *be* more orga-nized, and so will the discussion. You will also encourage your stu-dents to take notes on the discus-sion and help them learn how to do it. It is a technique they find hard

to master.

To help students put the upcom-ing discussion into perspective, be-gin with a brief review of the last class period. But draw the high-lights out of the students by posing questions like "What are the major points we covered last time?" Let students refer to, and thus review, their notes.

Igniting the exchange. Sev-eral proven strategies can launch a discussion (McKeachie, 1986; Mc-Keachie et al., 1994). One is to start with a common experience, which you can provide with a video, film, demonstration, simulation, or role play. Another sometimes hot ignition switch is to stir up a con-troversy. You can set up a student debate in advance (see Chapter 17) or play devil's advocate yourself. As students can interpret your rep-resenting the devil as manipula-tive, untrustworthy, and occasion-ally confusing, it is crucial that you explain what you're doing in ad-vance. While you're assuming the role, you might even wear a hat or a sign with "Devil's Advocate" writ-ten prominently on it.

Of course, the most common way to stimulate a discussion is to ask the first in a series of questions you have planned in advance. As we rely on this strategy so exten-sively, and for good reason, the en-tire next chapter is devoted to ques-tioning techniques.

Waiting for responses to in-crease participation. No matter how you launch and direct a discus-sion, always allow sufficient time for students to respond--at least ten to 15 seconds, depending upon the difficulty of the challenge. While a few students may jump at the chance to say anything, even if it is incorrect, most need time--more time than we might expect--to think through and phrase a response they are willing to announce.

If the question is particularly difficult, lengthy, or involved, you might advise students and give them time to outline their answer first. Again, having a response written in front of them will enhance their confidence and courage. You may also get higher quality answers. This way, too, you can feel free to call on anyone, as all are equally prepared.

Watch for non-verbal cues of students' readiness to respond, especially changes in facial expression. Still, you might refrain from calling on anyone *until you see several raised hands or eager faces.* When you have many possible students from whom to select, you can spread the attention and participation opportunities across students who haven't spoken recently.

Encouraging non-participants. It is a good idea to monitor participation in every class, especially if it's a component of your students' grade. Then actively encourage it where it's lacking. If one side of the room seems too quiet, you can make it a point to say so, and direct a question exclusively to those in that area. If an individual is not contributing, use the same tactic, but be extra gentle; you want to avoid putting that person too much on the spot.

Another ice-breaker with quiet students is to call on them to read a passage of text, a question, or a problem aloud. This technique is particularly effective where a narrative or play is involved, but it can be useful in many contexts. You might then follow up by asking the student to comment on the reading.

Persistent non-participation may be a symptom of a deeper problem that calls for a private approach. It is a good idea to have the student see you in your office, and tactfully ask why he has been so quiet in class. Accept any answer as legitimate, then encourage him to become involved. One way to help a student overcome fear is to give him one or more discussion questions in advance of the next class and let him rehearse his answer with you.

Dealing with dead silence. When no one says a word after a generous wait time, you might break the silence and tension with a touch of humor: "Hello, is anybody out there?" But you should definitely find out the reason for the silence. Perhaps your question was ambiguous, or students didn't understand it, or they misunderstood it. For your own benefit, ask them to identify the specific points of contention.

Responding to student responses. Give approval, verbal or non-verbal, to *all* student contributions, but do so with discretion and discrimination. Students want to know how correct and complete their own and their classmates' answers are. But they also want your judgment to be delivered in a diplomatic, encouraging way.

Approval can take the form of a nod, an interested or accepting facial expression, the simple act of recording the response on the board, or appropriate verbal feedback. Here are some verbal response options you may wish to use:

When the answer is correct,

praise according to what it de-serves.

When the answer is correct but only one of several correct possibilities, ask another student to extend or add to it. Or frame a question that is an extension of the answer. Avoid premature closure.

When the answer is incomplete, follow up with a question that directs the student to include more--e.g., "How might you modify your answer if you took into account the _____ aspect?"

When the answer is unclear, try to rephrase it, then ask the student if this is what she means.

When the answer is seemingly wrong, follow up with one or more gently delivered Socratic questions designed to lead the student to discover his error. For example: "Yes, but if you come to that conclusion, don't you also have to assume...?" (See Chapter 13, the section on the Socratic method.)

When the answer is incomplete, unclear, or seemingly wrong, invite the student to explain, clarify, or elaborate on it. Or ask other students to comment on or evaluate it. Avoid identifying and correcting errors yourself for as long as possible.

Directing traffic. As some of the above response options suggest, sometimes you best facilitate by doing and saying very little, acting only as the resource of last resort. You should step in only if no student supplies the needed clarification, correction, or knowledge or if the discussion strays off track. In fact, the most successful facilitator's primary task is to direct traffic--that is, signaling students to react to other students' contribu-tions.

In addition to inviting students to comment on and extend each others' answers, ask them to address their comments to the class-mate to whom they are responding, to actually look at that person and address him by name. For the first few weeks, name tags or placards may be essential. The goal is to get the spotlight off you and on the students.

Don't forget to invite your students to help *you* out as well. When you sense that you aren't explaining a point or answering a question effectively, ask them to give their version. Students speak one another's language.

Transitioning and wrapping up. Before moving the discussion on to the next topic, be sure the current one is settled. You might ask if anyone has something to add or qualify. If no one does, ask a student to summarize the main points made during the discussion of the topic. *Then* move on, making a logical transition to the next topic.

Watch the clock and try to re-serve time at the end of class to wrap up and summarize the discussion. Again, ask one or more students to give the highlights, and add as necessary. A review at the end encourages students to check their notes and fill in important omissions. It also keeps them on common ground.

An alternative is to close on a classroom assessment technique (see Chapter 26). Probably the most popular and easiest to administer is the one-minute paper. Ask the students to take out a piece of paper and write down the one, two, or three major things they learned during the class and any questions that remain. Collect their responses, but allow them to remain anonymous. Then you can review them with an eye toward correcting misconceptions and addressing their questions at the beginning of the next class.

Discussion appeals most strongly to the auditory learning style (see Chapter 12), and even discussion can get monotonous after a while. So consider varying your participatory formats to better serve other learning styles, as well as to add spice to life. The various student-active, experiential, and cooperative learning formats described in Chapters 17 and 18 offer stimulating alternatives to the all-class discussion. These include brainstorming, debate, change-your-mind debate, the press conference, the symposium, the panel discussion, role playing, simulations, field and service work, and various small- group activities.

Of course, engaging questions and sound questioning techniques can keep the discussion format lively and challenging for weeks on end. They can also inform your quizzes and exams so you can better assess the level of thinking you're trying to teach. So let us turn now to crafting questions.

Questioning Techniques for Discussion and Assessment

Questioning is a central teaching skill and has been for millennia. Socrates honed it to such a fine art that an entire method of questioning is attributed to him. The college teaching literature offers several schema for classifying and organizing questions, the major ones of which will be summarized here.

Sound questioning techniques can enhance instruction in four ways:

1) Questions launch and carry discussion, one of the most commonly used student-active teaching techniques (see Chapter 15).

2) They stimulate the exploratory, critical thinking on which the discovery method, including Socratic questioning, is based (see Chapter 13).

3) When used for classroom assessment, our questions yield answers that help us gauge what students are learning and whether to review a topic or to proceed to the next (see Chapter 26).

4) Questions are the means by which we evaluate and grade our students' learning; the better our questions reflect what we've been teaching, the fairer and more useful our testing and evaluation procedures (see Chapters 27 and 28).

Questioning schema and techniques fall into two major categories: those that suggest leading students through a more or less orderly *process* of inquiry and those that classify questions into more or less useful *types*. This chapter couches the material in the contexts of discussion and discovery, but later chapters will return to these schema and techniques in assessment contexts.

Questioning as a Process of Inquiry

The Socratic method. Described in Chapter 13, the Socratic is perhaps the most spontaneous questioning technique. You may begin with a planned question to open a dialogue on a given topic, but you shape your succeeding questions in response to the answers the students give. Of course, with experience, you may be able to anticipate the blind alleys and misdirections your students will take on specific topics and develop a general discussion plan.

Most instructors don't feel comfortable with such a spontaneous, unstructured format for an entire discussion period. Students don't either; they have a hard enough time taking notes on the most structured discussion.

"Working backwards from objectives." A second strategy, one that has gained the status of a "conventional wisdom," is to work backwards from objectives. It involves advance planning. First, jot down your objectives for the day: the one, two, or three points you want your students to understand by the end of class. Then, for each point, develop the key question that the point will answer. (This step resembles a game of "Jeopardy.") Finally, for each key question, develop another two or three questions that logically proceed and will prepare students for the key question. In other words, work backwards from the key points you want your students to understand through the questions that will lead them to that understanding. (The next section gives pointers on how to write *good* questions for stimulating a lively discussion.)

When class begins, launch the discussion with one of the last questions you framed. You can lend structure to the discussion by writing all the questions (key ones last) on the board or an overhead or by handing out copies of them (preferably with note-taking space below each question). Still, unless you frame too many questions, you can afford to be flexible. You can allow the discussion to wander a bit, then easily redirect it back to your list of questions.

Bloom's taxonomy of questions. A third approach is to follow Bloom's (1956) taxonomy of questions, guiding your students up through his hierarchy of cognitive levels, where *knowledge* (recitation) represents the lowest thinking level and *evaluation* the highest. This schema first appeared in Chapter 3, where it was applied to developing course objectives. The lists of verbs associated with each cognitive operation are just as useful here for framing questions.

To structure a discussion as a process of inquiry, you might start off with *knowledge* questions on the highlights of the last lecture or reading assignment. This factual recall exercise serves as a mental warm-up for the students and gives those who did not attend the lecture or did not do the reading a chance to pick up a few major points and at least to follow if not participate later. Avoid questions that call for one- or two-word answers, however; aim for multi-sentence responses.

Fair warning: Do not spend more than several minutes on this level. The boredom potential aside, students will not answer many recitation questions because they fear their classmates seeing them as apple polishers--"bailing you out," so to speak. More important, whatever our field, our educational mission is to develop more sophisticated critical thinking in our students.

Therefore, rapidly move the discussion up the hierarchy through *comprehension*, so you can find out whether your students understand the material and can put it in their own words. If they understand it, they should be able to answer *application* questions and use the material to solve problems, devise examples, or correctly classify your examples. If they can do this, they should be ready to progress to *analysis* of the material: pulling apart its elements to draw comparisons and contrasts; identifying assumptions, causes, effects, and implications; and reasoning through explanations and arguments.

Once students have found their

way *through* material, they are prepared to step *outside* of its confines and attempt *synthesis*. This type of question calls for integrating elements of the material in new and creative ways, composing or designing something new with them or combining elements from two different sources. When students can synthesize material, they have mastered it well enough to address *evaluation* questions. They now can make informed judgments about its strengths and shortcomings, its costs and benefits, its ethical, esthetic, or practical merit.

Bloom's taxonomy helps rein in students from leaping into issues they aren't yet prepared to tackle. Often students are all too eager to jump to judging material without thoroughly understanding it first. In addition, if you teach the taxomony to your students, they acquire a whole new metacognition on thinking processes and levels. If you label the level of your questions, you maximize your chances of obtaining the level of answers you are seeking. Students also quickly learn to classify and better frame their own questions.

The taxonomy should be used flexibly, however. Some discussion tasks, such as debriefing a case (see Chapter 19), may call for an inextricable combination of application, analysis, and synthesis. Moreover, a comprehension question in one course may be an analysis issue in another. How any question is classified depends on what the students are given as "knowledge" in lectures and readings.

Types of Well Constructed Questions

There is more to constructing questions than turning around a couple of words in a sentence and adding a question mark. Well-crafted ones take thought and creativity and in turn require the same of students. They all have one feature in common: They have *multiple respectable answers*. Therefore, they encourage broad participation and in-depth treatment.

Often, too, multiple-answer questions spark debate. Welcome the conflict and let students argue it out. Before letting the issue rest, ask for possible resolutions and/or analyses of the conflict if they don't evolve on their own.

McKeachie's categories. McKeachie et al. (1994) suggests three types of fruitful, challenging questions. *Comparative* questions ask students to compare and contrast different theories, research studies, literary works, etc. Indirectly, they help students identify the important dimensions for comparison.

Connective questions challenge students to link facts, concepts, relationships, authors, theories, etc. that are not explicitly integrated in assigned materials and might not appear related. These questions are particularly useful in cross-disciplinary courses. They can also ask students to draw and reflect on their personal experiences, connecting these to theories and research findings. When students realize these links, the material becomes more meaningful to them.

Finally, *critical* questions invite students to examine the validity of a particular argument, research claim, or interpretation. If the class has trouble getting started, you can initiate the discussion by presenting an equally plausible alternative argument. This type of question instills in students an appreciation for careful, active reading. When you ask the class to comment on what a student has just said, you are also posing a critical question. Used in this context, it fosters good listening skills.

These three types bear resemblances to Bloom's analysis, synthesis, and evaluation questions. But McKeachie does not order them as a process. Use the typology you find most straightforward.

Andrews' "high mileage" types. Andrews not only developed categories of questions but also conducted classroom research to identify their relative "mileage"--that is, the average number of student responses each type evokes (Gale and Andrews, 1989). Using his results, we can learn how to ensure our discussions are lively. Here are his top mileage types, all of which can be pitched at high cognitive levels:

Brainstorm questions, found to yield 4.3 student responses per question, invite students to generate many conceivable ideas on a topic or many possible solutions to a problem. For example: "What issues does Hamlet question in the play?" "What trends starting in the 1960s may have negatively impacted American public education?" "How might the public be made to care about ecological imbalances?"

Typically the instructor, acting as facilitator, records all responses on the board, an overhead, or a flip chart. Only after all brains stop storming do the students begin editing, combining, eliminating, grouping, etc. It is best to let them sort and evaluate options using criteria they generate themselves.

Focal questions elicit an even higher 4.9 responses per question. They ask students to choose a viewpoint or position from several possible ones and to support their choice with reasoning and evidence. Students may develop and defend their own opinions, adopt those of a particular author, or assume a devil's advocate stance. For example: "Do you think that Marx's theory of capitalism is still relevant in today's post-industrial societies?" "To what extent is Ivan Illich a victim of his own decisions or of society?" "Is the society in *Brave New World* a utopia, a nightmare of moral degeneration, or something between the two?"

A variation on a focal question is for you to play devil's advocate on an issue. Alternatively, you can make a contentious, controversial statement and invite your students to react against it. But as recommended in Chapter 15, be sure to let your class know exactly what you are doing.

Playground questions hold the mileage record with 5.1 responses per question. They challenge students to select or develop their own themes and concepts for exploring, interpreting, and analyzing a piece of material. For example, "What do you think the author is saying in this particular passage?" "What underlying assumptions about human nature must this theorist have?" "What might happen if (present a counterfactual)?" When posing such open-ended questions, however, be aware that this type of question tends to veer the discussion into other topics.

Types of Poorly Constructed Questions

It is difficult to fully appreciate highly effective discussion questions without examining the less effective types as well. Andrews' categories and classroom research provide valuable insight and information on this latter kind, too. These questions tend not to encourage broad participation and/or higher-order thinking.

Analytic convergent questions may elicit complex, analytical thought, but they have only one correct answer. So they make students edgy and cut the discussion short as soon as someone gives the right answer. It is little wonder that they evoke only 2.0 answers per question. Typically 1.0 of the attempts isn't exactly that right answer. Analytic convergent questions are best used sparingly as knowledge and comprehension warm-ups. At least they get students talking.

Programmed-answer questions are only *implicitly* closed-ended. Although they may have more than one appropriate answer, the instructor (perhaps unconsciously) conveys having only one specific answer in mind. Students regard this type of question as an unwelcomed challenge to read the instructor's mind. Some even consider it manipulative and closed-minded.

Rhetorical questions are those with an obvious answer, usually too obvious for students to take seriously. At best, they inspire a few nods and agreeing facial expressions. While this type of question has its place in a motivating or persuasive speech, it is mainly a momentary time-filler in teaching.

Quiz show questions have a one- or two-word correct answer-- e.g., a name, a date, a title--but they only pay off on television. Usually they elicit only factual recall, and they serve poorly as warm-up questions for genuine discussion. Their average mileage is 1.5 responses per question, suggesting that the first "contestant" guesses wrong about half the time.

Dead-end questions are even less stimulating; they're quiz show questions with a yes-or- no answer. Students simply place their bets. These questions can easily be transformed into useful types in one of two ways. First, you can often change them into true-false items, having students rephrase false statements to make them true. Better yet, restructure them into relational questions by beginning them with a why or a how. With thought now required, students are more likely to participate.

Fuzzy questions are too vague and unfocused for students to know how to approach them. They may be phrased unclearly, such as "Who else knows what else falls into this category?" Or they may be too global, like "What should we do about the breakdown of the family?" Students loathe taking the risk required to begin to answer such a grand question. Other common fuzzy questions represent a well-meaning attempts to help: "Does everyone understand this?" and "Any questions?" You may occasionally get an honest response, but all too often you find out later that not everyone *did* understand and quite a few students *must* have had questions. It is usually better to use classroom assessment techniques (see Chapter 26) to answer our concerns.

Chameleon and *shotgun* questions are both a series of weakly related questions "fired off" one after the other in hopes that one will hit with the students. Chameleons change their topical focus through the series until the last one barely resembles the first one, leaving students not knowing which one to try answering. Shotgun questions, on the other hand, may all go off in the same general direction, but they make the instructor look like a "bad shot"--either desperate for a response or confused about the issues. Students in turn become confused and disoriented in the murk of the inquisition, not knowing which in the series to dodge and which to address. The average series yields only 2.3 responses.

Put-down and *ego-stroking* questions are two sides of the same bad attitude. The former type of question implies that students ought to know the answer and/or shouldn't have any more questions--e.g., "Now that I have explained this topic completely and thoroughly, are there any more questions?" The latter type assumes the superiority of the instructor to the discouragement of the students' individuality. A request to "rephrase the answer the way I would say it" douses students' creativity, self-expression, and often their motivation to answer at all.

Handling Problematic Types of Student Questions

Generally you welcome your students' questions as warmly as you welcome their informed responses to yours. You hope to clarify their misconceptions and encourage their curiosity and exploration. But just as students don't respond well to certain types of instructor questions, instructors find some types of student questions annoying, frustrating, and even aggravating. Responding to them "appropriately" is always a challenge. Some of the strategies recommended below are drawn from Watkins (1982).

Questions you've already answered. A student asks you about the procedure for doing an assignment that you've already explained. No doubt you think that you have more than adequately described your expectations and requirements, and you feel justified in responding with a put-down ("Where were you when I gave the assignment?"). But to maintain a good rapport with all your students, you're best off holding back and just answering the question civilly. To minimize repeating yourself, refer that student to the written instructions you've provided and ask exactly which aspect of the assignment needs clarification.

Wheedling questions. Occasionally students try to wheedle answers out of you to avoid having to work out the answer for themselves. In class, you can invite other students to suggest leads and possibly get a discussion going. But one-on-one, the best way to avoid giving in is to answer each of the student's questions with another question that should help him think through the answer. In fact, this occasion provides the perfect opportunity to use the Socratic method (see Chapter 13). A student who is asking questions solely to pry answers out of you will soon tire of your questions and go away.

Argumentative questions. A student who tries to entrap you in an argument just for the sake of arguing usually wants attention. This touchy situation will repeat itself regularly if you allow it, so the first or second occurrence calls for firm, quick, and decisive action. Just acknowledge the student's input and quickly move on. To lower oneself to the bait jeopardizes your credibility with the class. If another incident occurs, ask the student to "bring the issue up later" in your office. After class, make an appointment and inform the student that you do not appreciate such disruptive behavior in your classroom.

Loaded questions. The rare nefarious student may design a question just to embarrass you and put you on the defensive. Like the argumentative student, this type is also probably seeking attention and respect from their peers. You can often turn the loaded question back on the student asking it:

Student: You're not really saying...?

Instructor: What I'm saying is....Now, what is your perspective on this topic?

Hostile questions and complaints. When hostility arises, it is usually over a grade. Your objective is to neutralize the emotion and delay dealing with the issue until the student calms down and you can arrange a private meeting. It is a good idea to schedule an appointment in your office at least a day or two later. Then open with a positive, empathetic statement: "I understand your frustration. Let's take a look at your paper and talk about the grading." Try to agree with the student wherever possible. If necessary, disassociate the grade of the paper from the student's worth as a person. Even if you

can't turn the student's opinion around, you can reduce both your anxiety levels by showing yourself to be an ally (at least partially).

It is extremely rare that an instructor feels physically threatened by a hostile student, and it invariably happens when others are not around. While verbal hostility calls for a private approach, the physical version requires quite the opposite: Try to move yourself and the student into as public a place as possible, even if just the hallway.

Rambling questions. A long-winded student seems to meander endlessly trying to frame a question, boring and frustrating not only you but the rest of the class as well. You can take control by seizing the chance to interrupt the student and paraphrase whatever meaning you can salvage. Then supply an answer and move along. Alternatively, you can defer answering it for the sake of "saving class time" by advising the student to raise it during your office hours.

Questions you can't answer. Even experienced instructors can forget--and new ones find it hard to believe--that students do not expect us to be walking encyclopedias. We know so much more than they do and rank so high in their eyes that we can afford to feel completely secure with all our cognitive limitations.

So if you happen not to have an answer to a student's question at your fingertips, just say so. It is not worth the risk of trying to pull the wool over your students' eyes by bluffing your way through an answer. It shows courage and professionalism to say that you don't know the answer but will make the effort to find it out. Then make good on your promise. If you're in class, you might ask if another student knows the answer.

Making the Most of Student Questions

The person posing the discussion questions need not always be the instructor. If you model good questioning techniques and spend a little time teaching your favorite questioning schema, you can have your students develop discussion (and even test) questions as a homework assignment. You can use the best ones in class (or in an exam) and even grade them if you choose. The quality of these questions also tells you how diligently your students are doing their reading.

The next chapter offers other teaching formats that put the spotlight and the responsibility for learning on students.

FROM STUDENT-ACTIVE TO EXPERIENTIAL TEACHING FORMATS

This chapter covers a potpourri of teaching formats that allow students to "discover" knowledge on their own. These formats rank even higher than discussion on a continuum of student involvement, ranging from moderately student-involving to extremely high. We start with the former and move to the more experiential.

Research documents that more discovery-oriented and student-active teaching methods ensure higher student motivation, more learning at higher cognitive levels, greater appreciation of the material's utility, and longer retention of the knowledge. They also meet a wider range of instructional goals than do more passive methods (see Chapters 3 and 13).

Match-up Exercises

Give each student a piece of information that requires a second (or third) piece of information to make complete sense, and have students walk about the room to find the classmate(s) with the complementary information. Then ask the resulting pairs (or triads) to explain to the rest of the class how their information matches. For example, to help students learn how to read topographical maps in geology, have them match maps with cross-sectional views of the same terrain. In math, have them match word problems with equational set-ups. In the lab or social sciences, have them match theory with hypothesis, or hypothesis with appropriate research design and methodology.

Student Presentation Formats

These formats add pizzazz to student presentations. In each case, you assign or have students select the topic, research area, position, role, school of thought, etc. that they will represent. Usually, such formats require advance research, some even a paper. But you can set up some of them spontaneously in a well prepared class. Before you "turn students lose," so to speak, to investigate, represent, and/or question different sides of a controversy, be sure they understand rhetorical structure, the basic rules of evidence, and logical fallacies.

Debate. Every field has topics amenable to a two-sided, fact-based argument. The format need not be any more complex than statements of the affirmative and the negative, plus rebuttals, each with a strict time limit. It is best to assign sides to student pairs or triads.

A variation that involves the entire class is a *change-your-mind debate.* You designate different sides of the classroom as "for the affirmative" or "for the negative," with the middle as "uncertain/ undecided/neutral." Before the debate, students sit in the area representing their current position and change their seating location during the debate as their opinions sway. After the debate, lead a debriefing discussion focusing on the opinion changers ("What changed your mind?") and the undecided students, who are likely to provide the most objective analysis of both the debate and the issue at hand.

"Expert" individuals or teams. Designate individual students, pairs, or triads to be the course experts on a certain topic, geographical area, body of theory or research, etc. Following your bibliographic leads, students do outside readings and turn in weekly, annotated reading lists on their area of expertise. Regularly query the "experts" in class, asking for informational updates or about the relevance of their area to the day's discussion.

Dunn (1992) applied this format very effectively in his World Affairs course, where he paired off students as "briefing teams" charged with keeping up on the current affairs of nine world regions. On some days he played the role of a political leader dependent upon his students' briefings, especially to lighten the mood when he felt the need to cajole his class into working harder.

Panel discussion. Four or five students briefly present different points of view on a topic, either their own or one they are representing. Panel members can even play different noted scholars (e.g.,

Freud, Jung, Adler, Skinner, and Rogers in a psychology course). Then the class addresses thoughtful questions and challenges, preferably prepared in advance, to various panel members.

Press conference. You or a student assume the focal role, posing as a noted scholar, a leader in some realm, or a representative of a particular position or school of thought, while the rest of the class plays investigative reporters--each student with an assigned audience/readership (e.g., local residents, residents of another area or country, a special interest group, a specific company or other organization, etc.). These "reporting" students ask probing, challenging questions of the focal person.

Two planning caveats are in order. First, the focal role should represent a broad-ranging, controversial decision or stance. Finding such a role is easy in political science, but in other fields it requires more creative thought. In psychology or sociology, for example, you might set up a scenario of a criminologist or criminal psychologist whose testimony leads to the probation of a violent convict. The focal role may be the testifying expert or the psychologist or sociologist whose theory justified the probation. In economics, the focal role may represent an uncertain intervention strategy. In the sciences and medical fields, it may stand for a controversial environmental or public health position--perhaps on the ozone layer, endangered species preservation, prescription drug restrictions, or the like.

Secondly, in addition to assigning audiences/readerships to the students playing reporters, you should require them to research and write out their questions and challenges in advance. Having them then write a mock article incorporating the press conference is an optional follow-up assignment.

Symposium. Individual students or student teams present their independently conducted, outside research or papers that express their own ideas. The rest of the class asks questions and gives constructive criticism, especially useful if students can revise their work. Additionally, for each class period, you may assign one or two discussants to interrelate and critique the research/papers. Discussants should have at least a day or two to review the symposium products in advance.

Role Playing

You assign students roles in a true-to-life, problematic social or interpersonal situation that they act out, improvising the script. When one player is not supposed to know the full story about another player's intentions, problem, or goals, you should provide written descriptions for each role. You also must decide what information to give to the rest of the class. Following the enactment is a class discussion of how the players felt at crucial junctures and what behaviorial patterns the other students observed.

This technique is used successfully in therapy as well as in instruction, especially in the humanities and social sciences. While it relies on make-believe scenarios in the classroom, students learn experientially by identifying with the roles they play and observe. You may also play a role, especially when you want to model certain

behaviors (e.g., how to conduct a family therapy session, how to negotiate a contract, how to mediate conflict).

In structuring an original role play, the only rule is to incorporate conflict among the roles and some need for the players to reach a resolution (Halpern, 1994). Here are some applications to inspire your own ideas (Nilson, 1990):

- Professional (doctor, lawyer, pastor, etc.) and client disagree over an approach to the client's problem.
- Executive promises union negotiator (or up-start worker) a major promotion for keeping quiet.
- Worker representatives try to convince executives not to close an unprofitable plant.
- Human resources executive must make a tough hiring decision among various male, female, minority, and non-minority candidates with different job qualifications and personalities.
- Politician experiences role conflict between partisan and administrative roles or between ideological stance and the need for campaign funds.
- Couple or family argues over money, (un)employment, discipline, authority, autonomy, communication, moving, domestic violence, alcohol or drug use, etc. This scenario may include a social worker's, physician's, or therapist's role.

If you teach a foreign language, feel free to make a role play of any situation your students may encounter while traveling. While they may not learn much through empathy, they will get useful, conversational practice in the target language. If you teach literature, consider casting students in the roles of the characters and letting them play out a hypothetical scene that extends the piece of literature.

Simulations and Games

With computer technology imitating life, two distinct types of simulations are available. The new computerized type is on tutorials programs (CAI) and multimedia CD-ROM discs (see Chapter 21). One software package on hydraulics, for instance, allows students to solve complex canalization problems by varying the delivery, inflow, outflow, and power of various pumps. In electrical engineering, they can manipulate the performance of an electrical network and study overloading, breaks, and the like. Medical software simulates diagnostic situations, presenting students with a hypothetical patient's symptoms and even a patient's answers to questions the students ask--all through interactive technology (Pregent, 1994).

The traditional type of simulation is a human enactment of a hypothetical social situation that, while not necessarily realistic, does abstract key elements from reality (Mitchell, 1982). Only a thin, grey line distinguishes it from role playing. Similations usually cast the entire class in roles and run longer, sometimes for many hours. In addition, they portray grander, more macro situations, which usually can't be re-enacted in real time or in realistic detail.

Human simulations developed a strong faculty and student following through the 1970s and the early 1980s. So did academic games, variants that are exclusively competitive and somewhat more abstract (they rely on boards, cards, dice, etc.) At the time, they were the most student-involving instructional techniques that were widely available. They were not easy for instructors to develop themselves, however; simulations of societies, formal organizations, markets, cultures, world politics, and other grand realms are extremely complex and require an array of supporting materials. So an extensive market of hundreds of simulations and games sprung up.

To this day, few other formats can bring material alive in the classroom as effectively. They allow students to "live out" the hypotheses and implications of theories, giving them intense emotional, cognitive, and behavioral experiences that they will otherwise never have. Therefore, simulations and games still have their place in instruction.

Star Power, Bafa Bafa, and Simsoc are classics in psychology, history, anthropology, sociology, and political science. The Prisoner's Dilemma is an excellent social science "frame game," that is, one that can be played with different scenarios and pay-off rules to illustrate different points. Hyman (1978, 1981) developed several variations.

More recently, Karraker (1993) presented a mock trial frame simulation with suggested real cases on which to base it. Depending upon the case you choose, your students can conduct a trial addressing issues like environmental protection, industrial safety, medical technology, religious practices, securities markets, affirmative action, community development, or individual rights. Thus the simulation has cross-disciplinary applications.

To find out about simulations and games in your subject areas, see your own field's teaching journals and the following journals (Mitchell, 1982):

Simulations/Games for Learning: The Journal of the Society for Academic Gaming and Simulation in Education and Training (SAGSET) (contains reviews)

Simages (contains reviews)

Simulations and Games: An International Journal of Theory, Design, and Research

Simgames: The Canadian Journal of Simulation and Gaming

Journal of Experiential Learning and Simulation

Problem-Based Learning (PBL)

Seemingly a cross between a role play and a simulation, this relatively new method is more experiential than either. You assign large-scale problems to teams of five to eight students to solve. The problems should be realistic ones like those that students are likely to encounter in the career for which they are studying--problems in administrative communication, poor organizational morale, unfavorable public relations, a moral dilemma, a challenging policy implementation, or an undefined problem to be discovered during the PBL project.

The students play professionals, often members of a committee, with one assuming the role of project leader, another facilitator, another recorder, and the rest, team members. To tackle the problem, they follow a systematic series of procedures (Bridges, 1992; Pregent, 1994, pp. 86-87):

1) Review the problem as a group and clarify the meaning of terms they do not understand.
2) Analyze and formulate the problem. (You provide guidance.)
3) Identify the knowledge they need to acquire to solve the problem.
4) Classify this knowledge.
5) Establish objectives for outside research. (You may give references.)
6) Divide the work.
7) Conduct the assigned research individually by agreed-upon deadlines.
8) Continue to meet, share research findings, and conduct additional research as needed.
9) Merge all useful research findings into a solution in a finished product.

It is your responsibility, of course, to teach your students these procedures and to monitor their first time through them. But the teams should work as independently as possible. Each devises its own internal organization and decision-making rules for evaluating alternative formulations of and solutions to its assigned problem. Members not only draw from course materials but also conduct outside library and field research. The solution takes the form of a lengthy memo, report, budget, plan of action, or oral presentation before a hypothetical administrative or executive body.

Pedagogically, PBL has impeccable credentials. It activates prior knowledge, imparts new knowledge in the context in which it will later be applied, and builds in enough redundancy to ensure the knowledge is well understood and retained (Bridges, 1992). It is based on the well-tested principle of having students learn by doing, and even the simplest projects have them do a variety of things: lead, facilitate, record, compromise, cooperate, schedule, conduct meetings, discuss, prioritize, organize, plan, research, apply, integrate, evaluate, make decisions, persuade, negotiate, and resolve conflict. In fact, you decide and determine what they will learn to do in your project designs. To supplement the basic repertoire of activities, you can incorporate the need for additional role plays and mini-simulations, such as conferences, interviews, field observations, in-basket exercises, and progress presentations.

The realism of problem-based learning is grounded not only in the problems, the roles, and the activities, but also in the time factor. Each project proceeds in real time. Solving one problem can entail weeks of lengthy meetings, inside and out of class. In fact, a substantial problem can absorb most of a term's class time. But you can design and pose problems that take only a couple of weeks to solve.

This description of PBL couches the method in organizational or administrative subject matter. In fact, one of the finest sources on using it is Bridges (1992), who gives detailed accounts of educational administration projects. But PBL is applicable in any field where people work in teams to solve a problem, such as organizational studies, business administration, management, engineering, even the sciences. Medical schools started using it widely in the 1980s (Kaufmann, 1985; Kaufmann et al., 1989; Jonas et al., 1989), and law schools have used a variant, moot court, for decades.

Service Learning (SL): The Real Thing

Nothing teaches experientially like direct experience. If you want students to understand the characters in a piece of modern literature, let them talk with the real human counterparts. If you want them to comprehend the dynamics of inequality, let them work with the poor and the homeless. If you want them to appreciate the problems of another country, let them help the emigres and refugees. If you want them to understand prisoners, children, whomever, let them spend productive time with them.

Service learning is a method by which students acquire knowledge while working in volunteer, community service. The current generation of college students is distinguished by its service orientation, which may explain service learning's growing popularity. But it also raises ethical questions: Should the service be for charity or for social change? Should students be required to give service, even if their current politics and morals don't warrant it? What about the potential liability risks if a student is injured in service?

According to SL proponents, instructors, and "graduates," service learning is almost uniformly a positive, life-changing experience for students--the kind they never forget. As with problem-based learning, it imparts new knowledge not just in the abstract but in context--with service learning, in the real-world context in which the phenomenon occurs. If you are interested in incorporating SL in a course, peruse Kendall et al. (1990) for inspiration, exemplars, and instructional advice.

COOPERATIVE LEARNING

"The real challenge in college teaching is not covering the material for the students; it's uncovering the material with the students."

- Karl Smith, 1994

Every class conveys two lessons: one in the content and another in the teaching method. Student-active techniques send the message that with expert guidance, learners can actively discover, analyze, and use knowledge on their own. With this participatory "empowerment", students come to understand that they must assume greater responsibility for their own learning.

One particularly powerful student-active method is cooperative learning, defined as "a structured, systematic instructional strategy in which small groups of students work together towards a common goal" (Cooper et al., 1993). The lesson it conveys is that when people work together, they can accomplish much more than they can as individuals working apart--that is, two heads are better than one, three heads are better than two, and for some tasks, four or five heads are best.

The Case for Cooperative Learning

While cooperative learning is not that new a concept, the educational world has been slow to pick up on its well- researched benefits and applications. According to Johnson et al. (1991), nearly 600 studies have been published in the past 90 years comparing the effectiveness of cooperative, competitive, and individual approaches to teaching. Many of these studies found overwhelming support for cooperative learning as the best approach, and even those that didn't could not identify any detrimental effects to using it. Johnson et al. conclude that it just takes time to change deeply ingrained paradigms, much as it took over 200 years for the British Navy to adopt the simple but proven citrus cure for rickets.

In general, the research on cooperative learning has focused on three fundamental dimensions: achievement/productivity (i.e., learning), positive interpersonal relationships, and psychological health. Cooperation produces positive results on all of them (Johnson et al., 1991). Astin (1993) studied the effects of 192 environmental factors on various educational outcomes of 27,064 students at 309 institutions. His results indicate that the top two influences on academic success and satisfaction are interaction among students and interaction between faculty and students, each a key component in cooperative learning strategies. In fact, both factors ranked significantly higher than curriculum and content variables. Light (1990, 1992) reported similar results in the Har-

110

vard Assessment Seminars.

Johnson and Johnson (1989) surveyed 193 studies comparing the effects of cooperative and traditional techniques on student productivity/learning. More than half the literature reported cooperative learning to have a stronger impact, while only ten percent found individualistic methods more powerful. In addition, cooperation enhanced interpersonal attraction in 60 percent of the studied cases, while competition did so in only three percent. A similar literature survey by Cooper et al. (1993) concluded that cooperative learning is more effective than traditional methods in improving critical thinking, self-esteem, racial/ethnic relations, and prosocial behavior.

The superiority of cooperative learning seems to hold at all levels and across student backgrounds. Johnson et al. (1981) reported that cooperation increases academic achievement more strongly than does competition from elementary school through adult education. Frierson (1986) documented that minority nursing students who studied cooperatively for their board exams performed significantly better than those who studied alone. After instituting cooperative, out-of-class enrichment programs for calculus students at-risk at UC Berkeley, Treisman (1986) found that black students in the program received course grades over one letter grade higher than their non-cooperative counterparts.

However, cooperative learning should not necessarily supplant lecture, discussion, and other more traditional formats and methods. Not all learning activities have as their goal to improve critical thinking, problem solving skills, social relations, and self-esteem. More-

over, the research cited above indicates that cooperative learning need not be used all the time to have positive effects on student achievement.

It may be helpful, then, to consider cooperative learning a *supplementary* technique (Millis, 1990) and a *format* for various classroom activities. As a *supplement*, it can serve as a student-active break between segments of a lecture (see Chapter 14) or a jump-start for class discussion (see Chapters 15 and 16). As a *format*, it is useful for social and subject-matter icebreakers (see Chapter 7), experiential learning activities (see Chapter 17), case debriefing (see Chapter 19), foreign language proficiency exercises (see Chapter 23), problem solving exercises (see Chapters 24 and 25), classroom assessment techniques (see Chapter 26), and help and review sessions (see Chapter 28).

Changing Methods, Changing Roles

Introducing greater cooperation in the classroom requires role shifts for both students and instructors (MacGregor, 1990; Johnson et al., 1991; Rhem, 1992). Students must move:

- from passive listeners and notetakers to active problem solvers, discoverers, contributors, and transformers of knowledge;
- from low/moderate to high expectations of preparation for class;
- from a low-risk, private presence to a high-risk public presence;
- from personal responsibility for attendance to community expectation and responsibility;
- from individualistic competition

among peers to collaboration among group members whose success depends upon one another;

- from formal, impersonal relationships with peers and instructors to genuine interest in one another's learning and overall well-being;
- from viewing instructors and texts as sole authorities to seeing themselves, their peers, and their community as important sources of knowledge.

Young freshmen, in particular, can have a hard time making the adjustment, as they may have developed negative associations around cooperation in high school. There, cooperating with authority may have denoted blind or deferential obedience; cooperating with peers may have evoked the suspicion of cheating; and group work may have been mismanaged (MacGregor, 1990).

The instructor's role changes, too. No longer is it focused on sorting, classifying, and screening out students. The primary goal is to develop students' competencies and talents. Millis (1990) humorously notes that cooperative learning also recasts the instructor as "a guide on the side" instead of "the sage on the stage." In other words, the role shifts from expert/authority figure to facilitator/coach, one who unobtrusively circulates, observes, monitors, and answers questions. Instructors often have what Finkel and Monk (1983) colorfully term the "Atlas complex"; they feel wholly responsible for the success of the course and their students. Cooperative techniques call for placing much of the responsibility for learning squarely on the students' shoulders. Of course, relinquishing control can be difficult at first for an instructor.

Crucial Elements of Cooperative Learning

Cooperative learning techniques share a number of essential features that you must ensure are built into or provided for in the way you assemble groups, design tasks, manage activities, and determine grades (Feichtner and Davis, 1984-85; Kagan, 1988; Millis, 1990; Johnson et al., 1991; Cooper et al., 1993; Smith, 1993).

Positive interdependence. For a group to function effectively, each member must feel a sense of personal responsibility for the success of his or her teammates. In addition, each member's success must depend at least in part on the group's success. In brief, members must feel they need one another.

To ensure this element, you can do one or more of the following: assign a group product with a group grade (you can also separately grade individual contributions); give group (as well as individual) quizzes and exams; allocate essential resources or pieces of information across group members, requiring them to share (materials interdependence); assign each member a different part of the total task (task interdependence); randomly select students to speak for their group; and/or assign group members different roles.

Among the possible group roles are recorder, spokesperson, summarizer, checker/corrector, skeptic, organizer/manager, observer, timekeeper, conflict resolver, and runner/liaison to other groups and/or the instructor.

112

Individual accountability. All members must be held responsible for their own learning as well as for the learning of other group members. At the same time, no member should feel that he or she is giving more (or less) than an equal share of effort to the group task. In other words, no freeloaders or hitchhikers allowed.

You can build in this element in several ways, some of which overlap with those above: base final grades predominantly on individual quizzes, tests, papers, and other assignments; randomly select students to speak for their group; assign group members different roles; and/or base a significant portion of the final grade on peer performance evaluations.

This last strategy deserves elaboration. It can be used only when groups have stable memberships over weeks or months. At the end of the semester or the group-work unit, have each group member either give each of their teammates a letter grade for group contributions or allocate a limited number of points across their teammates. If you use points, you may want to forbid students to allocate points equally across teammates.

It is essential that you give students a list of criteria on which to grade their peers, such as attendance, preparation, promptness, leadership, quality of contributions, quantity of contributions, and social skills. These criteria and your peer evaluation policies and procedures merit explanation on the first day of class. The peer portion of the final grade should reflect the amount and importance of group work in the course--at least ten to 20 percent but no more than 60 percent.

It is not unusual for students to give their teammates almost uniformly high peer performance evaluations. This tendency, however, reflects the fact that cooperative learning motivates students to prepare and perform more effectively than perhaps any other teaching format. Students will do things for one another and in response to social pressure that they simply won't do for us. However, they also are merciless in penalizing freeloaders, sandbaggers, ego-trippers, bullies, whiners, martyrs, saboteurs, and other group pathological types. In other words, they grade each other pretty much the way we would grade them (Ferris and Hess, 1984-85; Murrell, 1984-85; Jalajas and Sutton, 1984-85).

Appropriate group composition, size, and duration. Heterogeneous groups in terms of ability, race, gender, and other characteristics help develop students' social skills and foster understanding among individuals of differing social backgrounds. Research also finds that heterogeneous groups help all students learn the material better (also Heller et al, 1992; Heller and Hollabaugh, 1992). When group composition is diverse, specifically in ability and/or knowledge background, the slower students learn from the quicker ones--often better than they do from traditional methods because students seem to speak one another's language. The quicker ones in turn benefit because, by teaching the material, they learn it all the better. (Of course, if a class is extremely diverse in knowledge background and ability, very slow students can also hold back the very gifted.)

The research also indicates that students should not form their own groups if these groups are to last any longer than a segment of one class session. Such a composition only reinforces existing cliques and encourages discussion of extracurricular topics.

Optimal group size varies with the open-endedness of the task. Several cooperative activities described later in this chapter and in Chapter 14 rely on pairs. But most other activities require groups of three to five (no larger) to ensure lively, broad participation and to prevent freeloading. Three is optimal for mathematical and scientific problem solving tasks with alternative means to one correct answer (Heller and Hollabaugh, 1992). Four or five is best for tasks with multiple respectable answers involving brainstorming, interpretation, and problem solving of a "focal" or "playground" nature (see Chapter 16).

It may be wisest to avoid mixing females with a male majority. Heller and Hollabaugh (1992) found that males tend to dominate and overshadow the female(s) when in the majority.

Ideal group duration also depends on the task. Long-term group assignments facilitate major projects and ongoing tasks, since duration fosters group loyalty and refines members' cooperative skills. On the other hand, students can get acquainted with more classmates if groups change with each short-term project or every several weeks. What often happens, however, is that students develop group loyalties quickly and plead to keep the same groups throughout the term.

Ever-changing *ad hoc* groups or pairs, based solely on seating proximity, may be sufficient for occasional problem solving and discussion assigments. In large classes where space is short and chairs are immobile, you may feel limited to these *ad hoc* groups. But you can overcome such limitations by assigning seats.

Face-to-face interaction. Cooperative learning requires that instructors allocate class time to group meetings. Experience reveals that you cannot rely on students to meet and collaborate face-to-face outside of class. (Instructors who do find that group members divide the labor and go their separate ways, defeating the whole cooperative purpose and its benefits.)

Genuine learning and challenge. The cooperative task must make students *learn* something, not just *do* something. It must require alternative means to an answer and/or multiple answers and pose a genuine challenge that only more than one mind is likely to meet within the given time limit. In brief, it should be a harder task than you'd assign to students working alone.

Explicit attention to collaborative social skills. Working together effectively requires certain behaviors of all the individuals involved: listening actively, taking turns in talking, not interrupting, encouraging others, cooperating, sharing resources, being open-minded, giving constructive feedback, tactfully defending one's views, compromising, and showing respect for others.

These are acquired skills that you must explicitly foster in at least some of the following ways: modeling them yourself; praising when you see or hear them practiced;

114

having the class brainstorm and discuss them; including them among your objectives for group work; including them among your peer evaluation criteria; and, especially, allowing students time to reflect upon and process the quality of the day's or week's group interactions. Processing may be individual, group, or class and can include questions such as these: How well did I listen? How well did I play my assigned role? Did we include all group members in our discussions? How high quality was our task performance? How could we accomplish our task more effectively? How could we function as a group more smoothly?

Management Tips

Beyond the essential elements above are several standard operating procedures that help ensure success and make the management of group activities easier and more predictable for you (Feichtner and Davis, 1984-85; Millis, 1990; Johnson et al., 1991; Cooper et al., 1993; Smith, 1993).

First and foremost, **start small.** You might begin by trying out a small-scale, pre-tested technique (like those in the next section) in the class where you feel the most confident. Expect it *not* to work perfectly--any technique can fall short the first time tried--and plan for your time allocation to be off one way or another. A safe launching pad is an optional help or review session.

Second, **use cooperative learning only with a criterion-referenced grading system** (see Chapter 29). Grading on a curve, or "norm-referenced grading," undercuts the spirit of cooperation and the prospect of group success

on which cooperative learning relies. An absolute grading scale gives all students an equal chance at achievement.

Third, **introduce the activity to your class by explaining your rationale for using it.** Without getting too technical, you might mention some of the research that documents its superior effectiveness. Perhaps list the crucial elements of cooperative learning and your objectives for the group work. Also reassure your students that they will not jeopardize their grades nor be accused of cheating (see Chapter 9) by helping each other.

Fourth, **give groups a very specific, structured task that requires a written product to show at the end.** The major reasons for group-work failure are the lack of organization and specificity in the assignment and the students' confusion over its purpose and expectations. The written end-product may be no more formal than handwritten notes for the group's verbal report at the end of the group session. It may be a problem solution, a group exam answer sheet, or notes for a group presentation. Or it may be a major group paper or project that students have met for weeks to complete.

A word of warning is in order, however: Feichtner and Davis (1984-85) present evidence that large-scale, formal group assignments are more problematic than smaller-scale and less formal ones. Specifically, they caution against assigning more than one major group presentation and more than three written papers or reports per semester. Otherwise, students are more likely to report having a negative group experience. Group exams, however, tend to generate positive experiences.

Fifth, **set and enforce tight time limits and deadlines for task completion,** even for short tasks that pairs or groups can complete in a couple of minutes. It is helpful to bring a timer or stopwatch with you to all cooperative class sessions. For tasks of five to 50 minutes, you might give appropriate ten-minute or two-minute warnings. Larger-scale assignments call for firm deadlines for the completion of various subtasks (prospectus, data collection, data analysis, outline, first draft, etc.). It is best to schedule all final product deadlines comfortably in advance of the end of the term. Tight time limits and deadlines help keep groups on task.

Sixth, **ensure the assignment of individual roles within each group.** Many possible roles were listed above in the section on positive interdependence. At the very least, each group of three or more needs a recorder/spokesperson. Role assignments should rotate at least weekly among the members of stable groups. You can make the first role assignments randomly, or use the following technique for assigning roles in *ad hoc* groups: After breaking students into groups, tell them to point to one fellow member on the count of three. Assign the student receiving the most "points" the task of appointing the recorder/spokesperson and any other necessary roles. The element of surprise makes this technique humorous.

Seventh, **set the rule of "three before me."** That is, you can insist that students take their questions to each other first and not to you until they have asked at least three other students. Or accept only group, not individual, questions.

Eighth, **set rules to control noise levels and maintain order.** Among the most popular ones are "no unnecessary talking" and "only one group member talking at one time." Another helpful hint is to bring the classroom to silence by informing students that you will signal when time is up by raising your hand. They should then stop talking and raise *their* hands as soon as they see yours up. This technique enables you to silence a huge lecture hall in seconds.

Ninth, to ensure that groups have a genuine learning experience, **conclude each group session with a means of assessing students' progress or mastery of the material.** You might ask for a one- or two-minute presentation or progress report from each group. Or you can administer a brief quiz or classroom assessment technique (see Chapter 26). If a quiz, it is advisable to set a high standard of mastery that all group members must meet before any of them can leave class. Alternatively, you can select a member from each group at random to take the quiz for the group.

Tried and True Cooperative Learning Strategies

If you are interested in trying or extending cooperative learning in your classroom, you might try some of the popular formats described below. While the levels of success and usefulness vary by discipline and instructor, you can adjust them or create your own versions to serve your needs. The following sampler comes from several sources, including Kagan (1988), Millis (1990), Johnson et al. (1991), Cooper et al. (1993), and Smith

116 (1993). Many work well between lecture segments as student-active break activities (see Chapter 14). Although a few may sound adolescent, they have all been used effectively at the post-secondary level.

Think-Pair-Share. Give students a question or problem and ask them to think quietly of an answer or solution. Have them discuss their responses with their neighbor, then share them with the class. Set a time limit of one or two minutes for the pair exchange. Chapter 25 describes how Harvard physics professor Eric Mazur uses this activity in his large lecture classes as both a student-active break and a classroom assessment technique.

Pairs Check. Partners coach each other on worksheet problems and/or check notes for completeness and accuracy. This activity is similar to *Pair and Compare* in Chapter 14 and takes only two minutes.

Three-Step Interview. Students form pairs and one partner interviews the other on a predetermined topic for two or three minutes; partners switch roles. Then pairs combine to form groups of four. Each group member introduces his or her partner, sharing the information from the original interviews. This exercise serves well as an icebreaker activity and fosters active listening skills.

STAD (Student Teams-Achievement Divisions). After a lecture, video, demonstration, etc., teams of three or four receive a worksheet to discuss and complete. When members feel that they have reached acceptable solutions, you give a brief oral or written quiz to the group, a representative, or each individual member to assess their mastery of the material.

Jigsaw. Each member of a "base group" is assigned a minitopic to research. Students then meet in "expert groups" with others assigned the same minitopic to discuss and refine their understanding. Base groups reform, and members teach their minitopics to their teammates.

Constructive Controversy. Pairs in a group of four are assigned opposing sides of an issue. Each pair researches its assigned position, and the group discusses the issue with the goal of exposing as much information as possible about the subject. Pairs can then switch sides and continue the discussion.

Group Investigation. Assign each group or let each group choose a different topic within a given subject area. Groups are free to organize their work and research methods and even to determine the form of the final product (e.g., a video, play, slide show, demonstration, presentation, paper, etc.). To ensure individual accountability, monitor and grade individual contributions, as well as the group product.

Numbered Heads Together. Each member of a team of four is assigned a number. Pose a thought question or problem, and allow a few minutes for discussion. Call out a number, designating only students with that number to act as group spokesperson. This exercise promotes individual accountability.

Roundtable. Groups of three or more members brainstorm on an assigned topic, with each member taking turns to write down one new idea on a single piece of paper. The process continues until members run out of ideas. When time is up, the group with the most independent ideas wins recognition.

Talking Chips. This method ensures equal participation in discussion groups. Each group member receives the same number of poker chips (or index cards, pencils, pens, etc.) Each time a member wishes to speak, he or she tosses a chip into the center of the table. Once individuals have used up their chips, they can no longer speak. The discussion proceeds until all members have exhausted their chips. Then they reclaim their chips and begin another round.

Co-op cards. Each partner in a pair prepares a set of flashcards with a question or problem on the front and the correct answer(s) on the back. One partner quizzes the other until the latter answers all the questions or problems in the set correctly. Then they switch roles and use the other set of flashcards. This activity helps students memorize and review.

Send a Problem. Similar to *Co-op Cards,* each member of a group writes a question or problem on a flashcard. The group reaches consensus on the correct answer(s) or solution and writes it on the back. Each group then passes its cards to another group, which formulates its own answers or solutions and checks them against those written on the back by the sending group. If groups disagree, the receiving group writes its answer as an alternative. Stacks of cards continue to rotate from group to group until they are returned to the original senders, who then examine and discuss any alternative answers or solutions given by other groups.

Preparing Students for Life

Younger college students are intent on learning about the real world they are about to enter, while older ones want to know how they can function more effectively in it at a higher level. No doubt, among your objectives as a instructor is to help prepare your students for this rapidly changing world--to make them more knowledgeable citizens, consumers, social participants, appreciators of the arts, and/or science watchers and supporters, as well as more successful professionals and businesspersons in their careers. You select your content with this goal in mind. But the methods you choose may reinforce or override your verbal messages.

To prepare students for full participation in our society and the world, it is obvious that student-active techniques are more effective than traditional ones. To prepare students for the business and professional world in particular, cooperative learning is an essential part of their college experience.

European and Japanese industry achieved remarkably high productivity, creativity, and employee satisfaction and loyalty by reorganizing work into participatory, cooperative tasks during the post-World War II period. Industry in the United States has followed of late. Perhaps the idea of team work originally went against the American grain, which so stresses

118 individual competition at every level of education and business, relegating team cooperation to sports. Whether between individuals or athletic teams, traditional American achievement has been a zero-sum game in which others must lose for one to win.

But as W. Edward Demings (1993) points out--and the American work place recently discovered--greater gains are ensured for *all* by cooperating. "People pulling in opposite directions on a rope only exhaust themselves: they go nowhere," says Deming. "Every example of cooperation is one of benefit and gains to them that cooperate. Cooperation is especially productive in a system well managed." This cooperative ethos characterizes the business and professional environment in which today's students will build their careers.

The Case Method

The case method exposes students to problematic, real-world situations and challenges them to apply course knowledge to analyze the issues and formulate workable solutions. It is based on real or realistic stories that present problems or dilemmas without a clear resolution. Cases (or "vignettes," as short cases are often called) are usually printed, but some are available dramatized on videotape and on interactive CD-ROM.

You need not depend on "canned" cases; you can write your own to suit your own instructional purposes at no cost but your time. Anyone with the least bit of flair for story-telling should find case-writing an entertaining activity. This chapter provides guidelines for writing as well as selecting cases.

The Effectiveness of the Case Method

Aside from the fact that students enjoy the case method, good cases are rich educational tools.
- They require students' active engagement in and use of the material.
- They help make up for students' lack of real-world experience.
- They accustom students to solving problems within an uncertain, risk-laden environment.
- They foster higher-level critical thinking and cognitive skills such as application, analysis, synthesis, and evaluation.

- They demand both inductive and deductive thinking, compensating for higher education's focus on the latter.
- They serve as excellent homework assignments, paper topics, and essay exam questions, as well as springboards for discussion, review, and cooperative group problem-solving.

On the student-involvement continuum from didactic methods on the low end (e.g., lecture) to experiential methods on the high end (e.g., service learning), the case method falls somewhere in the middle, depending upon the case. The more it resembles a simulation, the more experiential the learning.

A case more closely approximates a simulation when it is written in the second person (placing the student in the story's key role), in the present tense (happening now), and in extended stages (see "Extended Cases"). On the other hand, the second person and the present tense may undercut the realism of a hypothetical case, and they obviously don't belong in a "real" case. No matter how they are written, cases are unlike truly experiential formats (see Chapter 17) in that students don't act them out. However, interactive CD-ROM cases blur the distinction.

Appropriate Subject Matter

Not all subjects or courses can employ the case method. They must have a context for *application* or *use*. This is why professional schools have adopted it as a central instructional method. Business and law did so decades ago; in fact, the Harvard Business School built a whole curriculum and publishing company around it. Medicine, nursing, clinical psychology, educational administration, and pastoral studies have followed. Engineering specialties with incomplete knowledge bases have recently discovered cases.

Faculty and TA development has also embraced the method. It uses cases portraying problems that instructors may encounter with classes and individual students, for example: challenges to authority, hostile reactions to sensitive material, accusations of discrimination, grading and academic honesty disputes, and difficulties implementing new techniques.

The case method has a place in many arts and science fields as well, some of which already use it to some extent: philosophy (e.g., ethics); music history (Chiaramonte, 1994); economics (e.g., macro, legal aspects); political science (e.g., policy analysis, public administration, constitutional law); sociology (e.g., social problems, criminology, organizations); psychology (e.g., clinical, abnormal, or-ganizational behavior); biology (e.g., resource management, ecology); and scientific methods in general (e.g., design a research study to test a given hypothesis).

What Makes a *Good* Case

A good case may be written in the second or third person and in present or past tense. It may be as brief as a paragraph or two or as long as a short monograph; the many hundreds of management and business administration cases advertised in the Harvard Business School Publishing catalog range from a couple to over 40 pages. What is important is that a case have the following qualities.

Realism. Real or hypothetical, a case should depict a currently relevant situation with which students can empathize or identify. Realism is further enhanced by technical detail, character development, historical context, and extension over time or a decision-making process (see next section).

Opportunities for students to synthesize course material. Cases should require students to draw on accumulated kowledge of the subject matter to analyze the problems and formulate solutions. Without some review built into the situations, students may forget to apply the basics in real decision-making situations in their careers.

Uncertainty and risk. While some solutions will be better than others, a case should offer room for multiple solutions and valid debate. Several solutions may be viable, but you may require students to select just one course of action and to justify their choice. Or you may ask them to rank-order their solutions. The uncertainty surrounding the solutions may be due to uncertainty in the knowledge base (a trait of all bodies of knowledge), information missing in the case (as it often is in reality), and/or the genuine validity of different approaches to the problem.

Further, the decisions students make must have some importance, even if it is only hypothetical, e.g.: a character's employment, health, or life; an organization's survival or success; a country's welfare; the loss of a legal case; social justice or public security.

Extended Cases

Continuous cases tell an unfolding story in segments over real or condensed time. As real-life situations usually evolve and change over time, this structure adds realism. For instance, some faculty development cases describe an instructor's shifting relationship with a class over a term, with each mini-chapter presenting different issues to consider. Some medical and nursing cases follow the progression of a disease or a pregnancy in a hypothetical patient.

Sequential-interactive cases lead students through a process of narrowing down their solutions/decisions by providing additional information *as the students request it.* Like those on CD-ROM, these cases approach the experiential realism of a simulation and problem-based learning. They cast students in the key decision-making role throughout, requiring that at least their minds act it out.

Here is an outline of how such a case may be structured across subject matter, with the medical or clinical variant in parentheses:

1) Students study a case giving limited information on the nature or root cause of a problem. First, they brainstorm all interpretations/causes (diagnoses) and their solutions (treatment plans). Then they rank-order the interpretations/causes (diagnoses) according to the ease and feasibility for verifying or eliminating them (ease and safety of testing).

2) Students request specific, additional information, beginning with what they have ranked as the easiest/most feasible to obtain (easiest and safest to test), to help them narrow down the possible interpretations/causes (diagnoses).
3) The instructor provides the information they request in turn. (One should have additional information in hand for any likely request.)
4) Students rerank-order the possible interpretations/causes (diagnoses) in light of the new information and repeat step 2.
5) The instructor repeats step 3.
6) Students select the most likely one or two interpretations/causes (diagnoses) and their solutions (treatment plans).

Depending upon the subject matter and the problem, you may also want to include the ease and feasibility of implementing a solution (treatment plan) as a rank-ordering criteria. After all, if students identify widespread poverty as the root cause of a problem, they may not be able to develop a workable, action-oriented solution. Alternatively, you may wish to focus attention on the relative importance or likelihood of a cause. The case method is extremely flexible.

Debriefing Cases

For cases to function well as homework assignments, paper topics, essay exam questions, or discussion springboards, you must guide students through a productive debriefing. That is, you have to challenge them with good questions about the case--questions that engage them in application, analysis, and synthesis of the material, plus

122 critical evaluation of their proposed interpretations and solutions. Brainstorm, focal, and playground questions admirably serve these purposes (see Chapter 16).

The simplest formula for debriefing a case is Problems-Remedies-Prevention, that is: "What are the problems?", "What are the solutions?", and "How could these problems have been prevented?"--the last of which is optional. The structure for sequential-interactive cases given above follows this basic formula.

While the problems and solutions are the essential issues, you might ask other questions to direct students back to the course material to find answers. Good cases often contain other matters and important details well worth students' consideration, e.g.: possible reasons behind a character's action or inaction; reasons why such action or inaction fails to solve or even worsens a problem; the impact of the historical context, the organizational culture, or financial constraints; or how the situation might play out if one ingredient were different. Just as you would print up and hand out all your questions for an assignment or an exam, it is helpful to do so for a discussion as well. Otherwise, case debriefings tend to run off in several directions at once.

You can launch a case discussion with the entire class (see Chapters 15 and 16) or in a cooperative learning format (see Chapter 18). This latter option presents still more options:

1) All groups can work on the same case with the proviso that each group reach a consensus on its answers (otherwise majority rules). This format works well only with cases that can gener- ate widely different interpretations.

2) All groups can work on the same case, but with each group addressing different questions.

3) After a general class discussion identifying the problems in the case, half the groups address solutions and the other half preventions.

4) Each group works on a different case and presents a descriptive summary and debriefing to the rest of the class. This option allows the instructor to allocate cases according to the groups' varying interests and knowledge backgrounds.

A Postscript for Pioneers

If the case method is rarely, if ever, used in your field, but you can see a place for it in your course, realize that trying it involves very little risk. It is a tried-and-true method in many fields, and course evaluations show that students find it both highly instructive and enjoyable. The key is in the quality of the case. You might show drafts of your own creations to colleagues before using them in class. Remember, too, that you can continue to improve your cases over time.

WRITING-TO-LEARN ACTIVITIES AND ASSIGNMENTS

Why have your students do in-class or homework-related writing exercises, even those that you don't grade? The reasons are well grounded in research. For starters, writing about the material helps students learn it better and retain it longer--whatever the subject and whether the exercise involves note-taking, outlining, summarizing, recording focused thought, composing short answers, or writing full-fledged essays (Hinkle and Hinkle, 1990; Ambron, 1987; Langer and Applebee, 1987; Young and Fulwiler, 1986; Kirkpatrick and Pittendrigh, 1984; Newell, 1984). The power of writing is that it forces students to *actively think* about the material.

Secondly, because practice makes perfect, any writing can improve writing skills. You can reap this benefit, whatever your field, as long as you explain the appropriate writing format and provide models, practice assignments, and plenty of feedback (Madigan and Brosamer, 1990; also see Chapter 22).

A third reason to have your students write is for classroom assessment (see Chapter 26)--that is, to find out *quickly*, while you're still focusing on a particular topic, exactly what your class is and isn't learning. This way you can diagnose and clarify points of confusion *before* you give the next exam and move on to other topics (Cross and Angelo, 1988; Angelo and Cross, 1993). In fact, the student feed-back and questions that writing exercises provide can practically plan a good part of your classes for you. Reading short, informal writing assignments that do not require grading takes no more time than any other type of class preparation.

Finally, many writing exercises give students the chance to learn about themselves--their feelings, values, cognitive processes, and their learning strengths and weaknesses. Younger students in particular need and appreciate opportunities for self-exploration (Ambron, 1987).

This chapter covers a number of writing-to-learn activities and assignments that have proven instructional value (from references above, especially Cross and Angelo, 1988 and Angelo and Cross, 1993).

Free Writes

Students write about a predetermined topic for a brief, specified number of minutes (one to three) as fast as they can think and put words on paper. The objective is to activate prior knowledge or to generate ideas by free association, disregarding grammar, spelling, punctuation, and the like.

Free writes serve as effective warm-up exercises in almost any discipline. Usually students come to class "cold," having forgotten the last class, the week's reading, and the lab manual instructions. Assigned regularly, free writes also put them on notice that they'd better be keeping up with the course. Here are some possible free write topics:

- "Write down all the important points you remember from last Wednesday's discussion."
- "From what you recall from the lab manual, write down what is to be done in lab today, any procedures that confuse you, and what the experiment is expected to create or show."
- You write three key words on the board from the last class or reading and ask students to explain their importance.
- You write a "seed sentence" on the board--that is, a major hypothesis, conclusion, or provocative statement related to class or readings--and ask students to write their reactions.
- You can also use exam review questions for a free write exercise. It will help prepare your students for a tightly timed essay test.

While it is best not to grade free writes, you might collect them and check off those that demonstrate evidence of the student's having listened to the lecture or discussion, done the assigned readings, or studied the lab manual. Free writes can count toward class participation.

Revision Groups

Students either do a free write assignment in class or bring in their drafts of an assigned essay, lab report, short paper, or proposal. You break them into groups of three or four, and each student in turn reads her written work to the rest of the group. After each reading, the other members jot down their comments and questions, starting off with their praise, and give these comments to the reader. (To keep the noise level down and to speed the process, no unnecessary talking is permitted.) Students then have a basis on which to begin a revision before you ever see their products.

During a review session, revision groups also help students prepare for essay exams. Each member of a group can write an answer to a different review question and receive the benefit of group feedback.

The One-Minute Paper

With books and notebooks closed, students summarize the "most important" or "most useful" point(s) they learned from a particular lecture, reading assignment, laboratory, or discussion. Time permitting, they also write down questions that remain in their minds. While called a "*one*-minute paper," the exercise usually requires two or three minutes. It works best to have students write about something they just experienced, such as a lecture or a discussion.

Just as free writes can function as a warm-up, a one-minute paper can serve as a "cool-down." It helps students absorb, digest, and internalize new material, moving it from short-term and mid-term memory into long-term. It also makes them think about the material, especially what they didn't understand, which is precisely what you need to know before wrapping up a topic.

As one-minute papers are not graded, they are usually anonymous. You might collect and read each one to find out how well the students grasped the new material.

Their summaries and questions will tell you what to review and clarify in your next class.

Journals

Students write down their intellectual and emotional reactions to the lectures, discussions, readings, laboratories, their solutions to homework problems, or other written assignments. They do this regularly at the end of each lecture, discussion, or lab and/or while they are doing their assignments outside of class. To save time, some instructors require just one weekly journal-writing session, either in-class or as handed-in homework, on any or all aspects of a course. Students should have a special notebook solely for their journal.

Journals help students keep up with the course as well as to read and listen *actively*. They also make students think about the material and what they are learning. It is best, however, to provide students with guidelines on what their journals should address. Here are some sample questions:

- What is new to you about this material?
- What did you already know?
- Does any point contradict what you already knew or believed?
- What patterns of reasoning (or data) does the speaker/author offer as evidence?
- How convincing do you find the speaker's/author's reasoning/data?
- Is there any line of reasoning that you do not follow?
- Is this reasoning familiar to you from other courses?
- What don't you understand?
- What questions remain in your mind?

Journals should be collected and checked off regularly or intermittently, but they usually are not graded. (If they are, they should not count very much toward the final grade.) You might write comments in the students' journals, thus developing a personal, one-on-one dialogue with each student.

One-Sentence Summaries

As an in-class activity or a short homework assignment, students answer these questions on a specific topic in one (long) grammatical sentence: Who Does/Did What to Whom, How, When, Where, and Why? (WDWWHWWW) The topic may be a historical event, the plot of a story or novel, or by substituting another What for Who/Whom, a chemical reaction, a mechanical process, or a biological phenomenon.

This technique makes students distill, simplify, reorganize, synthesize, and "chunk" complex material into smaller, essential units that are easier to manipulate and remember. It is advisable that you do the exercise first before assigning it and allow students twice as much time as it takes you. You can collect and comment on the summaries yourself or have your students exchange them and write comments on each other's.

Learning Logs

After each lecture, reading assignment, and/or problem set, students write two lists: one of the major points they understood and the other of the points they found unclear. Later, at regular intervals, they review their learning logs to diagnose their learning strengths and weaknesses (e.g., reasons for repeated errors) and to brainstorm ways to remedy these weaknesses. This diagnostic process can be conducted in class where students can discuss their learning pitfalls and share study and problem-solving techniques.

Learning logs serve several worthy purposes. Students isolate and review major points presented in the course. They also identify what they aren't grasping. Finally (and most important, for some students), they learn about their own learning styles, as well as ways to enhance their learning. This technique is especially valuable in cumulative subjects in which students do similar, graded assignments on a frequent, regular basis.

Learning logs should be collected and checked off intermittently to ensure students are keeping them up. You might grade them if they comprise a major course assignment.

Directed Paraphrasing

In their own words, students summarize the content of a reading assignment, a lecture, a discussion, or a lab. Restrict the assignment to a specific length, and define a specific audience and/or purpose for the summary. Students can pretend they are writing to laypersons for purposes of public education, to public policy makers for purposes of social change, to practicing scientists for purposes of research needs, etc.

As students must paraphrase material, they must work to truly understand it and internalize it. Also, since they are writing to a specific audience, they must consider the persuasive and political facets of knowledge--for example, what facts and arguments are important or irrelevant to a given group.

Directed paraphrasing assignments may be major or minor, in-class or homework, graded or just checked off. Students can also present them orally, and the rest of the class can role play the audience.

Dialectical Notes

Students read and take notes on a relatively short, important, self-contained passage from course readings. (You must carefully select the key passage.) On the left side of their note paper, they write down their reactions to the text as they read it: where they agree, where they disagree, where they are unsure, where they are confused, where they have questions, etc. At some later time, they review the passage and their left-side notes and write their reactions to these notes on the right side of their note paper.

Students can take dialectical notes either in class or as a fairly short homework assignment, or both. You can assign the first part (passage reading and reactions) as homework and do the second part (reactions to reactions) in class. Leave some time between the two parts, however--anywhere from a few days to 20 minutes of classroom discussion.

Dialectical notes encourage students to read a text carefully, to analyze it critically, and to reevaluate their initial reactions to it. These notes also demonstrate the nature and value of scholarly dialogue and debate. In addition, they make superb springboards for discussion. After students get used to the exercise, you might consider collecting and grading their notes.

This technique is especially useful in courses that require close readings of difficult texts, such as philosophy, literature, history, political science, religious studies, law, social theory, ethnic studies, and women's studies. It also adapts easily to mathematics, economics, engineering, and physics problem solving. Students work the problem in mathematical symbols on the left side of the paper and explain in words what operations they are performing and why on the right side. Later in small groups students can read and discuss each other's various approaches and solutions.

Letters Home

Students paraphrase in informal language what they are learning in a course in the form of a letter to one's parents, a sibling, or a friend. This technique helps students see the relationship between course material/projects and their everyday lives. It also gives them the opportunity to describe the material in their own words, thus to internalize and remember the major points. Its value as a pre-exam review exercise is obvious.

Sociology professor David Laquinta at Nebraska Wesleyan University devised the assignment for his sociological research course. He had his students describe the research they were conducting for the course, with their letters counting for one sixth of their final grade (*The Chronicle of Higher Education*, February 26, 1992, p. A35). Letters should at least be collected and checked off.

Question Writing and Follow-up Activities

Students are regularly required to bring a specified number of written questions (one to five) to every or almost every class. Their questions should address points in the previous lecture or discussion, the week's readings, or an assigned problem set that are "sincerely" confusing, unclear, incomplete, etc.

Question writing motivates students to keep up with the course and to read and listen actively. Since students bring their questions already prepared to section, they don't need a lengthy warm-up, and the first part of your class practically prepares itself. Your planning task involves *what to do* with these questions, and it is *not* advisable just to collect them and answer them yourself. This is too "instructor-centered" a teaching strategy.

A better, student-active approach is to engage students in discussing and answering each other's questions. One way is to pair them off and have them trade questions. Together, they answer as many of their questions between them as they can. Answers may be exchanged orally or in writing. Then after five, ten, or 15 minutes, they can pair off with other students and again answer as many remaining questions as they can. You only need address the questions that students can't answer among themselves after two or three different pairings.

A second way is to break the class into groups of three, four, or even five and again let the students

128 answer as many questions among themselves as they can. You might circulate and field lingering questions.

Still a third way is the "question chain." Student A presents his/her first question to Student B, who has presumably raised his/her hand. Then Student B answers it and asks a question of Student C, and so on. A variation on this theme is to redefine the type of question that students compose: The first few can be questions to which students *should* know the answers, in which case Student A need not wait for a fellow student's hand to go up. After covering everyone's "review" questions, students can raise their "sincere" questions.

In a smaller class, you'll be able to see which students do and do not have written questions in front of them. In a larger class, you may want to collect them to check them off. (Do not collect the class's written *answers*, as students will need them for later reference.)

Some of these writing-to-learn techniques, sometimes called "informal writing," will merit mention again in Chapter 26, as they also provide valuable assessment feedback about your students' learning. Chapter 22 deals with teaching your students more formal modes of writing in your discipline.

Tools of the Trade: Making the Most of Instructional Aids and Technology

Teaching at its finest demands that instructors consider every educational tool at their command--various techniques, formats, aids, and technologies--to give their students the richest educational experience possible. From focusing on the former two types of tools, we now turn to the latter two.

As Chapter 12 points out, students rely on different learning modalities to different extents. Some students learn best by listening and discussing, some by reading and writing, others through graphic representations, and still others by hands-on experience. Since the traditional college classroom is strongly geared to the digital and auditory learning styles, students who are more visually or kinesthetically oriented are often at a disadvantage. Visual aids and simulated experiences, ranging from low-tech chalkboards and flip charts to the most advanced computer simulations and interactive learning modules, help these students excel while reinforcing everyone's learning.

This chapter is organized starting with the lowest-tech, most readily available visual aids to the (currently) highest-tech, more time-intensive instructional technology.

The Ubiquitous Board

You and your students grew up with it. It's in every classroom in the nation (though no classroom seems to have enough of them). You might even have one in your office. It now comes in a few colors and a modern, glossy white version with marker pens. In fact, it's so familiar to all of us in the educational sector that we rarely consider about how to use it most effectively. All we notice are the times when it's used *in*effectively, which is usually when we can't see it.

Below are a few guidelines for board use, perhaps all of which are intuitive yet all too often forgotten (Bartlett and Thomason, 1983):

- **Write neatly, legibly, and large,** as much as possible on a horizontal (vs. diagonal) line, and only on areas visible to all students. If board writing is not your forte, shift to printing. Be very careful with your spelling, especially if you hold students responsible for theirs.
- **Use thick chalk in a large classroom,** such as "railroad crayon."
- **Use different color chalks and markers** for complex diagrams and drawings to facilitate students' visual understanding of the parts of a process, stages of development, sections of a specimen, etc.
- **Write what you can before class** to save time and energy during class.
- **Outline material on the**

board rather than writing sentences, and use symbols and abbreviations wherever possible. Not only does this practice save you time and board space, but it also helps students increase their note-taking efficiency. In addition, strive to write quickly so you don't lose students' attention.

- **Use the board as an organizational tool.** It is best to work from far left to right, numbering points as you develop them. Divide different topics with lines or spaces, but do connect related ideas with lines as well. Underline new terms when defining them. During pauses, step back to evaluate your board work, and correct and clarify points as required.

- **Be complete in your presentation,** defining critical new terms, giving all steps in a solution, and labeling all parts of your diagrams and technical drawings.

- **Practice writing while looking over your shoulder towards the class.** At least try to avoid spending much time with your back to the class. During the moments that you must, don't bother talking; your students may or may not hear you. It is better to pause, turn around, and explain the material while you are making eye contact with the class.

- **Ask students occasionally whether they can see your board work.** Over an hour, your handwriting may change, or the glare from the windows may settle on different spots.

- **Coordinate your words and your board work to reinforce each other.** It is best to introduce new material verbally,

then outline it on the board, then explain what you've outlined. If you've written out major topics or questions, point to each one as you shift the discussion to it. Also refer to the board regularly to reinforce important points.

- **Use the board to record discussion contributions.** You can reduce redundancy and help your students learn to take notes on discussion.

- **Ask the class before you erase** to ensure that everyone has been able to copy what you've written. (Remember the horror story of the math professor who wrote on the board with the right hand and followed closely with an eraser in the left?) If someone needs an extra moment, you might move on to a different part of the board, if available, or use the pause productively to ask or answer questions.

- **Bring students to the board to display their answers** to problems, discussion questions, and the like. They will be less shy about coming up if you begin this routine early in the semester and if you assign the problems/questions to small groups. Students don't mind publically presenting a group solution.

- **Avoid wearing very dark clothes on a heavy chalkboard-work day.** Or judiciously try to avoid leaning against the chalkboard. They may call it "dustless" chalk, but it isn't!

The Flip Chart

Heavily utilized at conferences and in boardrooms, the flip chart is rarely seen in a classroom. Yet it has great potential as a teaching tool in a smaller class. Some of the same guidelines for board use apply.

Despite its smaller size, it has three advantages: 1) You can write out much of your material in advance and in any color marker. 2) You can preserve material, both what you prepare and what evolves during a class, from semester to semester. 3) Rather than erase, you can tear off pages and tape them wherever you want. It may be worth the minor investment to buy your own flip chart or large pad and easel.

The Overhead Projector

The guidelines for overhead use are similar to those for board use. For instance, if you use marker pens on your transparencies, make sure that the colors you select are easily discernible and that any glare in the room does not obscure the images you are projecting. Also be careful to allow students adequate time to assimilate and take notes on the projected material.

The overhead projector has additional intricacies and guidelines for effective use (Head, 1992; Rogers, 1993). (These suggestions are worth keeping in mind the next time you give a conference presentation or an invited lecture.)

- **Design your overhead transparencies to project horizontally** on the screen rather than vertically, if possible. The horizontal format fits better on the square screen. In fact, the screen often crops off the lower fourth of a vertical transparency.
- **Use visuals and graphics freely.** The overhead medium is perfect for symbols, graphs, charts, pictures, tables, and diagrams.
- **Focus on one and only one concept in a transparency.** And keep the images as simple as possible. A transparency becomes cluttered and difficult to interpret with more than three or four graphic images.
- **Use key words as heads and subheads,** not complete sentences, to focus students' attention on concepts and relationships.
- **Keep the information on each transparency to a minimum.** The amount of information on one transparency should not exceed seven lines of seven words each. More than this is difficult to process. Furthermore, the print should be large and clearly legible--at least 3/16" character height. Smaller print may be hard to read from the back of even a small room. For a substantial data set, you may wish to project just a title and to distribute handouts with the actual data--the same for complex graphs, tables, and diagrams.
- **Consider using overlays for sequential diagrams,** such as when you want to illustrate a sequential development, or when you want to reuse some of your transparencies in other contexts. Mathematics, physics, and economics present excellent opportunities for overlaying transparencies: Start with the basic axes, add the curves, then add symbols and explanations. The biological sciences often use overlays to show a succession of specimen sections.
- **Use a pointer,** such as a pencil or a laser, rather than your finger. And it is better to **use it**

on the overhead projection plate rather than moving around in front of the screen. The shadowed image of even a pencil is very sharp, and it commands your students' attention without your making distracting gestures.

- **Eliminate glare by using color transparencies** instead of the standard clear ones. Several colors are available, including a soft yellow film that is particularly easy on the eye. Brighter colors such as green or red can be interjected for emphasis.
- **Never stand between the projector and the projected images.** Doing so blocks the image and is distracting to the class.
- **Turn off the projector lamp when not in use,** even if you are still talking. This way, students stay focused on what you are saying instead of the empty screen.

The Slide Projector

Professional produced "2 x 2 (inch)" slides are available for many subject areas, and even amateur photographers can make high quality slides. The rules of thumb for using 35 mm slide projectors resemble those for overhead projectors, but with a few unique twists. Daniel (1975) and Head (1992) offer some useful tips:

- **Learn how to load slides correctly.** Many an excellent presentation has been marred by an upside down or backwards slide. To load a slide properly, first examine it to find the way it should be viewed on the screen. Then place a dot or "thumb spot" in the lower left corner of the frame. Your right thumb will cover the thumb spot if you are loading the slide properly.
- **Learn how to use the slide projector *before* your presentation.** For instance, know how to focus the image, advance the carousel, and clear any jammed slides, as well as how to replace a blown lamp bulb. A few minutes of preparation can save a lot of lost class time spent troubleshooting technical problems.
- **Begin and end your presentation with a black or grey slide.** Bright flashes of light on a white screen can annoy and distract students. If you have a long explanation in the middle of your presentation, insert another neutral slide for the time during which you will be speaking.
- **Visually vary your presentation.** If your slide show consists of photographs or diagrams, break up a long sequence with a slide of text.
- **Keep the show rolling.** For a class, even a minute on one slide can drag the pace of a presentation, unless the image is very complex.

When to Consider High-Tech Alternatives

Low-tech visual aids have proven their teaching effectiveness. But according to Albright and Graf (1992), the days of "chalk and talk" are nearing an end in many disciplines. Instructional technology (IT) has taken on a new, broader meaning that encompasses computer assisted instruction (CAI), computer-controlled multimedia presentations, and distance learning on electronic mail.

These new alternatives give you greater latitude in designing your courses, but also greater responsibility for choosing and using the various technologies appropriately. You are ultimately your own instructional developer and technologist. (Only when you consider unfamiliar techniques and technologies do you typically turn to professionals for advice.) So it is important to view classroom computer technology as only a tool, and only one of many tools. We can become so fascinated with the bells and whistles that we forget lower-tech ways to accomplish the same objective. What is crucial is to base any computer application on sound pedagogical principles (Knapper, 1982; Albright and Graf, 1992).

What are *appropriate reasons* for using high-tech instructional tools? Lewis and Wall (1988) cite six *good* reasons that faculty give. First, a certain technology may achieve certain course goals and facilitate certain instructional tasks that are impossible to accomplish otherwise. For instance, interactive video technology allows students to experience distant times, places, and events to which they lack direct access.

Second, a certain technology may provide the only realistic means for you to demonstrate a phenomenon. For instance, in chemistry and physics, faculty can use a computer simulation or display program to show an atomic structure or a chemical or physical force interaction. Such applications are particularly effective when the phenomenon in question is too large, too small, or too dynamic to convey with printed media, static diagrams, or hand gestures.

A third appropriate use of a technology is to allow students to drill and practice at their own pace. No one instructor can regularly give every student individual instruction, although we try to do so when necessary. Computer tutorials can function in our place, without the time and patience limitations that afflict us mere mortals.

Fourth, computer technology specifically can help students acquire the technological literacy that their future occupations will certainly require. By learning to use word processing software, spreadsheet programs, statistical packages, layout and design software, engineering programs, etc. *now*, students overcome their anxieties as well as their ignorance and broaden their job placement prospects.

Fifth, both you and your students can appropriately use technology to enhance your productivity--in particular, to reduce the time spent on routine record-keeping and communication. Course records for large classes, for example, are most easily managed on a standard spreadsheet. Putting a class journal on electronic mail permits nearly instantaneous responses, and e-mailing assignments saves class time. Word processing software streamlines writing and editing tasks. You can even word process your comments on written assignments and essay exams, as students' papers and answers often display similar strengths and weaknesses.

Finally, computer technology, specifically electronic mail, can give you and your class some of the conveniences of distance learning with none of the costs. For instance, a student who misses a class or an office hour can make network contact with the professor or TA and confer, ask questions, submit assignments, and even edit materials directly on the computer interface.

Let us now take a look at some of the most exciting and useful types of high-tech instructional tools.

Presentation Software

While not interactive, presentation software can enhance the visual quality and impact of lectures and professional presentations. Such software allows you to create and project text integrated with images, animations, and videos--all in full color--while playing sound.

Even if you intend to display only text and images, presentation software gives you greater flexibility than overhead transparencies or the traditional slide show. For instance, at any given moment you can highlight the text or zoom in on the section of the image that you are explaining. In addition, you can save the presentation for students to review later.

The same rules apply to text in presentation software as in lower-tech instructional aids: Focus on only one concept per slide; use key words rather than complete sentences; and keep the information on each slide to an absolute minimum. Such software provides templates to help you arrange your information in a logical and pleasing way.

An additional rule also applies: Restrain yourself from getting too elaborate with color combinations, backgrounds, clip art, slide transitions and builds, and other design options and special effects. In instruction, usually the fewer the glitzy distractions and the simpler the visuals, the better. It is also advisable to keep the same colors

and backgrounds throughout a presentation. When in doubt, yellow text on a dark blue background is easiest to read in a dark classroom.

Text is quite easy to produce with presentation software alone. Inserting images, sound, animation, or video requires additional software and equipment (e.g., a scanner, a microphone), as well as a great deal of computer memory for storing these very large files. On your first time through the process, it is highly advisable to obtain the help of an experienced colleague, knowledgeable student assistant, or IT consultant.

Groupware for Discussion and Collaboration

No longer is conversational exchange confined to face-to-face situations like class time. Now instructors have their choice of three different electronic forums for class discussion and collaboration: electronic mail-based communication (simple e-mail and "listservs," also called "mailing lists"), Usenet News (also called "newsgroups" or "bulletin boards"), and conferencing software. Each has its own special features and strengths.

Whatever the forum, electronic interaction can augment classroom learning in several important ways. The fact that it is somewhat anonymous and not face-to-face reduces many students' self-consciousness and defensiveness, thereby enhancing their involvement and participation. Corporate experience with electronic brainstorming software (EBS) indicates that problem-solving skills and creativity may also be enhanced (Gallupe and Cooper, 1993). EBS software, which allows for total anonymity among participants, has been tested against face-to-face interaction and found to generate more and better ideas. Gallupe and Cooper (1993) surmise that the anonymity and absence of "evaluation apprehension" among participants explain EBS's success.

Some studies suggest that electronic interaction also fosters clearer and deeper thinking. Probably because students have to write their responses, the medium encourages them to think more carefully and critically. In addition, as they must frame their messages for clarity and conciseness, students enhance their writing and communication skills (Bellman, 1992). But perhaps most obviously, electronic interaction both extends your students' learning time and space beyond the classroom and ensures that the learning is student-active.

Your institution's instructional technology or computer center can set up one system or another for your course and advise on how to get your students subscribed. (You can set up one of the group options below on your own.) Do bear in mind that, to ensure broad participation, you may have to devote one or more classes to training your students to use the protocol. If you are uncertain of the finer points of the system, you may want to arrange for a software specialist to provide the training.

E-mail and listservs. E-mail is a one-to-one (the simplest version) or one-to-many (the listserv) communication system by which a sender accesses a mainframe system and leaves a message to be read by one or more receivers at remote locations. This communication is called "asynchronous" because a receiver can read the message at any time after it is sent.

Most e-mail is transmitted over store-and-forward systems like the Internet.

One-to-one e-mail with your students can serve the same purposes as your office hours and after-class exchanges but without the restrictions of time and place. It also saves class time that would otherwise go to individual student questions, concerns, and Socratic dialogue. With training in using the attachment option, students can e-mail you homework assignments and papers done on the computer as well.

A listserv or mailing list, on the other hand, permits out-of-class discussion among you and all your students. If you wish, you can require a minimum degree of participation and easily monitor it. You should be prepared to initiate and at times encourage or guide the discussion. This medium also allows you to save class time by sending housekeeping messages, reminders, study questions, and even entire assignments. Students can exchange messages among themselves as well, greatly expanding the time available for peer review and project collaboration.

Unless you ask your programmer to build in another arrangement, every message sent from one member goes out to all the other members. Membership requires subscription. Therefore, you can ask all your students to subscribe to your course listserv individually (and hope that they do by your deadline), or you can subscribe all your students at one time. Of course, any late subscribers to the list will miss all the earlier messages.

Another communication option that falls somewhere between simple e-mail and listservs is to set up your e-mail system to send messages to your entire class at once. Just ask your students to activate their own e-mail accounts and to give you their addresses. Then type in all their addresses under a course "nickname" (an option available on most e-mail software). From that point on, you can e-mail announcements, reminders, assignments, etc. to all your students at one time. In turn your students can reply to you individually and confidentially with their questions, to which you can reply individually. If you distribute the list of addresses, your students can also communicate with one another, but you will not be able to monitor them unless they "cc" their messages to you.

Newsgroups. In this medium members send messages to a common Internet location for later retrieval. Unlike with e-mail-based systems, those who join a newsgroup late will find earlier messages waiting for them. Newsgroups are designed for group discussion, and instructors can monitor student participation. But any one-to-one communication must go through e-mail.

Your course newsgroup need not be one of those many thousands of very public topical forums with titles that start with "alt," "comp," "misc," "rec," "soc," etc. Your programmer can set one up with restricted access. Depending upon your set-up, your students may require newsgroup or Web browsing software (or at least easy access to computers with it) to interface with the newsgroup protocol.

Conferencing software. A medium now coming into its own in higher education, this type of sys-

tem has stiffer software requirements than newsgroups as all participants must use the same program. However, some pioneering software can be downloaded for free if a college, school, or university network subscribes.

Most conferencing software allows instructors and students to set up topical folders, to hold private and small-group conferences, and to transfer any type of computer file within a conference. It also permits real-time, private conversations among synchronous users--ideal when students are collaborating on a project from different locations or when they need their instructor's help to solve an immediate problem.

Courseware I:
Computer Assisted Instruction
(CAI)

CAI is also known as CMI for "computer mediated instruction" and CAL for "computer assisted learning." Some of the most popular applications are simulation and analysis programs for the biological sciences, certain engineering specialties, the foreign languages, religious studies, accounting, and mathematics.

Quite a few instructors across the country have successfully adapted popular commercial software, such as spreadsheet and statistical packages, to their courses. Others have developed the computer savvy to write their own programs. In general, CAI is most helpful in teaching factual material and subjects in which the exercises and problems call for one correct or one clearly best answer.

Before venturing into CAI, do become very familiar with the package you intend to use, as either you or another course staff member must teach students how to use it. When instructors just turn students loose on a new package and expect them to figure it out on their own, its effectiveness drops dramatically. In addition, some students resent having to master an alien, complex program while struggling through the material as well. So it is best to select a simple, user-friendly package that requires only basic instructions. Only if students can easily navigate through a program can they reap the potential educational advantages.

If simple packages are not available for the level of your course, consider using one you like for demonstration purposes only. The imaginative, high quality graphics that some programs provide are invaluable teaching tools in themselves, especially for visually and kinesthetically oriented students.

Courseware II: Multimedia Technology

In the 1970's and into the 1980's, multimedia generally implied a presentation comprised of slides and sound. Now, multimedia has become "organized access to text (words and numbers), aural (sound effects, music, and speech), and visual (still images, video, and animation) elements, synthesized into a single, integrated presentation system controlled by a computer" (Lamb, 1992). Also called hypermedia instruction, it is one of the most exciting recent developments in educational technology.

Hypertext or hypermedia environments are different from the traditional text format in that they are nonlinear and interactive. Students can select different paths for learning based on the choices and decisions they make during the presentation.

Since most instructional users choose this technology to supplement their text or sound materials with video or high resolution images, high quality video displays are a must. Stereo sound systems are also helpful. Most multimedia systems rely on CD-ROM technology for storage. A single compact disc stores more than 650 megabytes of digital information--effectively more than the content of a complete encyclopedia. Future multimedia iterations will continue to introduce more and more educational applications, which no doubt will become more and more affordable.

Excitement and glitz aside, how pedagogically sound is multimedia technology? Actually, it offers tremendous instructional benefits. Communicating knowledge and skills via multisensory channels has been proven more effective than using any single channel alone (Lamb, 1992). This general finding is called the "cue summation" principle, which states that multiple sensory input channels, those allowing various graphic, symbolic, and auditory cues, allow learners to select the cues that best fit their own needs and abilities. Multisensory media, then, accommodates the full range of learning styles (see Chapter 12).

A host of other advantages also accrue (Lamb, 1992). Interactive learning takes less time than learning by traditional methods. Cost per student for the technology decreases with the number of students participating, since the primary expense is initial development and installation. Consistency of instruction also improves, as human instructors have their bad days and over time can grow tired of repetition. Finally, interactive systems give learners more control over (as well as responsibility for) their education. With more control, students feel greater ownership of the material.

The applications of multimedia technology are becoming increasingly refined and impressive. Science students can perform "experiments" that are too expensive or dangerous to carry out in the lab. (N.B.: While this use is attractive, it should only supplement hands-on work. There is no substitute for experience.) Business courses can incorporate software that engineers case studies into an interactive, multimedia format (Davenport and Harber, 1991). The Perseus Project at Harvard integrates history, archaeology, art history, religion, and linguistics into a multidisciplinary study aid for studying ancient Greece (Crane, 1991). Similarly, the Shakespeare Project at Stanford combines textual studies with real-time video of performances of the Bard's works (Friedlander, 1988). The Civil War Interactive, a cooperative project between documentary director Kenneth Burns and George Mason University, takes students on a tour through history, interweaving period photos, maps, text, and graphics with context-sensitive coaching (Fontana, 1991). Vanderbilt University's Learning Technology Center has developed multimedia applications for teacher education in mathematics, reading, and special education.

So why not tailor a hypertext to one of your own courses? It is possible, and some people find authoring software relatively easy to master. Not everyone does, however, and you should ask your institution's IT or computer center about the training and assistance they can provide. In addition, your development costs and your time investment can be steep (MacCrate, 1993).

Web Resources and Courses

The World Wide Web offers multimedia instructional resources, as well as a place to develop and publish your own multimedia course materials, without entailing the costs of purchasing or producing CD-ROMs. The available Web materials that you find valuable for a class and those that you yourself put on the Web may or may not be interactive, and they may or may not feature eye-catching images, sound, animation, and video. Even so, they have two major benefits. First, they are accessible to students from any computer terminal with a Web browser anytime and anywhere. Second, they (presumably) contain links to additional information or knowledge located elsewhere in the same document, at another Web site, or at a gopher site. Thus students can select their own pathways to learning and pursue further the topics of greatest interest of them.

The Web and its Internet companions, gopher and Usenet News, contain a wealth of sites that you may want your students to read/view/hear as an assignment or for course-related research. The only problem is that this electronic space is so vast that you cannot possibly know when or whether you've located the best resources. Your campus library or Instructional technology center may offer Web-search workshops that can save you hours, even days, of roaming around on a Web browser.

Of course, colleagues are invaluable with respect to specialized areas. You may want to broadcast your request for recommended sites on one of your area's listservs or bulletin boards.

Here are just a few homepages from which to start a search for instructional resources:

- http://www.nosc.mil/planet_ear th/everything.html--a huge image map featuring about 175 subject categories, including academic disciplines, the arts, the professions, and geographical regions.
- http://ets.cac.psu.edu/catalog/-- the gateway to more than 40 of Penn State's Faculty Technology Projects representing a broad range of courses, many with exciting instructional materials.
- http://tilt-www.acns.nwu.edu/ lecturehall.html--the doorway to the World Lecture Hall, a vast compendium of pages created by faculty worldwide for their online courses. Materials include course syllabi, lecture notes, exams, assignments, and multimedia "textbooks" in almost 30 academic and professional disciplines, from anatomy to religious studies. Valuable to students for supplementary course materials and *in*valuable to instructors for Web course models.
- http://www.tile.net/tile/listserv/ index.html--a starting point for finding topical listservs for yourself or your students.

Courses on the Web are an integral part of distance learning (along with video conferencing and local area network television). But increasingly instructors not involved in distance education are putting parts of their courses on the Web either in addition to or instead of meeting in traditional classroom settings. These Web pages may include as little as the syllabus and some biographical information about the instructor and TAs, or as much as all the lectures, homework, exams, multimedia shows, and links to assigned readings and viewings.

In selecting materials to put on the Web, it is wise to consider the impact of doing so. If you publish your syllabus and later want to make changes in it, how will you know that your students will go back to the syllabus and notice them? You may still want to announce the changes in class and/or on your course groupware. If you include your detailed lecture notes, will your students still come to class to hear your lectures?

But consider the exciting possibilities of making your lectures an outside reading/viewing assignment: You have liberated hours and hours of class time for all the discussion, writing-to-learn exercises, cooperative learning activities, and other student-active formats that you may have wanted to integrate into your course but never had the time to include.

Assuming, then, that you are meeting with your class on a regular basis, the course materials to put on the Web should be supplementary to, not redundant with, your in-class activities.

Putting up just basic text materials requires only a Web browser, a working familiarity with HTML (hypertext mark-up language) or a text editor program, and a publication agreement with a capus Web server. HTML lessons are widely available on the Web and in print.

As with presentation software,

140 adding other features, such as images, clickable image maps, sound, animation, video, and forms (for homework and exams on which students can type their answers), requires additional software and equipment, plus advanced HTML, abundant machine memory, and plenty of time and patience. For most people, an experienced colleague, a knowledgeable student assistant, or an instructional technology consultant is essential on one's first time through the process.

To be sure, people new to this level of computer technology have widely differing reactions to it. Some take to it naturally and become comfortable with it quickly, while many others do not. Instructors interested in experimenting with IT should never hesitate to ask for help. They might consider taking IT training workshops, even those on other campuses, to help them acquire advanced skills. It is important to remember that IT is a complex, specialized field in which expertise and proficiency require a B.S. or M.S. degree. Few people can pick it up on their own. The technology is a rapidly changing one as well; the "best" software this year may be upgraded or superseded by another the next.

The World Lecture Hall (URL above) is just one place to find Web course models. Your institution's home page may be a take-off point to many others close to home. Several additional sites provide information on the many other forms and directions that IT can take:

- http://www.educom.edu/--an introduction to Educom, an organization of institutions of higher education that are spearheading the use of IT in the college classroom.

- gopher://ivory.educom.edu/stories.101--access to descriptions of 101 successful IT applications in dozens of disciplines at various colleges and universities.
- http://www2.ido.gmu.edu/aahe/Welcome.html--the home page of the American Association for Higher Education with links to its ongoing national projects on technology, teaching, assessment, and faculty roles and rewards.

Looking Ahead

We can reasonably expect the lower-tech instructional tools, such as the board and the overhead projector, to be around in basically their present form for years to come. But ironically, the higher-tech sections of this chapter may be obsolete by the time you read them.

In a few years from now, your homework assignments may consist largely of computer tutorials, possibly different packages for different students. Publishing houses may be sending you hypertexts for your consideration. Students may routinely e-mail their assignments and papers to you--and you, your comments back instantaneously. By the same medium, you may coach students through the process of revising their papers.
All we know for certain is that higher education is entering a new electronic world of instructional possibilities. You can keep abreast of the latest high-tech advances and products by reading the "Information Technology" section of *The Chronicle of Higher Education.*

PART IV.

DISCIPLINARY

DIFFERENCES

TEACHING STUDENTS TO THINK AND WRITE IN THE DISCIPLINES

A major reason that students can't write well in a given discipline is that they don't know how to *think* in the discipline. While thinking may not always be expressed in writing, writing is *always* an expression of thinking. In fact, writing instruction specialists contend that *writing **is** thinking*. Therefore, when you teach your students to write in your discipline--assuming they already know the basic rules of sentence structure, syntax, grammar, and the like--you are teaching them to *think critically* in your discipline.

Crossdisciplinary Commonalities

Not surprisingly, all the academic disciplines share a common ground of thought and expression, and the writing-across-the-curriculum movement defined that territory. Toulmin, Reike, and Janik (1984) offer a particularly useful model of crossdisciplinary reasoning and writing. First, all scholarship states a *claim* of some kind: a hypothesis, a thesis, a solution, or a resolution. Secondly, it presents *data* related to that claim --factual evidence that may take

the form of numerical results of an experiment, inferential statistics from a survey, historical documentation, or quotations from a text. Third, it makes a *warrant*--that is, as persuasive an argument as possible that the data justify the claim and/or make this claim superior to competing claims. Scholars then debate the validity of a given claim in terms of the applicability and the quality of its supporting data and the strength of its warrant.

The claim-data-warrant model is simple enough to teach to undergraduates, and it sensitizes them to the need to include all three elements in every piece of formal writing they do. (Student writing is often missing one or two of them.) It also gives them an easy-to-use framework for evaluating scholarly, rhetorical, and expository writing in general, including that of their peers (Neel, 1993).

However, this crossdisciplinary common ground does not extend very far. The disciplines diverge on the language used, the placement of these elements in relation to each other, the forms of data considered respectable, the standards for an acceptable warrant (Walvoord and McCarthy, 1991).

Teaching Critical Thinking Through the Discipline's Metacognitive Model

Craig Nelson, a biology professor and a leader of the college-level critical thinking movement, claims that critical thinking has no universal definition or rules. Rather, it is the usually unspoken "series of conventions on argumentation and evidence in a given discipline." It is the "disciplinary dialect" that a field speaks, the "disciplinary scaffolding" on which the profession constructs knowledge, the "metacognitive model" on which the discipline operates (Nelson, 1993). Thus, one field's critical thinking may be another field's logical fallacy or unjustified conclusion.

This is not a problem in itself. The problem is that *we fail to articulate our discipline's metacognitive model to our students* (Nelson, 1993; Langer, 1992). Maybe it never crosses our minds. Maybe we are so wedded to our model that we forget it isn't common knowledge or common sense. Maybe we assume that students will simply pick it up by osmosis. Some eventually do, of course. But not all do so easily, not without getting C's and B's along the way. And many students *never* do. They major in another field with a disciplinary dialect that they somehow *do* pick up.

Why not explain your field's metacognitive model up front to your students, especially in introductory courses, where their concept is the sketchiest and often the most mistaken? Writing is the natural context for doing so for three reasons:

1) Writing is the most formal, concrete expression of a student's understanding of the discipline.

2) Most courses give graded writing assignments.

3) These assignments afford students quick feedback on their attempts to communicate in the disciplinary dialect.

Metacognitive Differences among Disciplines

By way of introduction to disciplinary differences, consider the short answer or essay question command that so often appears on tests and written assignments: "compare and contrast." In the laboratory sciences, this typically means "to list" as many similarities and differences as possible. In the social sciences, it implies "to discuss" as many as possible, referring to theoretical texts and/or research findings to buttress one's "argument." In literature, however, the command has yet another translation: "to analyze" *one critical similarity* and *one critical difference* at length, staying close to the texts.

It is little wonder then when a literature major in an introductory biology course writes an elegant essay comparing and contrasting plants and animals and never understands why it barely gets a passing grade. Similarly, the biology major in a literature course may be just as puzzled about why his lengthy list of similarities and differences between *The Grapes of Wrath* and *The Sun Also Rises* receives a D. In fact, it is surprising that as many students figure out these disciplinary nuances as they do.

Based on interviews with college instructors, Langer (1992) outlines the major metacognitive differences among three major disciplinary groups, especially as these differences pertain to the written products expected of students:

Sciences. Students are supposed to apply hard facts and reliable data to a problem solving situation, to consider possible outcomes, to hypothesize the most reasonable prediction, to perform a tightly controlled experiment to test the hypothesis, to measure the results meticulously, and to come to probable, carefully qualified conclusions based on the resulting evidence. Student opinion has little or no place in the process, and students should establish the validity of the source when citing someone else's published opinion.

A lab write-up or report has a specific format, much like a recipe, that students receive instructions to follow. The task involves selecting the relevant information from lab notes and placing it in the proper categories, according to the format. Students are expected to include tables, charts, graphs, drawings, and the like to clarify, simplify, and/or abbreviate the presentation. They should carefully construct and label these visuals. What writing is necessary should be clean, concise, and impersonal with relatively short, non-complex sentences. Under certain circumstances (e.g., lists), incomplete sentences are perfectly acceptable. Sometimes use of the passive voice is recommended.

Many subfields in the social sciences and psychology follow a similar model, specifically those that rely on the experimental method and the quantitative analysis of large data sets.

History-based disciplines. Here the focus is on explaining the relationships between contradic-

tory developments and conflicting documentary evidence. Students are expected to examine concrete historical circumstances and to develop defensible stands on controversial issues, drawing on detailed supporting evidence based on valid documentation. Part of this process entails viewing the conclusions of others with a critical eye, distinguishing true from false positions and main points from subpoints.

In essence, the challenge in writing a paper is to argue clearly and convincingly a historical interpretation using concrete factual, contextual evidence. Content is of greater importance than format. As one history instructor describes the rule of thumb, students should "give at least three different types of reasons relevant to the issues and... details to support those reasons" (Langer, 1992, p. 79).

The fields within this model include art, music, dance, and literary history, some philosophical studies, the historical specialties in the social sciences, and, of course, history.

Literature. As in the history-based disciplines, students are supposed to interpret, but in literary criticism this means something distinctly different. The interpretation is of the meaning of a piece of literature, how it allegorically or metaphorically reflects some aspect of real life. To infer intelligently what an author may intend, students should draw on the major themes and motifs in literature. But personal opinion is an integral aspect of interpretation. In fact, originality of opinion is prized. Still, an opinion must also have validity, and validity is derived from specific, supporting references to the text. Points in the text are the

145

data or evidence of literary interpretation.

Students are also expected to analyze and evaluate an author's literary style, to compare and contrast it with those of other authors. They must incorporate a historical understanding of literary genres and traditions so they know which comparisons and contrasts are interesting. For example, examining stylistic differences between Chaucer and Hemingway might yield an extensive list, but a boring one belaboring the obvious. Of much greater interest are the fewer and more subtle differences between authors who occupy the same or similar literary worlds.

An excellent paper then begins with a novel but thematic slant on a piece of literature and/or a credible analysis of its place within an identifiable tradition, both strongly supported by details and quotations from the actual work. Thus content is critical. But more than in other fields, so is the writing style in the paper itself. After all, literature *is* writing, much like science is the scientific method. Those attracted to literature should be extremely literate and literary themselves.

Along with English, foreign language, and comparative literature, the arts and much of philosophy follow a similar model, perhaps with less exacting standards for students' writing style.

Making Students Better Thinkers and Writers

The purpose of this summary was not to tell you what you already know about your field. Rather it was, first, to heighten your awareness of very different heuristics that students may bring into your course from other courses they have taken outside of your discipline. Secondly, it was to help you determine what facets of the disciplinary dialect and scaffolding that you already share with your students and what else they may benefit from learning. Certainly, the more they know about your discipline's conventions of argumentation and evidence--the more they can "think" like a colleague--the better they will perform in your courses, especially in their writing assignments.

While you can explain these conventions to your students, Nelson (1993) suggests a one-hour, in-class exercise that allows students to "discover" your discipline's metacognitive model on their own, inductively. Pass out a brief essay-type question along with copies of four different answers ranging in grades from A to D/F, but with comments and grades removed. (Past exams are excellent sources.) Then break students into small groups and have them figure out which answers are better and in what ways. After they develop a list of criteria (which you should verify in class discussion), assign another essay for them to write, either in class or as homework, following these criteria.

According to Nelson, students who have done this exercise report higher-than-expected grades not only in the course in which it is administered but also in their other courses. For many students the experience gives them a whole new gestalt on what disciplines, knowledge, scholarship, and higher education are all about.

Teaching Students to Write for Their Futures

Except for those students who become academics, few of the writing conventions you teach them will carry them into their careers. College graduates spend an average of 20 to 30 per cent of their time in the workplace on writing tasks, and even more as they advance through the ranks (Spears, 1994). So if any of your courses can accommodate it, you may want to give your students some experience in business/administrative writing. Such assignments fit in naturally with extended cases, simulations, problem-based learning, and some service learning experiences (see Chapter 17 and 19).

You can build assignments around several different forms: relatively brief memos and letters; lengthy proposals for new policies, procedures, projects, products, services, and the like; and progress reports on projects and transitions. While the briefer forms make excellent individual tasks, proposals and projects reports are often collaborative products in the business/administrative world and thus should be in a course as well.

This type of writing has distinct features not shared with scholarly kinds (most from Spears, 1994). Let us examine them in detail.

Specific audience pitch. As it is always directed to a specific individual or group, either you or your students must clearly define the audience for each assignment. Students then target their message accordingly.

Language and style. Since the audience is usually a non-specialist in a hectic, pragmatic environment, the language must be non-technical, accessible, concise, and direct enough to be skimmed. The preferred words and phrases are clean, short, essential, and powerful--chosen to be quickly persuasive.

For instance, wherever possible, adjectives and adverbs replace prepositional phrases; briefer constructions such as "before" and "if" replace "prior to" and "in the event that"; active voice replaces passive.

Purpose. With few exceptions, business/administrative communications ask the audience to take some form of action, whether it be simple approval, change, or funding. Even progress reports may ask for more time or continued funding or faith.

Evidence to justify purpose. Standard evidence includes observations, repeated events, interviews, small-scale surveys, and printed materials, usually non-academic. Students can benefit from learning how to collect such data and familiarizing themselves with respected business and administrative sources.

Format. As in journalistic writing, the purpose and main points appear up front in the introduction. Longer communications such as proposals contain other read-friendly features: a title page; a table of contents; an executive summary or abstract (one page maximum) focusing on the purpose and the recommendations; short chapters and sections; abundant headings and subheadings; lists rather than text when possible; graphics such as charts, tables, diagrams, and illustrations to reduce text; a conclusion listing recom-

148 mendations; appendices with non-essential supporting information; and generous white space throughout.

Accuracy and timeliness. Finally, business/administrative writing must be error-free, which means checked for factual accuracy and carefully proofread, as well as submitted on time. If not, the credibility of the writer suffers or, worse, the proposal is not even read.

The workplace then has its own metacognitive model--yet another dialect, another scaffolding that most of your students will have to learn sooner or later. You can help them learn it "sooner" in your course, where the costs of error are comparatively low. No doubt your students will greatly appreciate your instructing them in a skill they will need and use a great deal.

Making a
Foreign
Language
Come Alive

This chapter reviews current methodology in the teaching of foreign languages, primarily at the beginning and intermediate levels, although some of the ideas can be applied to advanced grammar and literature classes. The purpose is not to present dogmatic prescriptives for teaching foreign languages but to give guidelines for adapting a proficiency-based methodology to your classroom.

A Brief History of Foreign Language Teaching Methods

If you observe a foreign language classroom today, you will see many different teaching styles, but the emphasis will certainly be on communication. That after all is the purpose of any language--to communicate ideas, wishes, feelings, needs, etc. Let us first consider how the field of foreign language teaching has changed over the years.

In the early days, the method used was called "Grammar-Translation." It was a tried and true method for learning Greek and Latin, so it was deemed workable for any language. Students memorized grammar rules and their exceptions. They then read a text illustrating the use of a partic-

ular rule and diligently translated into English or from English into the target language. This method produced fine scholars with excellent reading and writing skills but with poor speaking and listening skills because the target language was rarely used in the classroom. Time was spent on talking *about* the language rather than talking *in* the language.

In the 1960s, this method was rejected and new methods developed based on the stimulus-response theory of behavioralist psychology, which viewed language as a set of acquired habits. The Direct and Audiolingual Methods emphasized the "here and now." While pointing to a familiar object or a picture, the instructor repeated its name in the target language. Students then parroted what they heard and were praised if they correctly pronounced the word or "chastised" by the instructor's immediate correction if they did not. The approach stressed exact pronunciation and memorization of vocabulary and short dialogues, and intensive practice in the language laboratory. Instructors never used English, believing that students would "pick up" the language much like children do their native language--repetition and association of the word with the object and reinforcement of correct patterned responses. Grammar rules were to be "absorbed" inductively through continuous practice with the language.

But just as the Grammar-Translation Method neglected speaking and listening skills, the Direct and Audiolingual Methods often neglected reading and writing skills and did not allow for students' spontaneous contributions. The most serious flaw, however, was that often students had no understanding of what they were doing when they weren't given concrete examples to see and touch.

Arguably, some students did succeed in mastering the language with these methods, usually highly motivated ones who conceivably could have learned the language without any instructor's help. You will probably have a few of these students in your classroom who will learn no matter what you do or don't do. It is the less motivated and the linguistically challenged student for whom various methods are invented.

The new generation of educators suggests that the failure of the old methods was due in part to the fact that students never encountered "real life situations." They could correctly say that "there is a large green chalkboard in the center of the classroom," but this was not often a hot topic of conversation in the real world. What they learned was meaningless and, as a result, they forgot it as soon as they were tested on it.

Educators and researchers went back to the drawing board, replacing behavioralist theories with a cognitive approach, based on Piaget's and Chomsky's research. They theorized that children have an innate "linguistic coding device" that enables them to understand utterances before comprehending grammar or semantic structure, and perhaps this LCD would function similarly with second-language learners.

Proponents conducted experiments on every possible combination of strategies to find THE METHOD that would guarantee proficiency in the target language. The results produced Total Physical Response Method, the Natural Approach, Rassias' Dartmouth Method, the Silent Method, Suggestopedia, and the list goes on. And although no one method can claim 100 percent success, it appears that an eclectic combination of these methods develops the highest proficiency.

Total Physical Response (TPR) begins with a period of silent intake combined with physical movement. The instructor gives a command that she mimes and repeats several times until students associate the words with the action and indicate their comprehension. Students then perform the action. They are not required to speak until they are ready.

One of the most controversial and influential theories of language learning today is the Natural Approach (Krashen and Terrell, 1983; Krashen, 1985). The Natural Approach applies the principles of Krashen's Monitor Model theory, and imports into the classroom strategies similar to those used by immigrants in acquiring a foreign language without formal training. Student activities focus on communicative interaction in the target language, relegating grammar and structure to homework. As with TPR, in the beginning stages learners go through a "silent phase" during which they process what they hear. Given sufficient input, students acquire the language naturally, and output follows.

When students do begin to utter phrases, correction is minimal to encourage their attempts at communication. In fact, the entire classroom atmosphere is non-threatening. Instructors conduct "natural" activities, such as games, songs, problem-solving tasks, to concentrate students' attention on the meaning, not on the form, of the utterance. Krashen posits that, after sufficient exposure to the target language, learners develop a built-in monitor that eventually tells them when they have made a mistake. The theory, of course, has many critics, although many of Krashen's ideas still help frame today's classroom.

The Proficiency-Oriented Classroom

The latest research indicates that a combination of methods best helps students attain linguistic competence in a foreign language. As Omaggio-Hadley (1993, p. 78) argues, "It is not what activities are used so much as when and how they are used that distinguishes methods from one another." It is important that students understand grammar rules and structures, that they test out their hypotheses about the language by using it creatively and meaningfully, *and* that they understand how to communicate on a culturally acceptable level with native speakers of the target language. Thus, along with new methods, some portions of those methods previously discarded have re-emerged in the classroom.

The guiding organizational principle of the proficiency-based approach was first known as the "Functional Trisection": function, content/context, and accuracy. Littlewood (1991, p. 31) describes this tri-partite endeavor as follows:

1) Language is a structural system, that is "a system of 'signals' which enable us to convey meanings," and which students must learn to manipulate to communicate flexibly and creatively.

2) Language is functional in that it permits us to do things. "We have to relate words to the wider situation ... to express and understand the intended functional meanings and (through the choice of alternative forms) the social meaning which the forms carry."

3) Language is a process of social interaction within which "people interpret, question, clarify and respond to each other's messages," not a series of rigid one-way messages.

Rivers' approach to communication in the foreign language distinguishes between skill-getting and skill-using (1981). In the skill-getting phase, students analyze rules or structures of the target language, then through controlled pattern practice, they produce utterances that use the new concept. They then pass to the skill-using phase where they interact on a meaningful level with others, producing their own utterances. It should be noted that these two phases of language learning are not separate and distinct, but are interconnected and often function simultaneously, allowing students to explore and test their hypotheses and reinforce their understanding of how the language works.

What is revolutionary is that the class is *student-centered*, not teacher-centered. Not that the instructor keeps quiet, but students do most of the work and learn by doing. In addition, they start speaking on their own as soon as possible. Classroom activities progress from purely mechanical pattern practice to creative practice, giving speaking, reading, listening, and writing equal importance.

According to Omaggio-Hadley (1993), the proficiency-based method relies on minimizing the risk and the difficulty students encounter in communicating, yet allows just enough of both to encourage learners to stretch just beyond their competency level. Again, instructors give corrective feedback in a way that is non-threatening and non-intrusive to communication.

Another important element of the method, one that also reduces student frustration and anxiety, is providing a realistic context for all forms of communication, even mechanical drills. Context permits students to draw on their experience and knowledge of the world to hypothesize how the language works and what is happening in the material they are reading, watching, or hearing. Any knowledge learned in a context or a comprehensible series is easier to retain than unconnected bytes.

Developing a Syllabus and Daily Lesson Plans

By designing your syllabus using the Functional Trisection, you can prepare the whole semester and each day's lesson in an organized, efficient manner. Students also can look at the syllabus and see what is expected of them and what they will be able to do at the end of each chapter (see also Chapter 4).

First, examine the material in the text and the context in which it is presented. Note the grammatical structures, vocabulary, and cultural information, and determine the most logical sequence of presentation. Then decide what the students should be able to do with this information and how and when they should be tested on it. For each function (e.g., the past descriptive tense), design the context for presentation (memories of childhood) and accuracy tests. These tests may take the form of oral reports, short essays, dictations, or any other comprehension measuring device that shows that students know when and how to use the new function and recognize it when they hear it.

Plan activities to help students learn through broad, active participation. Outline each activity and about how much time it takes. To appeal to all learning styles (see Chapter 12), strive for a variety of activities that involve listening, writing, reading and speaking skills. As no perfect textbook yet exists, your best idea resource is other instructors. Here is a sample plan that, while geared toward a grammar function, can be modified to introduce literature as well.

Warm-ups. In beginning language classes, warm up with choral repetition of new vocabulary, tongue-twisters in the target language, questions and answers about the previous day's lesson, or even simple greetings. Warm-ups serve to get the brain "in gear" and loosen the tongue for working in the target language.

Presentation. Briefly present the day's lesson, preferably in the target language, with several examples to clarify the function. Use pantomime, overhead transparencies, the board, pictures--anything to get across the meaning without resorting to English. However, remember that a two-minute explanation in English is less wasteful of precious class time than a tortuous 30-minute explanation in the target language. Be creative but practical. The most efficient method, of course, is to insist that students read the grammatical explanation in their text and write out a few exercises before class so you can spend time on practice and fine-tuning.

Pattern Practice. Lead students through a series of brief mechanical drills that concentrate on one aspect of the new function. Conduct the drills first chorally with the entire class, then individually with a few students called on at random. Drills help students "feel" and "hear" the language, which is one of the processes necessary to internalize it. Rules that are consciously learned and memorized are eventually subconsciously applied in communication.

Practice: Controlled communication. Students then practice the function using the same pattern but with slightly different structures--e.g., substituting verbs or nouns to produce similar phrases but with different meanings. First, you model examples, then break students into pairs or small groups to construct other examples while you circulate to check for accuracy and to answer questions. Occasionally have students prepare examples to "teach" the lesson to their partner.

Reinforcement. Bring the class back together to go over any errors you noticed and to review what was not clear. Reinforce the lesson by giving short dictations, reading passages, or showing videos that illustrate the structure and enlarge the scope of the application.

Practice: Open-ended communication. End the day's lesson with open-ended conversations between students in pairs or small groups. Prepare "conversation cards" that will require them to use the new function in a more personal content. That is, they should supply meaningful answers that they might utter in real life. They can also create their own phrases and/or dialogues. Or use any number of games and communicative activities in this chapter to assure variety and ward off boredom. As Rivers emphasizes, "Students acquire ... precision of expression through performing rules, not through memorizing or discussing them. They acquire knowledge of the structure of the language through use" (1992, p. 310).

The importance of preparing a lesson plan cannot be overemphasized. To ensure a successful class, you must be prepared for all contingencies. Try to anticipate what problems and questions the students might have and experiment with different ways of illustrating the concepts. Even if you have taught the same lesson for years, take the time to review it. Are the exercises you did last time really worthwhile? Will they work better in small groups, in pairs, or with the class as a whole? What supplemental materials may reinforce grammar points or highlight cultural aspects? What about videos or other visual aids? Play out the class in your mind. What about the time allocations for various activities? Always have one or two additional activities planned in case one falls flat or takes less time than you thought. Every minute of class time counts.

Oral Correction and Accuracy

Successful language learning is, for the most part, based on the learner's motivation to communicate. Just as in natural settings, whether it be a child who is trying to express his desires to his parents or an immigrant who must make his needs known to native speakers, the learner must express himself in the language to the best of his ability. The first utterances may not be (and usually aren't) grammatically correct, but as long as the meaning is clear, communication takes place.

Early in language learning, this is all you can hope for, and you should encourage students by showing comprehension. If you insist on perfect grammatical and phonetic utterances at the novice level, most students, who are already anxious and insecure in dealing with a foreign language, simply freeze up and refuse to continue. This is exactly what you want to avoid, yet obviously, you don't want errors to become ingrained.

Most research indicates that students *do* benefit from error correction provided that it is done in a non-threatening way (Phillips, 1991; Herron, 1991). You can correct obvious errors by modeling, where you respond first to the meaning of the student's message and repeat the phrase correctly.

Then ask the whole class to repeat once or twice. A more indirect method is to note errors in student conversations as you are circulating, then later point out the errors and review the correct model orally and on the board. Student errors may reflect hypothesis testing or a serious misunderstanding of a particular structure.

A caveat is necessary here: When doing practice drills and pronunciation drills, do insist on correct responses. Here, students are focusing on only one functional element and are not attempting to communicate any particular meaning. So you should not permit sloppy pronunciation or errors due to inattention.

Activities for Developing Oral Proficiency

The activities in the proficiency-oriented classroom take into consideration the learning styles of all students. While some students may love role plays and inventing dialogues to enact before the class, others may not. Many prefer pair or small group work, where the pressure is less intense and they feel safe. Only a comfortable environment is conducive to successful communication. Here are just a few activities that are successfully used in language classes.

Map of unknown city. Pair work. Reinforces place-name vocabulary, directions, and asking questions. Prepare two sets of city maps, each one marked with names of places (library, park, museum, etc.) and street names, but with three or four "buildings" left unmarked on each map. Give students cards that indicate three or four specific places they must find on their map of the unknown city. Student A asks Student B to direct him to the library, for example, which is not on his map but is on Student B's map. Following the directions given by his partner, he then marks the location on his map. They then change roles so that Student A must now follow directions and find the missing places on his map.

Creating a story from a picture. Small group. Narrative description, verb tenses, adjectives. Divide the class into groups of three to five students. Give each group a picture showing a person or persons engaged in a particular situation--the stranger the better. Each member contributes to creating a story based on the picture, which each group writes out and shares with the class. In beginning classes, use a series of pictures (e.g., comic strips from the newspaper). Paste each image on cardboard, mix them up, and ask students to put the images in a logical order and to furnish a brief description of what is going on.

Biographical sketches. Whole class. Forming questions, family members and leisure activity vocabulary, adjectives. Prepare a series of cards containing bits of biographical information about three or four imaginary families. One card is distributed to each student, who must then interview other class members to find her "family" by asking questions about their address, favorite sports, family members, etc. For writing practice, students may then fill out a family tree to which they can add whatever they wish. For listening practice, each group can describe its "family" to the class as a whole.

Those listening must take notes and be prepared to answer questions.

Crossword puzzles. Pair work. Vocabulary words, verbs. You may use available foreign language crossword puzzles or devise a puzzle to be completed with vocabulary words, synonyms, antonyms, verb tenses, etc. Make these short enough for two students to do in about five challenging minutes.

Analogies. Whole class or large groups. Attributes, adjectives, vocabulary, comparisons and contrasts, negatives. In a section on transportation, for example, bring in pictures of various means of transportation. Hold up a picture of a car and ask students to describe the attributes of a car--i.e., what makes a car a car and not a train. Help with unfamiliar words, writing them on the board and repeating them several times. Students then identify another vehicle that shares several attributes with the car (wheels, a driver, a gasoline engine) but must then specify the differences between a bus and a car (carries many passengers, requires a ticket, is public vs. private transportation, etc.).

Role play. Small groups or pairs. Vocabulary, circumlocution, narration, cultural aspects. Role plays can include anything and everything from simple tasks (e.g., going to a restaurant or shopping) based on dialogues in the text to elaborate problem solving activities during which advanced students must show they can maneuver in the language. Role plays reinforce vocabulary and structures while simulating real situations students may encounter in the target culture. Have students write out their dialogues in class, then practice them at home so they can perform them in class without notes.

Synonyms/antonyms. Whole class or teams. Have students come up with synonyms or antonyms of current vocabulary words to help them acquire language flexibility.

Unknown words. Teams. Paraphrasing, describing. Teaching students how to paraphrase and use circumlocutions is often sacrificed due to lack of time, but it is an essential survival skill. Give students cards, each marked with an English word for which they do not know the foreign language equivalent. Keeping their word hidden from the rest of the class, they must describe the object or action in the target language while their classmates try to guess it.

Another variation for advanced classes is "Balderdash." Pair off the class and give one pair a completely unfamiliar word, which one member reads to the class. The other pairs invent and write down a definition, which they pass to the pair in charge. The pair in charge then reads all the definitions without identifying their source, including the real one that only they know. Other students vote on which is the right definition, and the pair whose definition gets the most votes receives points. When the real definition is chosen, the pair reading receives points as well as the pair who guessed it right.

Various games. Teams and small groups. Far from being a waste of time, classroom games can be very educational. Students can learn while having fun, and the relative freedom from stress induces even shy students to participate. A variety of games for which students already know the rules can be used for vocabulary, grammar practice, and cultural concepts. Among the most popular are Twenty Questions, Hangman, Jeopardy, Trivial Pursuit, Charades, What's My Line, and even The Price is Right for number practice. Competition can be fierce and using the language in context really boosts students' confidence.

Developing Listening Skills

Beginning language students often need "advance organizers" to give them an idea of what they are going to hear so they can focus on relevant information. They often panic because they don't understand every word and must learn that normal conversational speech in a foreign language contains a lot of irrelevant pause fillers, just as in their native language. If you are using the target language in class, students have an opportunity to hear authentic input and get accustomed to your particular intonation. But someone else's speech may sound like a completely different language to them. The problem with sending students to the language lab to listen to tapes is that you cannot know whether they really understand what they hear, and a lot of beginners become frustrated and tune out. This is why you should work on listening comprehension for a few minutes each class period.

For example, if the context of the lesson is about transportation, explain to students that they are going to hear a short announcement in a train station on the departure and arrival of several trains. They should listen for and note relevant information only about the train from Munich to Heidelburg. Or give them a transcript of a partial dialogue between two passengers to complete using information that you read to them. Alternatively, have them listen to an audio tape of authentic discourse, then ask them to explain what they heard in their native language. This avoids mere parroting and enables you to verify comprehension.

Visual aids are excellent devices for developing listening skills. Stevick (1986) contends that images that come to mind when listening to words can help students associate words and objects more effectively.

Here are some activities that combine visuals with listening. Show students a picture and describe it without pointing to anything specific. Then put it away and ask them to jot down what they remember hearing and compare notes with a partner. Show them a pair of pictures that differ in certain details. Then describe one of the pictures and have them decide which one you are talking about. Have them fill in graphs, charts, or maps based on dictated information. Show a video segment of a movie or advertisement without sound. Then ask students to describe the characters, where they are, and what facial expressions and body language might tell them about what is happening. Finally, replay the segment with sound and ask what they understood and if their hypotheses were correct. Replay it again and follow up with questions to verify comprehension.

Language instructors once thought that proficient readers could transfer their reading skills from one language to another, but this is often not true. Too often, students try to translate word for word, losing sight of the meaning of phrases. As in listening for comprehension, students need to know the *purpose* for their reading, what information they must listen for to perform a specific task. Using the following guidelines, you can teach them practical reading skills.

Pre-reading activities. To introduce the material, begin by asking questions to activate students' schemata. If they have a general idea of what they will be reading about, they can draw on their own experience to make hypotheses that will facilitate their comprehension. If the reading is about a restaurant, ask what kinds of restaurants they go to, what they have to do to get there, what foods are served in a fast-food restaurant as opposed to a three-star restaurant, what is on the menu, etc. Write their ideas on the board for future reference.

Skimming the text. For an initial assessment of the subject matter, have students rapidly skim the text to find clues about the subject. What form does the text have? Is it a train schedule, a classified ad, an interview, an essay? Are there any non-linguistic clues such as visuals that give clues as to the topic?

Scanning the text. Then ask students to find specific information in the text. List vocabulary that they mentioned during pre-reading. If

158 the text is an advertisement, what is being sold, what is the price, etc.? For train schedules, can they find the train that will get them to Paris from Rome before midnight on Thursday? If an essay, what words are used to indicate opinions? What comparisons are drawn?

Close reading. Finally, students read intensively to find main ideas or other pertinent information. On an application form, ask what they think is the most important piece of information to be supplied and why. Have them underline or list unknown words, then have the class as a whole guess what they mean. Show them how to use contextual clues, morphological clues, and their own knowledge about the world to help them figure out the meaning. For an advertisement, ask how is the product described. For an essay, ask them to find the main ideas and whether they support the author's conclusion. For reinforcement, tell students to put the text away and write a summary of what they remember from their reading. In pairs or small groups they can compare information and fill in gaps.

Done on a regular basis, this procedure helps students concentrate on global meaning, not on word-by-word translation. Follow-up activities include finding synonyms or antonyms of words they already know, analyzing the grammatical structures they just learned, and finding idiomatic expressions. These concrete examples of how the language works and is organized also help their writing skills.

To check comprehension, ask novice-level students to interview one another to obtain information to fill out a form or take a train.

Or give them several different advertisements to match with words indicating the purpose, such as selling/buying a car, apartment rental, maid services, etc. Challenge advanced students to outline an essay and, using the same form, write their own essay on a similar subject.

Developing Writing Skills

Of all the skills to be developed in the foreign language classroom, writing is the most difficult for you and for most students, but for different reasons.

You may think you are fostering writing skills by assigning written homework exercises. True, students do have to pay attention to form, structure, and spelling, but they are not really communicating. As Magnan (1985) and Terry (1989) point out, this form of writing is strictly practice, not creation. Students must learn how to form arguments, how to make relevant comparisons, etc.--in short, how to communicate ideas and information.

To develop students' writing proficiency, start them out with a sequence of small tasks that can extend into complex projects--for example: postcards followed by short notes, then formal letters; penpal letters with other classes; diaries of their daily routine, their likes and dislikes, etc. Ask students to create stories from pictures; to outline debates; to take notes on lectures or readings, then write papers. Just be sure they can write on a topic that interests them.

Evaluating their writing samples is often a source of anguish. You know that students are trying to express something important to them so you don't want to squash their attempts at creativity, yet you have to note grammatical and syntactical errors. If you grade writing only on grammar without regard for content, you will discourage and frustrate your students. (Remember how you felt the first time you got back a composition covered with so much red ink it looked like it had been through a war?) Further, it is debatable whether strictly structural and grammatical corrections help eliminate student errors (Krashen and White, 1991; Semke, 1984). Besides, students care what you think about their ideas and want your feedback.

The most equitable way to evaluate student compositions is to give a grade for both content and form. Assign points for content items, such as organization, novelty, reasoning, evidence, etc., as well as points for their manipulation of the language, such as variety of phrases, correct usage of grammatical structures, richness of vocabulary, etc. Show students the grading form you will use *before* they write their first composition so they know exactly how to approach the assignment and how to identify their weaknesses from your feedback.

Developing Cultural Awareness

American students tend to be unaware of the differences between their native culture and those of other countries. So you must familiarize them with the target culture on a much wider plane than just "tu vs. vous", "du vs. Sie" or "tu vs. Usted." Culture encompasses body language, intonation, word order, culturally correct pause fillers, and etiquette (Carroll, 1988). Attention to cultural awareness has produced a wealth of new activities and formats for students to become acquainted with other cultures: international fairs, study-abroad programs, interaction with native speakers, and cultural readings that underline the inherent differences in how other cultures perceive the world. These culturally communicative activities are just as important in the language learning process as are strictly grammatical activities.

Teaching the culture of another country can be a truly exciting experience for you and your students. Use everything at your disposal to introduce authentic cultural material in class: train schedules, museum tickets, television commercials, food, videos, movies, your own experiences abroad, and exchange students from the target culture who can talk about the differences they have observed. No doubt your institution's library subscribes to numerous foreign language newspapers and periodicals, and your media center can tape news broadcasts from SCOLA. Have students take advantage of these campus resources to research on some cultural aspect that interests them and that they can then present in class.

There is more to being a language instructor than simply knowing the language. You must get what you know across to the students. The key to successful teaching is organization. Plan your lesson to include practice on all four skills: reading, writing, listening and speaking. Devise strategies and incorporate activities that appeal to all students' learning styles. Decide what your objective is for the day and make this clear to the students so they know *why* they

160 are doing particular activities. This all requires time, patience, planning, and a certain amount of clairvoyance to anticipate problems. But with time, the rewards more than make up for the hard work.

TEACHING MATHEMATICAL PROBLEM SOLVING

One of the most difficult tasks that instructors face in mathematics, statistics, the sciences, engineering, economics, and business administration is teaching students to be good problem solvers. What does it mean to solve a problem in your discipline? How does it differ from solving problems in another discipline or in the real world? These are serious questions to consider as you reflect on how *you* approach problems and how you can best help your students to achieve proficiency in this vital skill.

The Problem with Most Problems

First, let us pose a central question: When is a problem really a problem? According to Zoller (1987), what you may often consider a problem in your courses is really only an *exercise*, since you often give students formulas and specific ways of finding solutions. By this way of thinking, a problem consists of a situation for which the student has no preconceived notion of how to find an answer.

Another important question to consider is whether or not your problem-solving assignments help your students acquire conceptual knowledge. In other words, do the problems you assign elucidate underlying disciplinary principles, or are your students merely "going through the motions," repeating the problem-solving pattern you showed them?

Nurrenbern and Pickering (1987) found that, on a chemistry test covering such standard materials as ideal gas problems and stoichiometry as well as conceptual understanding, students performed well on the math sections but demonstrated little comprehension of the physical chemistry behind the questions. Students picked up on a formula and used the "plug and chug" process of selecting the variables necessary to work a solution without understanding *why* they chose the variables they did. In essence, they were using nothing more than an algorithm, a set of mechanical rules, to compute the solution. So problem-solving facility does not necessarily foster concept understanding. For your students to truly develop in your discipline, both these facets must be balanced.

One of the most common methods of teaching students how to solve problems is modeling. You pose a question to the students and show them how to work it on the board. As only one method among many techniques at your disposal, modeling may be a good way to pro-

162 ceed in the early stages. But as an exclusive strategy, it has definite drawbacks.

Bodner (1987) notes that when you work a problem on the board, you are only showing students what experts do when they run through an exercise. You are not actually showing them how to attack a real problem. To accomplish this goal, you must model the cognitive processes involved in genuine problem solving. Only then can students appreciate what problem-solving techniques can do for them.

When students learn only to "plug and chug," several problems can result (Brookhart, 1990):

1) Students see only one way to arrive at a solution, even though there may be several viable alternatives.
2) They fail to understand the rationales behind the facts and rules that justify the steps to a solution.
3) Since instructors rarely make errors, students mistakenly conclude that those "meant for" the discipline easily work through problems with little more than typographical errors.
4) If a problem is at all difficult, it is unlikely that one's first attempt at a solution will be completely correct. But unless students are prepared for some failures, they become discouraged and stop trying.

A Systematic Approach to Teaching Problem Solving

Heller et al. (1992) identify two types of students who are struggling with problem solving in introductory physics. Some students claim to understand the material but not to be able to work the problems. They apparently believe that mathematical problem-solving skills are independent of the physics concepts being taught. Other students say they can follow the problem examples in the text but find the test problems too different and difficult. They seem to view physics as nothing more than a collection of mathematical solutions. Both types should sound familiar to you.

Novice problem solvers of both types often make the same tragic mistakes over and over: In their impatience to find a numerical solution, they dive into algebraic manipulations without fully examining and comprehending the whole problem. They neither qualitatively analyze the situation nor systematically plan a strategy for solving the problem. When they arrive at any solution, they are satisfied and don't take the time to check it.

To overcome the novice's poor tactics, the Heller team (1992) developed a method for teaching problem solving that is easily adaptable to any of the mathematical or quantitative disciplines. The heart of the approach is to teach students a five-step problem-solving strategy that requires them to systematically translate the problem into different representations, each more abstract and more mathematically detailed than the last. Similar methods have been proposed by Schoenfeld (1985), Bodner (1987), and Samples (1994).

Step 1: Visualize the problem. Sketch or diagram the main parts of the problem. Identify the known and unknown quantities and other constraints. Restate the question in different terms to make it more understandable.

Step 2: Describe in writing the principles and concepts at work in the question. Then translate the diagram into symbolic terms, and symbolically represent the target variable.

Step 3: Plan a solution. Identify the equations necessary to solve the problem and work backwards from the target variable to see if enough information is available to arrive at a solution.

Step 4: Execute the plan. Plug in the appropriate numerical values for the variables and compute a solution.

Step 5: Check and evaluate your solution. Is the solution complete? Are the proper units used? Is the sign correct? Is the magnitude of the answer reasonable?

An Effective, Innovative Teaching Strategy: Cooperative Groups Solving Real Problems

Heller and Hollabaugh (1992) devised the idea of "context-rich" problems in physics as part of their approach to promote good problem-solving skills. These are problems that are more like those that students encounter in the real world. Since they are presented as short stories about real objects and realistic events, they offer a reason for doing the calculations and finding a solution. (One such problem involves planning a skateboard stunt, another deciding whether or not to fight a traffic ticket.) They may also have these additional characteristics:
- No specific reference is made to the unknown variable.

- Excess information above what is needed to solve the problem is given.
- Student must supply missing information from "common knowledge" or educated guessing.
- No specific mention is made of reasonable assumptions that may be necessary to reach a workable solution.

Context-rich problems are designed to be difficult, so students working alone often fail to derive satisfactory answers. Thus Heller and Hollabaugh (1992) recommend cooperative problem-solving groups to spread the thinking and reasoning load over several students. Groups provide a supportive atmosphere for students to discuss the physical principles behind the problems and possible strategies to reach a solution. Since students talk out their different ideas and evaluate alternative approaches, group problem solving develops *individual* problem-solving skills.

Before obtaining promising results with cooperative learning, the Hellers and their associates experimented with different group compositions, including random, homogeneous, and heterogenous on various variables. They eventually arrived at the most successful arrangement.

Initially, they assembled the groups randomly. Then after the first exam, they reconstituted the groups based on abilities, teaming together students of high, medium, and low abilities, as the cooperative learning literature advises (see Chapter 18). Generally, students in these heterogeneous ability groups developed their problem-solving skills as fully as did the homogeneous high-ability groups in previous experiments.

The optimum group size proved to be three, with members rotating among the roles of Manager, Skeptic, and Checker/Recorder. Pairs lacked the critical mass to arrive at more than one or two strategies and were more easily side-tracked on a fruitless path. On the other hand, groups of four or more gave some members the opportunity to freeload on other members' reasoning. Additionally, same sex groups or groups composed of two females and one male worked best, avoiding the dominance posturing of more than one male in a group (Heller and Hollabaugh, 1992).

Heller et al. (1992) also found that the students in their experimental program developed higher problem-solving expertise than those taught in the regular lecture and discussion section format with assignments of standard physics problems. As far as student learning is concerned, they concluded that cooperative problem-solving groups working on context-rich problems offer a preferable alternative to the traditional approach.

With students relying on each other to resolve their concerns and questions immediately as they arise, these groups also free the instructor to circulate and help the students in genuine need. Chapter 18 gives more information on cooperative learning research results and set-up methods.

Identifying and Correcting Problem-Solving Pitfalls

Black and Axelson (1991) identify the often ingrained, poor problem-solving habits that plague many students. They also outline a strategy for helping students break these habits in individual tutorial sessions.

1) Inaccuracy in reading:
- failing to concentrate on the meaning of the problem
- skipping unfamiliar words
- losing/forgetting one or more facts or ideas
- failing to reread a difficult passage
- starting to work the problem before reading it all

2) Inaccuracy in thinking:
- placing speed or ease of execution above accuracy
- performing a specific operation carelessly
- interpreting or performing operations inconsistently
- failing to double check procedures when uncertain
- working too rapidly
- jumping to conclusions

3) Faulty or careless problem analysis:
- failing to break down complex problems into easily manipulated components
- failing to draw on previous experience to clarify a difficult idea
- failing to refer to a dictionary or text glossary when necessary
- failing to actively construct diagrams where appropriate

4) Lack of perseverance:
- losing confidence and admitting defeat too easily
- guessing or basing solutions on superficial understanding
- using algorithms mechanically to arrive at solutions without giving thought to conceptual issues
- failing to carry out a line of reasoning to completion
- taking a one-shot approach and giving up if the singular attempt

fails.

Helping your students overcome these bad practices is best done during office hours (see Chapter 10). You might invite students who are having difficulty to see you individually and lead them through Black and Axelson's (1991) recommended procedure.

First, have your students read a problem aloud and specify what is needed to solve it. Then let them try solving it on their own, insisting that they think through the problem out loud. Talking to themselves makes them slow down and improves accuracy and explicitness. As they attack and proceed through the problem, pose questions to them like:

- What do you know about the problem?
- How can you break the problem into smaller steps?
- What are some possible ways to go about solving it?
- How did you go from step one to step two?
- What is your reasoning for this step?
- What are you thinking at this point in the process?

Given the dangers mentioned earlier, it is best to use modeling sparingly and to demonstrate only a part of the general problem-solving process, not how to get the answer to any specific problem.

Teaching Problem Solving in Traditional Formats

To teach problem-solving skills effectively, you need not completely overhaul your classroom nor tutor every student individually. Everything known about how to teach problem solving boils down to just a few insights: Students do learn problem solving by doing, but they don't learn by doing it wrong, and very few deduce the real *process of problem solving* on their own.

Therefore, most students need to be taught the process as a step-by-step, self-posed question-by-question procedure that incorporates the conceptual principles being demonstrated. Cooperative group work helps keep the process explicit and generates different problem-solving approaches, weaning students away from the mechanical use of algorithms and making them realize their multiple options. Finally, real-world problems that are meaningful to students furnish more interesting and challenging contexts for them to apply and hone their skills.

Traditional lectures and discussion sections can easily accommodate instruction in the problem-solving process. In fact, the interactive lecture provides an excellent forum for intermittent practice applications of the procedures you teach (see Chapter 14). Smaller classes, discussion/quiz/recitation sections, and help and review sessions readily allow for cooperative group problem solving on a regular or sporadic basis. You might even enjoy trying your hand at creating more relevant, updated word problems.

At the very least, it is wise to move away from the standard procedure of simply going over the homework or review problems and effortlessly modeling idealized solutions, while students passively watch. You have to see and hear how *your students* approached and either solved or failed to solve the assigned problems. You can find this out by having them write their solutions on the board or a trans-

165

Teaching Mathematical Problem Solving

166 parency and explain them to the
rest of the class. They can work
individually or in *ad hoc* pairs or
triads, as long as *they are doing the
work.* To save time, you might select only the more difficult problems for student presentation.
Then towards the end of class, give
students new problems to solve in
small groups.

SCIENCE EDUCATION:

DYNAMIC METHODS FOR FAST-PACED DISCIPLINES

Knowledge in the sciences is increasing at a phenomenal rate--doubling every decade, by some estimates. It is the formidable task of the science instructor to filter through the massive amount of information and distill the wisdom of the modern age into a few lectures. Teaching in an ever-changing field calls for dynamic methods of instruction.

As an educator, you must keep in mind both what brought you here and what drives students to or away from you and your discipline. At some point, you must have chosen science because of your sense of wonder over the complexity of the universe and the simplicity of its principles, the unity and diversity of life, and the harmony and discord of nature. But the very reasons why you selected your field may be the same reasons why some students stay away: Science fascinates you, but it also shocks you with disconcerting revelations about the world. The unknown can be particularly frightening.

In a truly enlightened society, people must be not only conversant but also comfortable with science. You play a crucial role in fostering such a society, for science is an essential element of a well-rounded university education.

In the introductory courses in every discipline, a substantial number of students enroll for one reason: to fulfill breadth requirements. Of course, some students are there to acquaint themselves better with their chosen field. But for either group, the introductory course can make or break a student's intent to continue in the field or in science at all. To ensure that students at this level and beyond have the opportunity to fully explore the discipline, science instructors must remain open to suggestion and experimentation.

The Limits of the Lecture

By its very nature, science engages in the discovery and identification of facts. The lecture format is often the instructor's technique of choice because it maximizes the amount of factual information that can be conveyed. It also feels comfortable and easy to manage, especially with large classes. The instructor exercises total control while the students merely--or hopefully--listen.

In all fairness, the lecture has its proper uses, and it appeals to auditory learners. But most science students favor kinesthetic processing (see Chapter 12). They learn best from physically acting out or performing the lesson, then inducing the conceptual point on their own. So in science especially, the Chinese proverb rings true: "What I hear, I forget; what I see, I remember; what I do, I understand." In addition, the lecture rarely allows students to understand and appreciate the sense of discovery enjoyed by the investigators whose work is under study. So as a singular method of science instruction, the lecture has serious weaknesses.

As science is a process and an activity, it may make better sense to focus on teaching students how to *think about* and *do* the discipline rather than testing their short-term memory of facts. It may be better to extend the boundaries of science education to exploring questions rather than constraining students' imaginations with the recitation of pre-conceived answers. Chapter 13 provides many science examples that broaden the instructional boundaries from factual recall to discovery and critical thinking.

The Role of the Laboratory

Many science courses already build in a premium student-active learning component, the laboratory. This is an excellent place to implement many innovative teaching techniques that allow students to interact with each other and to move toward discovery.

Too often, however, students see laboratory experiments as merely canned exercises that are irrelevant to their training. Unless you show them otherwise, the laboratory becomes a chore to be endured and not an exciting learning experience.

Given the time constraints of many lab exercises, you may be tempted to forego conducting a discussion of the principles to be illustrated and just introduce the day's work with a brief synopsis of the procedures. While this short-cutting gets students out of the lab quicker--and they typically appreciate it--it robs the lab of its educational value. Fortunately, there are ways to introduce the principles efficiently while simultaneously preparing students to perform the day's tasks.

It is advisable to begin a lab by asking students to review the previous week's material. You might have them do a two-minute free write to activate their memory (see Chapter 20). Use their summary responses to tie this particular lab to the course's progression of labs, sketching a unified "big picture." (A well organized laboratory curriculum should have a built-in sense of continuity.) Then you can introduce the day's principle, eliciting the experimental hypotheses and predictions from the students. After the exercises, you might ask students to share and explain their results and observations. Managing the lab this way actually leads students through the scientific process of observations and discovery. They are not left to sink or swim on their own.

Student Participation Formats

Commonly used in other disciplines, well directed class discussions and small group work add a participatory and cooperative dimension to the discovery process. You can launch a unit of instruction by introducing several analytical methods for investigating some principle. But once students understand the methods, they have the tools to address some central questions on their own in cooperative learning groups (see Chapter 18).

Consider a biology class in which an instructor presents the structure and function of DNA, the function of various enzymes involved in DNA synthesis and replication, and radio-labeling techniques. She then introduces the topic of DNA analysis by challenging the class with a brief case study: A rare blood disorder has been identified in a particular family in Europe. Divided into groups of three or four, the students are asked: 1) to devise possible methods to determine the disorder's cause and to locate the defective gene, and 2) to suggest diagnostic tests for identifying potential victims. After each small group reaches a consensus, the instructor directs a full class discussion evaluating the various methods suggested. In this scenario, students engage in discovery, the case method, and cooperative learning all at the same time.

Some of the nation's leading science departments commonly use cooperative learning. Eric Mazur, a physics professor at Harvard, employs an economical yet effective student-active technique in his large introductory courses (Simon, 1992). After introducing a new concept, he immediately challenges students with a multiple choice problem on an overhead transparency. For a minute or two, students work individually on a solution and rate their confidence in their answer. Then they briefly discuss and defend their answer with a partner, after which they can revise their answer and confidence rating. After students pair off, Dr. Mazur records significant

increases in correct answers and confidence levels. In addition, students demonstrate higher achievement than they did with lecture alone. (Simon, 1992, also shows two other cooperative learning formats used successfully by other Harvard science professors and TAs.)

Terry Hufford (1991) of George Washington University's Department of Biological Sciences has had success with another cooperative learning format. A decade of fairly low grades in an introductory biology course prompted him to radically redesign it. He reduced class size, refocused on critical thinking and complex reasoning skills, developed guidelines to help students with study and test-taking skills, and redesigned laboratory exercises to promote collaborative work on more novel experiments. In the lab groups, students coordinated specific tasks with other group members, much as they might cooperate in a professional setting, and shared data and observations. Then each group shared their results and conclusions with the other groups.

Hufford extended these lab groups to cooperative study groups that met outside of class. Their activities varied from memorization drills to deeper conceptual discussions to "what if" questions.

The results of this program were stunning. Holding constant test difficulty levels and grading scales, student achievement soared. The number of students receiving grades of "A" jumped from less than nine percent to more than 20 percent, while the number of failures fell from approximately 15 percent to less than three percent. Even more impressive, the failure rate for African-Americans, a group

170 originally identified as at-risk, plummeted from more than 50 percent to less than one half of one percent.

The Essential Elements of Successful Innovation

Innovative science instruction programs across the country share five key features.

- First, while some emphasize scientific process and others applications, they all involve students in hands-on experiences, decision-making and critical thinking (Penick and Crow, 1989).
- Second, they are tailored to the needs and interests of specific groups of students, as well as the professor's.
- Third, they feature laboratories as real scientific investigations that allow students to identify a problem, design an experiment, and carry it out under the instructor's direction. Students then present their results in a scholarly forum such as a symposium or a journal.
- A fourth essential feature of the innovative programs is their interdisciplinary approach. They bring in mentors from different fields to reinforce learning, especially for marginal students and "science avoiders." They also feature field trips to local community resources such as parks, zoos, and industrial sites.
- Finally, and perhaps most important, innovative instructors continue to change and evolve their courses. They have learned by experience that complacency and satisfaction with the status quo can be deadly to education and excellence. Only

by remaining open to new ideas have they been able to revitalize science at their universities. The morale of their stories is really quite scientific: Teaching strategies and course designs, like organisms, populations, and species, must either adapt or die.

Lab Safety

Safety in the lab is of paramount importance to you and your students. Since students have less lab experience, they tend to be more careless. So it is your responsibility to make them aware of lab safety concerns and procedures.

It is important to give explicit instructions on proper procedures, especially when working under potentially hazardous conditions. For example, if certain chemicals require special disposal protocols, explain them and the reasons for them in detail. It is best to demonstrate as well as describe the proper construction and handling of apparatus.

You must also be able to act promptly and effectively should an emergency arise. Know the standard procedures practiced by your department. If you are unsure of how to proceed in any given situation, ask a supervisor, lab coordinator, faculty member, or departmental safety officer.

In the event of a lab accident, rule number one is to REMAIN CALM. Make sure you know the location of the first aid kit, fire extinguishers, fire blankets, emergency showers and eye washes, bleach solutions, hazardous waste clean-up kits, etc. Familiarize yourself with the uses of each so that your emergency response will be swift and decisive.

First aid training may not be required of science instructors at your institution, but your knowing first aid principles is essential. At least study a first aid manual such as the one published by the American Red Cross. Better yet, take first aid and CPR certification training courses.

Here is one crucial rule of thumb: If a student is injured in your lab, assess the situation and take proper action. Small cuts and scrapes may be inconsequential, requiring nothing more than a bandage. But today, due to AIDS, it is best to treat all injuries involving loss of blood as hazardous situations. So do not touch a student who is bleeding unless you are wearing gloves. Isolate the blood spill area and immediately swab the surface twice with at least a 10% bleach solution. Label biohazardous materials accordingly and dispose of properly, as per your university's standards. Contact your institution's student health center for more information on AIDS and how to protect yourself.

Some General Principles of Lab Safety and Management

1) Be prepared. This motto should not only apply to Boy Scouts but to every lab instructor. Do a dry run of new or unfamiliar procedures. Be able to identify pitfalls and problems. Remember, students can tell whether or not you know what you are doing, and they will tell you on your evaluations.

2) Direct students to keep the lab as clean as possible. Not only is this good practice for them, but it also reduces the prep staff's work load.

3) Inform students of dress codes, including the use of safety equipment such as goggles and face shields, and enforce them. Typical clothing requirements include long pants, tied-back hair, no excessively loose cloth-

---

Chances are, you will be faced with some type of lab emergency sometime during your career. With a little procedural knowledge and preparation, you should be able to handle most situations. Quiz yourself on how you would respond to emergencies like these:

- A student tries to force a glass rod into a rubber stopper. The rod breaks, driving the sharp end into the palm of his hand.
- A student wearing a loose sweater is working with a Bunsen burner. As she turns away from the burner, her sleeve catches fire.
- A student spills 12 M HCl on his hand.
- A student tips over a boiling water bath, scalding his feet.
- In the course of an experiment, a student goes into respiratory arrest.
- A student is shocked while plugging the cord of a piece of equipment into a wall socket.
- A student splashes a large quantity of a corrosive chemical into her eye.
- Due to a student's error, a massive quantity of bromine gas is liberated in the lab.

ing, no encumbering jewelry, no shoes without tops, no bare feet, etc. Explain the reasoning behind these rules.

4) Students *must* read the lab manual carefully before coming to lab. Pop quizzes and cooperative learning group reviews (followed up with peer performance evaluations) help to insure that students prepare. The better informed students are, the better the conduct of the lab.

5) Be especially aware--and continually remind students--of any particularly dangerous procedures and how to avoid hazards.

6) Encourage student questions.

7) Discuss procedures thoroughly. It is perfectly acceptable to be redundant where safety is concerned.

8) Demonstrate proper techniques and correct students when necessary.

9) Move around the lab. While you can't be everywhere at once, be readily available for consultation.

On the next page, you will find a brief "quiz" describing several typical laboratory emergencies. You might use it to determine your own and/or your lab TAs' emergency preparedness.

Part V.

Assessment/

Measuring Outcomes

ASSESSING STUDENTS' LEARNING IN PROGRESS

No doubt you can recall class periods when you would have liked to have known what your students were learning from your lesson and whether or not you should proceed with the next one. Perhaps you found out what they missed from a test you gave three weeks later. Obviously, it is much more cost-effective to assess your students' learning while in progress, before their shortfalls in understanding adversely affect their grades and motivation. Such information can also help you determine, and ultimately enhance, your teaching effectiveness. It can even direct your students to the areas on which they need to focus their studying.

Classroom assessment techniques (CATs) were developed precisely to serve these purposes (Cross and Angelo, 1988; Angelo, 1991a). You can use them regularly or intermittently without violating the structure and content of your course and quickly identify trouble spots of an entire class or given individuals. Knowing what your students didn't absorb the first time through the material, you can turn around a bad situation.

Perhaps classroom assessment isn't all that much different from the informal, sometimes unconscious gauges you already use: reading students' expressions and body language, asking and answering questions, and the like. But these are unreliable and rarely encompass the whole class. CATs formalize and systematize the process, ensuring all students are included in your assessments.

Four-Dimensional Assessment

To assess students' learning, it is helpful to view it as four-dimensional (Angelo, 1991b). First, *declarative learning* is "learning what" -- that is, learning the facts and principles of a given field. In terms of Bloom's (1956) taxonomy of cognitive operations (see Chapters 3 and 16), declarative learning focuses on knowledge and comprehension at the lower end of the scale. *Procedural learning* is "learning how" to do something, from the specific tasks of a given discipline to universal skills such as writing, critical thinking, and reasoning. Its emphasis is application. The third dimension, *conditional learning*, is "learning when and where" to apply the acquired declarative knowledge and procedural skills. Too often taught only implicitly through example and modeling, it can be better taught *explicitly* using the case method, problem-based learning, role playing, and simulations (see Chapters 17 and 19). While conditional learning clearly entails application, it also involves analysis and synthesis. Finally, *reflective learning* is "learning why," which engages students in analysis, synthesis, and evaluation. It directs their attention to their beliefs, values, and motives for learning about a particular topic. Without this dimension, higher education is little more than job training.

Different CATs are designed to measure students' progress on different learning dimensions. So before selecting a CAT, consider which dimension you wish to assess.

Characteristics of Classroom Assessment

All CATs share these features (Angelo and Cross, 1993).

Learner-centered. While no substitute for appropriate teaching methods or graded examinations, classroom assessment aims to help students to learn better, whether by improving their study habits or by changing their metacognitive model of the discipline. In this respect, students take responsibility for their learning.

Teacher-directed. You have total freedom to decide what will be assessed, how it will be assessed, how the results will be analyzed, and how they will affect further actions. Be sure, then, that your CATs address factors that you are willing and able to change or improve.

Mutually beneficial. As students actively participate in the process of classroom assessment, CATs reinforce their learning of material. Like the student-active lecture breaks described in Chapter 14 and the writing-to-learn exercises covered in Chapter 20, good CATs make your students review, retrieve, apply, analyze, and/or synthesize the material from your lectures, classroom activities, and reading assignments as well as their prior learning experiences. Further, as classroom assessment underscores your interest in your students' progress, it also enhances their motivation. In turn, you benefit from the feedback on the effectiveness of your formats and methods. By working closely with your students, you enhance your teaching skills.

Formative. Unlike summative evaluations such as graded quizzes and exams, CATs are usually anonymous, ungraded, and geared strictly toward student learning.

Context-specific. CATs work differently in different classes. Since you know your class best, you can tailor CATs to its specific "personality" and needs, as well as to your discipline, material, time constraints, and informational needs.

Ongoing. Ideally, CATs provide a continual educational "feedback loop," informing you about your students' learning, to which you in turn adjust your teaching, back and forth until the end of the term.

Rooted in good teaching practice. Classroom assessment builds on current teaching practices, making them more systematic, effective, and flexible. For example, by using a simple diagnostic pre-test, you can find out how closely your students already meet your objectives. You can then pitch your presentations to their actual level, possibly covering more material than you might have otherwise.

Angelo and Cross (1993) suggest a three-step plan for launching classroom assessment. First, *start small.* Select one "friendly" class in which you are confident things are going well and a simple, short, low-effort CAT (e.g., the One-Minute Paper, the One-Sentence Summary, Directed Paraphrasing, and the Muddiest Point).

Second, *give detailed directions and a rationale.* It is best to tell students what you are doing and why. They will need explicit instructions on the board or overhead projector and assurance that their responses will be anonymous and used solely for mutual improvement. Allocate a few extra minutes the first time through any CAT.

Finally, *respond to the gathered information.* After you have reflected on your students' responses, it is advisable to take some time to share them with your class. If you decide to change your teaching formats or methods as a result, tell your students what you will initiate or do differently, and why. Equally important, give *them* pointers on how *they* can improve their learning.

Some Tried and True CATs

Chapter 20 introduced several popular CATs that also serve as writing-to-learn exercises: the *One-Minute Paper,* the *One-Sentence Summary, Directed Paraphrasing, Dialectical Notes,* and *Learning Logs.* Angelo and Cross (1993; also Cross and Angelo, 1988) describe dozens of other techniques, among which are the following:

Background Knowledge Probe. (Moderate instructor effort; low student effort.) This is essentially a diagnostic pre-test to administer on the first day of class and/or when you begin a new unit of instruction. It can consist of two or three short answer or essay questions or 15-20 multiple choice items about students' attitudes and understanding.

This CAT provides information not only on your students' prior knowledge but also on their motivation, beliefs, values, and, if you use open-ended questions, their writing skills. The results also tell you what material to cover and what existing knowledge you can use to map on new knowledge. Finally, probes activate students' prior knowledge, readying them for additional learning.

Focused Listing. (Low instructor and student effort.) You can use this technique to activate students' prior knowledge before you teach a topic and to help them review afterwards. Direct students' attention to a single important name, concept, or relationship and ask them to list as many related concepts and ideas as they can. You might limit the exercise to two to three minutes or five to ten items. With these constraints, the results give you a pretty accurate picture of the features students identify and recall as salient and not just those they think you want to hear.

Memory Matrix. (Moderate instructor effort; low student effort.) Memory matrices stress recall of course material, but they also require students to organize it in a framework you provide. Start by drawing a matrix with content-appropriate row and category headings. Leave sufficient space for several one-word or phrase responses in each cell. Distribute copies for your students to fill in, with a limit on the number of items they can write in each cell. This limit keeps students from stalling in search of the one best answer. Collect and examine the matrices for completeness and correctness.

Memory matrices show you how your students organize knowledge and whether or not they properly associate principles and concepts. Additionally, matrices help visual learners excel, facilitate students' retrieval of large amounts of information, and are easy to evaluate.

Muddiest Point. (Low instructor and student effort.) Very simply, ask your students to write down what they perceived as the muddiest point in a lecture, a homework assignment, a film, a demonstration, a discussion, etc. Reserve some time at the end of class to ask and answer questions, then collect the student responses. You can then clarify the muddy points during the next class.

Perhaps the easiest CAT to implement, it can be used on the spur of the moment. Struggling students who are not comfortable asking questions publicly find it to be a lifeline. Additionally, it enables you to see the material through your students' eyes, reminding you of the many ways they process and store information. Finally, knowing they will have to identify a muddy point induces students to pay closer attention in class.

Concept Maps. (Medium to high instructor and student effort.) Concept maps are diagrams that show the mental connections stu-

dents make among various concepts. For instance, you might ask your students to diagram the important features around racism, democracy, or natural selection and have them show how the features interrelate by drawing lines and arrows between them.

As few students are accustomed to drawing causal or associative models, it is best to work through your first concept map with your class. Start by writing a focal concept on the board or an overhead transparency, then spend a few minutes brainstorming related concepts and terms with the class. Begin with primary associations, then secondary and tertiary. Feel free to try different types of diagrams (e.g., concentric circles, a wheel with spokes, branching models, causal models, etc.)

Concept maps help visual learners get their minds around abstract relationships. Using low-tech materials, they also give you a graphic view of your students' conceptual association skills.

Paper or Project Prospectus. (Moderate to high instructor and student effort.) A prospectus is a detailed plan for a project or paper--perhaps even a rough draft--that focuses students on the topic, the purpose, the issues to address, the audience, the organization, the time, skills, and other resources needed--in fact, whatever guidelines you provide for the final product. First, students need to understand these guidelines, that is, the important facets and likely pitfalls of the assignment. For the prospectus itself, you might compose a list of three to seven questions that students must answer. Of course, advise students not to begin substantive work on their actual assignment until they receive feedback on their prospectus from you and possibly other students. As this CAT is a major assignment in itself, you may want to make it required and give some credit for good work.

The prospectus accommodates many different types of assignments and teaches crucial, transferable planning and organizational skills. In addition, it gives students early enough feedback to help them produce a better graded product.

Everyday Ethical Dilemmas. (Moderate to high instructor and student effort.) For this CAT, you begin by locating or creating a brief case study that poses an ethical problem related to the material (see Chapter 19). Then write two or three questions that force students to take and defend a position. Let your students turn in their written responses anonymously, thus giving you an honest overview of the prevailing class opinions and values. Students will need some time to think reflexively and to develop their arguments, so you might assign this CAT as homework.

Ethical dilemmas encourage students to "try on" different values and beliefs, thus helping them develop moral reasoning skills. This CAT also affords you probing, personal glimpses into your students' ethical and cognitive maturity. With these insights, you can foster their continuing growth by introducing values and opinions that they have not yet considered.

Self Confidence Surveys. (Low to medium instructor and student effort.) As the name implies, this CAT consists of a few simple questions about your students' confidence in their ability to perform course-related tasks. Design a brief, anonymous survey focusing on specific skills and tasks. Find the low-confidence areas in the results, and give additional instruction and practice accordingly. Self confidence surveys help you identify your students' areas of anxiety and establish the minimal levels of self confidence necessary for success in the course.

Punctuated Lectures. (Low instructor and student effort.) After your students listen to your lecture or demonstration, stop for a moment and ask them to reflect on what they were doing during your presentation and how it helped or hindered their understanding. Have them anonymously write out and turn in their reflections. After reading their responses, offer suggestions on how they can improve their listening and self-monitoring skills. Through your feedback, this CAT helps students hone these skills, both of which are highly transferable. It also better acquaints you with your students' processing styles and pitfalls.

RSQC2 (Recall, Summarize, Question, Connect, and Comment). (Low to medium instructor and student effort.) This technique assesses your students' recall, comprehension, analysis, synthesis, and evaluation of recent material. Begin by having students list the most important points they can remember from the last class (or the assigned reading). Second, ask them to define as many terms as they can in one-sentence summaries. Third, have them write one or two questions about each point that still confuses them. Fourth, ask them to connect each important point they identified either with other important points or with your course goals. Finally, have them write an evaluative comment about the course, the class period, or the material (e.g., "What I enjoyed most/least..."; "What I found most/least useful...").

Each of the five activities requires at least two minutes. If you can spare the time, let students compare their responses among themselves. Of course, feel free to pick and choose the activities you find most useful.

RSQC2 gives you timely feedback on what your students consider important material and what they value about your course. By having them recall the previous class and make connections, this CAT also builds bridges between old and new material.

Student Portfolios

While very different from anonymous, one-time CATs, student portfolios allow you to assess and document your students' progress across written products without attaching grades. A portfolio is a collection of samples of a student's work during the term, one that you and s/he have the option of assembling together. These samples may be the student's best work, the widest variety of his/her good work, and/or the "history" of one or more major pieces of work (e.g., notes, outlines, peer and instructor reviews, and multiple revisions in response to those reviews). You grade only the total portfolio, typically at the end of the term (Bernhardt, 1992).

Student portfolios became very popular among English instructors from primary through post-secondary levels in the 1980s. Those who use them testify that portfolios encourage constructive

dialogue between students and instructor and motivate students to attempt more varied and adventuresome writing, to take instructor and peer feedback seriously, and to revise their work, often several times. College-level instructors in many disciplines, even mathematics, have developed their own versions of the portfolio, most of which either permit or require much more creative demonstrations of learning than do traditional assignments and tests (Belanoff and Dickson, 1991; Crowley, 1993).

Consider, for example, the imaginative range of assessments artifacts that a mathematics portfolio can contain: samples of journal entries; written explanations for each mathematical step of a complex problem solution; a mathematics autobiography focusing on changing attitudes and new insights; multiple solutions to a challenging problem, each reflecting a different approach; an elegant proof, either intuitive or formal depending upon the student's abilities; student-developed lesson plans for teaching a particular mathematical concept; student-developed word problems; student-drawn visual representations of problems; student-made concrete representations; and reviews of mathematical books and journal articles--all in addition to examples of traditional student output, such as tests, quizzes, and homework (Stenmark, 1989, 1991; Crowley, 1993).

Portfolios are not without their problems, however. For example, postponing grades until the end of the term will not necessarily save you grading time. Quite the contrary. While you may not have to affix letters to students' work till the end, you will probably assign more and more varied writing projects and put more time and effort into writing formative feedback and holding student conferences on each project during the term. Without this detailed, personalized feedback, none of the potential benefits of portfolios will acrue. In addition, you will otherwise suffocate at the end of the term under an avalanche of notebooks and folders filled with only vaguely familiar writing samples. In the terms used above to describe CATs, portfolios entail very high effort on both your own and your students' part (Bernhardt, 1992).

Another serious problem for many students is the lack of letter grading during the term. Often they are anxious not knowing where they stand and how they are doing, and some need to know early in the term to decide whether to stay in the course. Academic regulations may not even allow such postponement of grades. Vanderbilt University, for instance, requires faculty to submit midsemester deficiency reports on students earning a "C-" or lower, and committees will not approve new courses unless a substantial part of the final grade is determined by the end of the seventh week.

A final problem with portfolios pertain to grading standards. If a portfolio contains only the students' best work, how can anyone in the class not receive a good grade? But the converse problem also arises: Some instructors resist assigning deservedly low grades to students who have worked so hard during the term. Even with herculean effort, some students barely pass a course, and it can be very difficult for some instructors to break the bad news to them after all the time they've spent talking with and working with these students.

Therefore, before adopting student portfolios, consider the following issues about delayed grading: how your students might respond to it; if your institution's academic regulations accommodate it; and whether you can uphold your quality standards in spite of it. Then ask yourself if you can make the time to give your students' writing the detailed, ongoing feedback that is required.

Extending Classroom Assessment to Classroom Research

If you are collecting and examining systematic data on the effectiveness of one teaching format or method over another, why not write up and publish your more interesting results? You already know how to conduct research. All you may need is an outlet.

There are well over a hundred journals on college teaching, as well as dozens of national newsletters. Some specialize in a given discipline, a few in a specific teaching method (e.g., cooperative learning, instructional technology), but most are general. Though each journal favors one or two types of articles, they collectively publish standard research studies, literature reviews with insightful conclusions, evaluative descriptions of teaching innovations (i.e., "how to" articles), philosophical statements, and analyses of current educational policies, problems, and trends (Nilson, 1992). You might skim several of these journals to find a few that publish pieces similar to yours. Look for such periodicals in your institution's main library, educa-

181

182   tion library, and teaching center library.

Cross (1992) points out that classroom research doesn't require a grant or committee approval. But she recommends enhancing your research by reading up on learning theory and by collaborating with colleagues who are teaching the same or similar courses.

Classroom research is not new. Decades before Cross and Angelo started promoting the idea, economics ushered in scholarly, scientific inquiry into student learning/achievement, the most important outcome we can assess. The field has been on the forefront ever since, largely because economists have been able to agree on the learning objectives for certain courses and to develop standardized tests to measure goal attainment. Until other disciplines can reach a similar consensus, their research will be limited to small classroom samples.

TEST
CONSTRUCTION

How does test construction fit into the overall scheme of teaching? As Chapter 3 explained, the process of teaching begins with developing instructional objectives. Your general and specific objectives direct your selection of presentation methods to produce the desired learning response in your students. It is best to construct your assessment instruments, then, to measure your success in meeting the objectives. So all three phases of instruction--objective setting, teaching, and testing--are woven into a multifaceted arrangement of interdependent parts, each strengthened by the others.

While instructors can evaluate student learning in many ways, graded quizzes and examinations are the most common way. This chapter examines the advantages and disadvantages of many of the popular types of test questions and suggests techniques for constructing meaningful tests.

Thinking about Testing

Before you begin writing a quiz or an exam, think seriously about what you are trying to accomplish with it. A test can assess merely students' short-term memory skills or their abilities to comprehend, apply, analyze, synthesize, and evaluate the material as well. (See Chapters 3 and 16 for details on Bloom's six levels of cognitive operations/questions.)

Review your course objectives and identify the levels of cognition each one represents. If your objectives focus primarily on knowledge, comprehension, and application, then so should your quiz and exam questions. Unless you have trained students to work at the higher levels, questions pitched at these levels will not measure their goal attainment. Your students will also be doomed to perform poorly.

General Testing Guidelines

The following suggestions were adapted largely from Lacey-Casem (1990) and Ory and Ryan (1993).

Test early and often. Early testing gives students feedback that tells them how to optimize their course performance. Frequent testing gives more opportunities for success, reducing the penalties for any single poor performance.

Compose test questions immediately after you cover the material in the class. The material and the cognitive level(s) at which you taught it are fresh in your mind. Practiced regularly, this strategy ensures you a stock of questions to use when quiz and exam times arrive.

Give detailed, written instructions for all exams and quizzes. Remind students about your and your institution's policies on academic dishonesty (see Chapter 9), and specify the test time limit, the number of each type of question to answer, the point values of different items, where to record answers, whether to show work, whether books, notes, or calculators can be used, etc.

Start the test with some warm-up questions. Asking a few easier questions at the beginning of a quiz or exam induces students to start thinking about the material and builds their confidence.

Proofread the test form for errors. Check for spelling, grammar, split items (i.e., items that begin on one page and continue on the next), format consistency, format errors, instructions for each type of question, and adequate space for constructed responses. It is best to have another set of eyes proofread it, too (e.g., a colleague, your TA or head TA, or your supervising professor).

Have another instructor evaluate the test for clarity and content, especially if you are somewhat inexperienced, but even if you are seasoned. You may have written a quiz or exam that seems crystal clear to you, only to find out later that certain items were double-barrelled, ambiguously phrased, or awkwardly constructed. Writing good test items is a hard-to-learn craft, and you needn't learn it all by bad experience.

Types of Test Questions

In general, there are two kinds of test questions (Ory and Ryan, 1993).

Objective questions. Multiple choice, true/false, and matching items measure knowledge and comprehension very effectively. Inexperienced instructors sometimes think that objective questions are easy to construct. In truth, a good, unambiguous multiple choice question takes time and thought. Professional test writers often produce only eight or ten good questions a day.

Constructed response questions. Completion, short answer, essay, and problem solving allow students to do more than just choose among given, possible answers. Here students write and often justify their own answers. (This type of question is commonly misnamed "subjective," a term that should not be used because it gives the impression that instructors have no clear standards for judging students' answers.) While easier to compose than the objective type, constructed response questions are much more difficult to grade. You must interpret students' sometimes rambling thoughts and judge among variable answers. Consider giving students a choice among several such questions. Having options lowers their anxiety and allows them to show you what they've learned best.

Each type of question has its place, and different students do well with different types of questions. Using a variety of questions on an exam allows students to feel more secure with the test format.

This section lays out the strengths and weaknesses of different types of tests questions, as well as construction guidelines (Lacey-Casem, 1990; Ory and Ryan, 1993).

Multiple Choice

Advantages:

+ Easy/quick to grade by hand or optical scanner.
+ Reduces some of the burden of large classes.
+ Can assess knowledge, comprehension, application, and analysis.
+ Useful as a diagnostic tool since student choices can indicate weaknesses.

Disadvantages:

- Difficult/time-consuming to construct.
- Encourages instructors to test trivial and factual knowledge.
- May be ambiguous; students often misinterpret.
- Particularly subject to "cluing," i.e., students can deduce the correct answer by elimination.

Construction:

- Estimate one to five minutes for students to answer each question.
- Address one problem or concept per question. Avoid questions with multiple correct answers, as these confuse students.
- Phrase items with clarity and internal consistency. The item stem should be a direct positive statement expressing a complete thought. The response alternatives or options should be brief and similarly structured. Avoid wordiness.
- Include any words in the stem that can be repeated in the response alternatives.
- Avoid items that merely ask a series of true/false questions.
- If you use negatively stated stems, italicize or capitalize the negative word(s) to avoid confusion.
- Use familiar language, i.e., similar to the language that you or the readings used to explain the concept, process, relationship, etc.
- Make sure there is one correct or best response.
- Minimize the use of "all of the above" or "none of the above."
- Use three to five alternatives per item.
- Make alternatives equally plausible and attractive. Absurd options only make guessing easier.
- Present alternatives in some logical order or alphabetize them to reduce your likelihood of falling into a pattern.
- Avoid grammatical cues to correct answers.
- Incorporate sketches and diagrams where appropriate.

True/False

Advantages:
+ Easy to prepare and to grade.
+ Can test a lot of material in a short time.
+ Can assess both lower and higher levels of cognition.
+ Can tap higher levels by having students correct the false statements.
+ Useful as a diagnostic tool if students correct false statements.

Disadvantages:
- High guessing factor for simple true/false questions.
- Encourages instructors to test trivial and factual knowledge.
- May be ambiguous.
- May include irrelevant clues.

Construction:
• Allow 30 seconds to one minute per item.
• Use only statements that are entirely true or entirely false.
• Focus each statement on a single idea or problem.
• Write positive statements. Negative and double negative statements are confusing.
• Avoid verbal cues to the correct answers. For example, questions with *usually, seldom,* and *often* are frequently true while those with *never, always,* and *every* are commonly false.
• Use familiar terminology.
• Balance the number of true and false answers.
• Avoid always making true statements long and false statements short, or vice versa. Students quickly pick up on these patterns
• Avoid direct quotes from lectures or readings requiring only rote memorization.

Advantages:
+ Easy to grade.
+ Assesses knowledge/recall well.
+ Relatively unambiguous.
+ Can test a lot of material in a short time.

Disadvantages:
- Difficult to construct a commo set of stimuli and responses.
- High guessing factor.
- Cannot assess higher levels of cognition.
- Not useful as a diagnostic tool.

Construction:
* Allow 30 seconds to one minute per item.
* Keep stimuli and responses short and simple.
* List possible responses in some logical order (e.g., alphabetical or chronological) to reduce student search time.
* Say whether response items can be used more than once.
* Limit stimuli and responses to 15 or less.
* Keep all stimuli and responses on one page.
* Have students identify their response choices using only capital letters to avoid ambiguity.

Completion (Fill-in-the-Blank)

Advantages:
+ Easy to prepare and grade.
+ Assesses knowledge/recall and vocabulary well.
+ Eliminates guessing.
+ Can test a lot of material in a short time.

Disadvantages:
- Cannot assess higher levels of cognition.
- Highly structured; requires an all-or-nothing response.
- Not useful as a diagnostic tool.
- May include irrelevant clues.
- Difficult to construct so that the desired response is clear.
- May be difficult to grade if more than one answer may be correct.

Construction:
• Allow 30 seconds to one minute per item.
• Use clear wording to elicit a unique response.
• Avoid grammatical cues. For instance, use a/an or was/were to reduce cluing.
• Omit only significant words from the statement.
• Omit words from the middle or end of a statement, not the beginning.
• Make all fill-in lines the same length.
• Place the response lines in a column to the left or right to facilitate grading.
• Use familiar language.

Short Answer

Advantages
+ Easy to construct.
+ Can assess levels of cognition from recall to analysis.
+ Requires a command of vocabulary and/or problem solving skills.
+ More useful as a diagnostic tool than any objective types.
+ Encourages instructors to give students individual feedback.

Disadvantages:
- Time-consuming to grade.
- Difficult to standardize grading due to variability across answers.

Construction:
• Estimate two to five minutes per item.
• Be very specific and concise in identifying the task students are to perform. See advice below for constructing essay questions.
• Indicate whether diagrams or illustrations are required or are acceptable in place of a written answer.
• Extend the cognitive process involved by asking for a case analysis, diagnosis, or hypothesis.
• Require students to show work for full credit on problems.
• Leave an appropriate amount of space for the answers. Too much space invites students to write too much.

Advantages:

+ Quick and relatively easy to construct.
+ Can assess all the higher levels of cognition.
+ Assesses students' abilities to logically compose and present an argument.
+ Encourages creativity and originality.
+ Requires students to really know the material.
+ Develops writing skills.
+ Encourages students to study in a more integrated/ synthetic manner.
+ Discourages last-minute cramming.
+ Encourages instructors to give students individual feedback.

Disadvantages:

- Time-consuming to grade.
- Difficult to standardize grading because of variability across answers as well as length of answers.
- Cannot test a lot of material on any one exam.
- Penalizes students who read or work slowly, have poor writing skills, or are non-native English speakers.
- May be ambiguous if students don't understand test verbs or don't read the entire question very carefully.
- Encourages grading protests because the scoring may seem subjective and inconsistent.
- Easy to make questions too broad for students to zero in on the answer.
- Allows students to pick up points for bluffing.

Construction:

- Estimate ten minutes to one hour per item.
- Estimate how long an answer should take to help students budget their time accordingly.
- Give the point value for each question.
- Give several shorter essay questions rather than one or two long ones. This strategy covers more material and spreads the risk for students.
- Use original problems, cases, diagrams, graphs, data sets, etc.
- Identify the key points that must be addressed in the answer.
- Be very specific and concise in identifying the task you want students to perform. Rather than beginning a question with an interrogative pronoun such as why, how, or what, start with a descriptive verb (see Chapter 28 for a list of common test verbs and their definitions) and specify exactly how elaborate the answer should be (e.g., "*Describe three ways* that social integration could break down in the modern world, according to Durkheim. Then *assess* how closely *each one* applies to the United States in the 1990s.").
- If a question is controversial or value-based, assure students that grading will be based on the validity of their arguments, the strength of their evidence, and/or the quality of their presentation-- not the opinion expressed.
- If you let students choose among several questions, limit the choices (e.g., to five out of seven rather than two out of five).

The time and effort invested in writing a good test are not without their rewards. It is heartening to see your students perform well on your challenging exam or to receive a compliment on it from a student. Both indicate that your test was probably a learning as well as a "fair" evaluation experience.

But even more important, the tests you design are the most important instruments you have for assessing *your* teaching effectiveness. So for *your* sake as well as your students', they should measure what you set out to teach. Student, peer, and self evaluations are other instruments, and student opinions of your success generally carry the most weight. But they merely take the place of the *only real teaching evaluation, which is how much students have learned.*

In the best of all possible educational worlds, each course exam would be tested to ensure high reliability and validity. Then student performance would be used to evaluate the instructor's teaching success relative to other instructors teaching the same course. Of course, such an ideal could only come to pass if faculty could agree on a standardized content and testing instrument for each course--an idea that goes against academic freedom and autonomy.

Still, how your students perform on well designed tests is your best data for your personal self-assessment of your teaching.

PREPARING STUDENTS FOR TESTS

Think back to your undergraduate days. Did you ever feel anxiety or a sense of dread when your professors announced an exam? Did you ever walk into a test feeling well-prepared, only to "freeze" when you saw the first question? Did you ever leave an exam feeling that you "aced" it, only to find yours at the bottom of the stack when the tests were returned? If even one of these questions made you feel a little uneasy, you can probably sympathize with some of the emotions your students are experiencing now.

The first question you usually hear when you announce an upcoming exam is "What will the test format be?" This is a valid question. We'd like to believe that students will perform well on any type of test with adequate study. But different types of exams call for different types of study strategies, and most students learn based on how they are tested (Wergin, 1988). Factual memorization for a recall-oriented objective test takes a different kind of study effort than that for analyses of problems or situations. It is that latter type of studying that helps students develop critical thinking skills, and students need experience in the higher cognitive processes of analysis, synthesis, and evaluation.

Preparation Techniques

If we accept that tests can be instruments of instruction as well as evaluation, then preparing students to perform well on tests is also an excellent teaching strategy. Here are some easily implemented ways to help students prepare for exams (some adapted from Lacey-Casem, 1990):

Study groups. Many of the chapters in this book (e.g., 17, 18, and 25) point out the teaching effectiveness of cooperative learning groups. Cooperative *study* groups that meet regularly outside of class are also very helpful (e.g., Hufford, 1991). Since student commitment can make or break them, you may want to formalize them by having students sign up for study groups very early in the semester. Then distribute a list of all the groups with their members' names and phone numbers.

Review sheets. This study aid helps many students, especially freshmen in introductory courses. You can make a review sheet as simple as an outline of important topics that you have emphasized or as elaborate as a sample exam. The sample test method involves much more time and effort, since you will not want to duplicate sam-

192 ple items on the real test. But you can use a previous test if it accurately reflects your current course.

Between the simple and the elaborate is the list of review questions. The questions should illustrate the variety of question formats that will appear on the test. If you plan to test with some objective multiple choice questions, ask some objective review questions. If you intend rather to test analysis and synthesis, develop review questions that require the same cognitive operations.

Review sessions. As do many instructors, you may wish to set up a special review session shortly before an exam. But it is likely to work well only if students have already made significant progress in their independent or small group studies. Therefore, you should make it clear that you will not be summarizing the last few weeks of lectures and readings nor giving out the answers to the review questions.

The most productive way to conduct a review session is to insist that students come prepared to 1) ask specific questions on the material and 2) answer the review questions on their own. With respect to their questions, always ask the class for answers before answering the questions yourself. With respect to the review questions, have the entire class participate in brainstorming and refining the answers, and assign different questions to small groups and have them develop and orally present their answers. Invite other students to evaluate the groups' answers, then offer your own assessment.

Chapter 14 describes another version of this format called

pair/group and review, in which student pairs or small groups develop and present their answers to the class, while you mock-grade them and explain your assessment criteria. You can also have the rest of the class mock-grade the answers to help students learn how to assess their own work.

Help sessions or course clinics. This method takes the review session one step further by establishing weekly meetings of two or more hours during which the professor or the TA answers questions. A regularly scheduled meeting encourages students to keep up with the course and not wait until the last minute to cram for a test. It also reduces stress by having students study without the impending threat of an exam.

Definitions of key test terms. Students, especially freshmen, often do poorly on a test because they are not exactly sure what a particular question, especially an essay question, is asking. So it may be safest to provide them with written definitions of common test verbs, along with review questions that give students practice in the operations. Consider sharing the definitions below with your classes (Ellis, 1985, p. 155; Lacey-Casem, 1990, pp. 41-42).

Analyze: Break something down into parts, such as a theory into its components, a process into its stages, or an event into its causes. Analysis involves characterizing the whole, identifying its parts, and showing how the parts interrelate.

Assess/Criticize/Evaluate: Determine or judge the degree to which something meets or fails to meet certain criteria. If not provided in the question, develop criteria for making judgments.

Classify: Sort into major, general groups or categories that you name or identify.

Compare/Contrast: Identify the important similarities and/or differences between two or more elements in order to reveal something significant about them. Emphasize similarities if the command is to compare and differences if it is to contrast.

Define/Identify: Give the key characteristics by which a concept, thing, or event can be understood. Place it in a general class, then distinguish it from other members of that class.

Describe: Give the characteristics by which an object, action, process, person, or concept can be recognized or visualized.

Discuss/Examine: Debate, argue, and evaluate the various sides of an issue.

Explain/Justify: Give the basic principles of or reasons for something; make it intelligible. Explanation may involve relating the unfamiliar to the more familiar.

List/Enumerate: Give essential points one by one in a logical order. It may be helpful to number the points.

Interpret/Explain: Say what the author of a quotation or statement means.

Illustrate: Use a concrete example to explain or clarify the essential attributes of a problem or concept.

Outline/Trace/Review/State: Organize a description under main points and subordinate points, omitting minor details and classifying the elements or main points.

Prove/Validate: Establish that something is true by citing factual evidence or giving clear, logical reasons.

Combating Test Anxiety

Some anxiety is normal before an exam and indeed has a motivating effect on students. Mealey and Host (1993) reviewed test anxiety literature and identified three categories of anxious students. Students of the first type lack adequate study skills and are aware of the problem. They are not well prepared for exams and worry about poor performance. The second category includes students who have adequate study strategies but become distracted during testing. Naveh-Benjamin et al.'s research (1987) confirms these first two types. The final group is composed of students who mistakenly believe that they have adequate study skills but do poorly on exams, then wonder what the problem could be.

Mealey and Host asked students how instructors reduce or heighten student anxiety before, during, and after an exam. They received four kinds of responses:

1) Students resent interruptions during an exam, even if they are to correct or to clarify test items.

2) Seventy-five percent of the students want the instructor to conduct some kind of review before the test. They feel more confident if they are sure they have correct information in their notes.

3) Students do not like an instructor to walk around the room and look over their shoulders. While it may keep cheating in check, it also raises the anxiety level of stress-sensitive students.

4) Students do not respond well to hearing how hard a test will be. They do not mind a challenging exam, but they would prefer to hear how they should study, followed by some words of reassurance.

Lacey-Casem (1990) suggests some other practical methods to help alleviate test anxiety:

5) Establish (in writing) your test schedule along with policies on missed exams.
6) Explain and keep to a clear grading system.
7) Test frequently. The more grades you have, the less a poor performance on any one exam will cost.
8) Allow students to drop one low test or quiz. Everyone can have a bad day.
9) Make sure your exams can be completed in the allotted time. It is discouraging to near the end of the hour and have many items unanswered.
10) Teach students to relax. Deep breathing exercises, counting to ten, and visualizing a successful test session (e.g., Hebert, 1984) are all useful ways to combat nervousness.

Occasionally, you may have a student for whom test anxiety is a debilitating problem. As with other emotional and psychological problems, refer such a student to your institution's counseling center and/or its learning skills/academic assistance center.

Preparing students for tests is one way to ensure your students review and synthesize the material. It can also help you organize and plan your exam. Whatever you can do further to reduce your students' test anxiety allows them to demonstrate more accurately their actual learning. And it is only by seeing their honest achievement that you can assess how effective *your teaching* has been.

GRADING:
TESTS, ASSIGNMENTS, AND COURSE PERFORMANCE

Grading is a task you may view with dread and disdain, but it provides essential feedback to your students on their performance and to you on your teaching effectiveness.

Historically, grading is a relatively new phenomenon in the academy (Hammons and Barnsley, 1992). Yale University was the first American institution to assign grades, starting in 1783. Professors used Latin descriptors ranging from the exceptional *optime* to the dismal *pejores* to classify student performance. In 1800, Yale adopted a numerical scale of 0 to 4, thus beginning the grade point average. Later, William and Mary adopted a similar scheme.

In 1850, the University of Michigan introduced a pass/fail system that set the passing grade minimum at 50 percent. Harvard began using letter grades in 1883. This system soon swept the country, but with tremendous disagreement on the grade cut-off points. For instance, Mount Holyoke set the failing grade at 75 percent, while Michigan maintained a 50 percent standard. Harvard's failing mark was a low 26 percent. Even with such broad discrepancies in the scale, higher education has made few major changes in this system, except to add +/- modifiers.

The Meaning of Grades

Pollio and Humphreys (1988) note that instructors, students, parents, and business people do not agree on the meaning of grades. For instance, when asked how long the impact of receiving a "C" vs. an "A" would last, a full 53 percent of the faculty respondents expected it would last at least two to five years. So did a third of the parents and business people. But only 14 percent of the students surveyed agreed, and 45 percent anticipated no impact at all.

While many students may not want to believe that grades are important to their futures, one of your major responsibilities is to evaluate their achievement and assign grades accordingly. In addition, you are responsible for upholding the value of the grading currency-- i.e., combatting grade inflation. So it is worth reviewing the level of performance each grade represents.

An "A" signifies an exceptional level of achievement. The student displays a superb command of the subject matter and can creatively apply it at many different levels. "A" students tend to be very committed and motivated.

A "B" indicates an above average but not outstanding level of achievement. "B" students demon

196 strate a good grasp of the material and the ability to apply at several but not all levels.

A "C" represents an average level of achievement. The student shows some mastery of the material and a narrow application range. This grade may indicate poor study skills or a lack of motivation or interest. Some "C" students get by on their decent test-taking skills.

A "D" means that the student has little or no true understanding of the subject area and may not be interested in learning any more.

An "F" denotes a performance below the level of random chance. The student may have a total lack of interest, motivation, and/or ability.

Summative Evaluations and Grading Systems

Pregent (1994) describes two types of evaluation: *summative* and *formative*. A **summative evaluation** is an assessment of the knowledge that has been accrued after the learning has ended, at the end of a part or all of the course. It typically follows one of two basic grading systems (Wergin, 1988; Hammons and Barnsley, 1992; Ory and Ryan, 1993; Pregent, 1994):

Norm-referenced grading (NRG). The first type of summative grading system evaluates each student's performance relative to all other students' performances. Usually called "grading on a curve," it places students in competition with each other for class ranking; the best and worst performances set the parameters within which other performances are judged. While this system assures any class GPA an instructor may want, it has some serious flaws. First, it statistically assumes a bell-shaped ("normal") distribution of student scores--a phenomenon that doesn't always occur. Second, the grades it yields are unrelated to any absolute performance standard. So if all students in a class perform poorly, some inadequate performances will receive an "A" anyway. Conversely, in a high achieving class, many excellent performances will unjustly get a "C."

Criterion-referenced grading (CRG). This second grading system eliminates such inequities (Wergin, 1988). It requires instructors to set absolute standards of performance (grading criteria) in advance, giving all students responsibility for their own grades.

Comparing these two grading schemes, you can see that the primary purpose of NRG is discrimination or selection, while CRG focuses on diagnosis and mastery. NRG tests general course objectives, while CRG assesses specific objectives. To be statistically viable as well as fair to students, NRG requires a wide variability of scores--an irrelevant issue in CRG. Finally, NRG yields only the students' relative class standing; CRG measures their actual learning and abilities.

To be sure, criterion-referenced grading has its drawbacks. In particular, it is difficult to develop meaningful, valid standards for assigning grades based on absolute knowledge acquisition (Ory and Ryan, 1994). Instructors who are unfamiliar with their student population may have no idea how scores may distribute on any given test or assignment. (As the nightmare goes, the scores may all cluster around 95 percent or all lag below

70.) But once you have a term's experience, criterion-referenced grading is the superior summative scheme, especially if you stress achievement, competence, and excellence in your students.

Formative Evaluations and Feedback Guidelines

A *formative evaluation* is an assessment of student performance at any point *during* the learning process, with the objective of helping the student to learn the material better (Pregent, 1994). While formative evaluations may involve grading, the scores are not calculated in a final grade; rather, they are intended as qualitative feedback to help the student improve. When you mark and comment on rough drafts of papers--or you train students how to assess each other's papers in small groups--you are providing your students with formative evaluations.

This type of feedback benefits both you and your students in several ways. For them, it encourages steady writing and work habits; it gives them criteria on which to revise and improve their papers and their writing in general; and it teaches them the real, professional writing process, which always involves extensive rewriting. For you, it yields much better student products, practically eliminates plagiarism, and changes your role from judge to facilitator.

These few suggestions will make formative evaluations of papers more productive:

- Strictly enforce deadlines for students' finding topics, gathering resources, developing an outline, and submitting a first draft. Formative evaluation takes time.
- Comment more on major writing issues, such as content, reasoning, and organization, and less on style and grammar.
- Make your comments constructive, personalized, and informal. Give praise where deserved, as students often do not know what they are doing right.
- Train your students to do small group evaluations of first drafts and informal assignments. Give your own detailed comments on the first drafts of the first paper, review your feedback methods with your class, then oversee students' comments on the drafts of the second paper. After that, the small groups should be able to provide good feedback on their own.
- Make sure students understand that formative evaluations focus on *major* problems in their papers and that making the suggested changes does not guarantee them an "A."

Accuracy, Consistency, and Learning Value

A sound grading scheme is *accurate, consistent,* and *valuable to learning.* Larger classes require special efforts to ensure these qualities, especially consistency. The following guidelines should help (Lacey-Casem, 1990):

Accuracy:
- A final grade based on many and varied assignments and tests.
- Well constructed quizzes and exams reflecting the course objectives and content (see Chapter 27).
- Point values that reflect the im-

portance of the concepts and relationships tested.

- Test keys and grading rubrics that allow for the possibility of multiple correct answers.
- An established grading standard appropriate for the level of your students.
- Careful evaluations of each student's performance.

Consistency:

- Objective testing methods that use optical scanning technology.
- Written guidelines for correct responses, particularly if multiple graders are involved.
- Two gradings of each essay or paper, the first impressionistic/holistic and the second detailed.
- Discussion of problematic answers among several graders to achieve consensus.
- Maintenance of student anonymity to avoid grading biases.

Learning:

- Accentuating the positive. Comment generously, including on what the student did right. Too many negatives are overwhelming and counterproductive.
- Identifying a few key areas for improvement and specific remediation methods. Once again, if you try to fix everything at once, students become overwhelmed and tune out.
- Directing comments to the performance, not the student.
- Being specific in your comments. Avoid a cryptic "what?" or "?".
- Allowing revisions of papers after formative evaluations of first drafts.

- Providing samples of exemplary work, and helping students understand what makes them excellent.
- Providing a detailed key with not only the correct answers but also the reasons why other responses are incorrect.
- Reviewing exams when you return them so that students understand what you wanted and how they can improve their performance. Focus on frequently missed items.
- Sharing studying, writing, problem solving, and test-taking techniques, and referring some students to your institution's learning skills/academic assistance center for special help.

Grading Constructed Responses and Papers

Grading answers to constructed response questions requires considerable thought and strategy to ensure accuracy and consistency within reasonable time frames. You can choose from two popular grading methods (Neel, 1993; Ory and Ryan, 1993):

Analytical scoring. Begin by developing a "rubric"--that is, considering and listing the components of an ideal response or paper. Then allocate point values among the components. As you read each student's response or paper, check off the components and total the point values for the grade. This method helps inexperienced instructors become accustomed to the grading process. It also makes grading disputes easier to handle.

While this approach may seem completely content-oriented and is often implemented that way, it can and usually should include other dimensions as well: organization, trueness to specified format, quality of data/evidence, documentation, logic of reasoning, clarity, style (sentence structure, word choice, etc.), and mechanics (grammar, punctuation, spelling, etc.).

Of course, you may only care about four or five such dimensions, and these will depend upon your discipline and the question or assignment. In reality, you can keep track of only four or five anyway. Each dimension you use can take on a different point value as well (e.g., 20 for content, 15 for organization, 10 for style, and 5 for mechanics, for a total of 50 points).

When you give the assignment or prepare students for your test, it is *imperative* to explain your evaluative dimensions and their point values to your class. Your students need to know and understand the criteria on which you will evaluate their work.

Global quality scoring. A little trickier to master, this method is based on comparative evaluations of your students' responses and papers. In one global quality schema, you read quickly through all the responses or papers for your holistic impression, placing each one in a stack designated high, medium, or low quality or "A," "B," "C," "D/F." Then reread each stack, subdividing the responses or papers into high/+, medium, and low/- and assigning grades accordingly. Your final task is writing comments.

Experienced instructors can implement this approach with high reliability, but it takes practice; global quality scorers of standardized essay exams undergo hours of training in the method. In addition, since it relies heavily on your experienced judgment, defending your grades to students can be difficult. Therefore, your comments are crucial.

With either scoring system, you can make your comments more accurate and meaningful by consciously trying to distinguish the various evaluative dimensions you have in mind. For example, try not to let a poor grammatical construction devalue a good idea (assuming, of course, you can decipher the idea despite the construction). You can limit your editorial and grammatical comments by correcting errors once and checking each repetition. Be sure to define your proofreading marks to your students; a handout may serve the purpose.

Identify students who are not native English speakers and be more patient in grading their responses and papers. You might refer them to your institution's writing program for special assistance.

Grading Lab Reports

While this is a specialized kind of grading for a specialized kind of writing, all guidelines for grading constructed responses still apply. Consider these questions as well:
1) How well is the problem understood and how properly is it addressed?
2) How clearly stated is the hypothesis?
3) How are the results presented? According to the instructions? Are all the results included?
4) How clear are the logic and organization of the assignment?
5) How strong are the analytical skills displayed in the results and discussion? How solid is the student's grasp of the scientific method?

It will help to provide students

with samples of quality scientific writing and to familiarize them with the proper format and content. You can also have them organize their reports with an outline or flow chart and practice-write the various sections.

Returning Students' Work

Grade and return tests and assignments as promptly as you can; students can't learn from your feedback on a piece of work they've long forgotten. To protect their privacy, return their work in random or alphabetical order--definitely not in grading rank--and record scores and grades inside the test packet or the paper--never where they can be seen. Under the provisions of the Buckley Amendment (the Family Educational Rights and Privacy Act), it is illegal to display publicly scores or grades with any information that may identify students, including Social Security numbers.

Allow class time for review, questions, and problem-solving exercises so students can learn what they didn't know for the test. It is best not to proceed to new material until students assure you that they understand what they did wrong.

When returning quizzes and exams, some instructors give a statistical grading summary showing the distribution of scores, the class mean, the standard deviation, and the cut-off lines for grades (already built into the CRG system). No doubt these data increase students' interest in elementary statistics, but they also encourage "point mongering," especially around cut-off lines.

This brings us to the unpleasant topic of grade disputes. No matter how carefully you grade, a few students will be dissatisfied with their scores, and it is wise to be prepared to deal with complaints. Here are some ways to prevent or resolve them (Lacey-Casem, 1990):

- Clearly state your grading policies at the beginning of the term in your syllabus and verbally.
- Include many graded quizzes, exams, papers, and other assignments to lessen the impact of a single poor performance, and/or let students toss out their one worst performance.
- Make your comments on students' work as specific as possible.
- Have students check your scoring arithmetic when you return their work.
- Explain how you calculated the grades. Review the problems in class or give a definitive key.
- Be willing to discard a disputed test question that practically all students missed; there is probably something wrong with it.
- Ask students to submit grievances in writing within a time limit. Those who cannot make their case within two weeks probably have a weak one.
- Let emotional students calm down before you deal with them. Schedule a meeting a few days later to discuss their complaint.
- Apprise a student with an unresolvable case of the proper procedures for pursuing the grievance further. Keep copies of the work until the case is settled.

EVALUATING AND DOCUMENTING TEACHING EFFECTIVENESS

Teaching effectiveness weighs more and more heavily in the faculty review process, including tenure and promotion decisions, at an increasing number of colleges and universities. By definition, teaching effectiveness is an instructor's degree of success in facilitating student learning. The more students learn, the deeper the cognitive levels at which they learn, and the better they can communicate what they have learned, the more effective an instructor's teaching.

While we measure our students' learning in tests and assignments, we rarely use standardized assessment instruments across different sections and semesters of the same course. Being required to do so would impinge upon academic freedom and autonomy. However, since we don't standardize our tests and assignments, institutions cannot directly measure teaching effectiveness nor directly compare the relative effectiveness of different instructors.

Student ratings and written comments about the course and the instructor are used instead. Numerical ratings in particular permit easy analysis and comparison. Relying on students' opinions to assess their learning may seem like a leap of faith. But a vast literature on the various types of teaching evaluations--research with which few instructors are familiar--finds that student evaluations are reliable and valid proxies for direct measures of student learning.

This chapter briefly summarizes the major research findings, concluding with guidelines on preparing a teaching portfolio to document your classroom effectiveness.

Peer, Administrative, and Self-Evaluations

Dozen of studies conducted in the 1970s and 1980s (e.g., Centra, 1975; Bergman, 1980; Greenwood and Ramagli, 1980) came to these conclusions about peer, administrative, and self-evaluations of teaching: 1) All three relate very little or not at all to student learning/achievement and only mildly to student ratings. 2) Among peers, interrater reliability (defined below) is low. 3) Peer and self-evaluations are much more generous than student evaluations. 4) Peer and administrative evaluations are so highly correlated as to be almost redundant; self-evaluations do not correlate much with any other type of evaluation.

The literature also consistently draws the implications that none of these three types of evaluations should be used as the sole teaching evaluation tool, nor should they replace student ratings and comments. But researchers also contend that peers and administrators can provide instructors with valuable, useful feedback in certain areas.

Student Evaluations: How Reliable?

Since administrators started adding them to faculty and TA dossiers in the early 1970s, student evaluations have been under a great deal of scrutiny. Numerous studies document that student ratings provide meaningful assessment data that should be used in instructor reviews. But they also recommend that other data be included as well (Cashin, 1988).

In assessing *reliability*, three criteria are very important: *consistency, stability,* and *generalizability*. First, how consistent are student evaluations? Interrater reliability increases from moderately high to very high with class size. In Cashin and Perrin's (1978) study, average item reliability in a class of ten students was .69, but increased to .89 in a class of 40. Thus more raters yield higher consistency.

Stability indicates the agreement between raters over time. In a longitudinal study conducted by Marsh and Overall (1979; Overall and Marsh, 1980), student ratings collected at the end of a semester were compared against ratings collected at least one year after graduation. The average correlation of the ratings was .83, showing a high level of stability.

Finally, generalizability is the apparent accuracy of the data as indicators of instructor teaching effectiveness. Marsh (1982) examined the ratings of instructors teaching the same course in different semesters and teaching different courses. Additionally, he examines different instructors teaching the same course as well as different instructors teaching different courses. The correlations for the same instructor/same course were quite high (.71) as opposed to the same course/different instructor (.14). An instructor's effectiveness apparently crosses course boundaries as well, since the same instructor/different course correlation was .52 vs. the different instructor/different course group correlation of .06.

Cashin (1988) recommends using data from multiple semesters and multiple courses to obtain a reliable picture of teaching effectiveness. If an instructor teaches only one course, then consistent ratings from two terms may be sufficient. For instructors with more responsibilities, however, ratings from two or more courses for every term taught over the past two or more years provide a better assessment. For fair and comprehensive instructor reviews, evaluations of courses with fewer than 15 students should be supplemented with other assessment material.

Student Evaluations: How Valid?

As to *validity*, two concerns are paramount: 1) the effectiveness of student ratings as an indicator of student learning/achievement and 2) any biases that may reduce that effectiveness. For example, Cohen (1981) reported that student achievement on an external exam correlated quite well with teaching effectiveness items in a student questionnaire. The best correlates with student achievement were the teaching skill dimension (.50), the organizational dimension (.47), and overall instructor effectiveness (.44). Less strongly related were instructor friendliness (.31) and the instructor interaction/facilitation dimension (.22).

Instructors often wonder how their grading may affect their evaluations. Actually, there is no statistically respectable method to draw definitive conclusions. Research finds that student grades (individual and class), motivation, and learning are not only all related to instructor/course ratings; they are also highly *inter*related--so much so that it is impossible to say which of the three truly explains their relationships to instructor/course ratings (Howard and Maxwell, 1982).

What about other biases? Cashin (1988) separates myth from reality in his comprehensive literature review. First presented are the variables that have been found ***not*** to affect student ratings in a statistically significant *and* consistent way.

Instructor characteristics:
1) gender
2) age and experience
3) personality (as measured by a personality inventory)
4) research productivity (r = .12).

Student characteristics:
1) gender
2) age
3) level (freshman, sophomore, etc.)
4) grade point average
5) personality (as measured by a personality inventory).

Course and administrative variables:
1) class size (Smaller classes have slightly higher ratings but possibly due to higher student motivation.)
2) time of day when the course is taught
3) time during the term when the evaluations are collected.

But some biases ***do*** exist (Cashin, 1988):

Instructor characteristics:
1) instructor status (Regular faculty are usually rated higher than TAs.)
2) expressiveness (if it can be considered a bias; in fact, expressiveness increases student learning even in the absence of tests and other extrinsic incentives.)

Student characteristics:
1) motivation (Students reporting high prior interest in the subject or taking the course as an elective give higher ratings. Conversely, those enrolled to fulfill requirements give lower ratings.)
2) expected grades (but only possibly, according to Howard and Maxwell, 1982).

Course and administrative variables:
1) course level (Higher level courses, especially graduate level, tend to receive higher ratings.)
2) discipline (Some studies indicate that humanities courses receive higher ratings than social science courses, which in turn receive higher ratings than science and mathematics courses. But it is impossible to say how much these differences are due to varying student

motivation, interest, and anxiety, especially in applying complex, quantitative reasoning skills.)

3) content, workload, and course difficulty (Contrary to popular belief, more *demanding* courses receive *higher* ratings--findings that strongly support the validity of student ratings.)

4) student anonymity (Signed ratings are higher than anonymous ones for obvious reasons.)

5) presence of the instructor (The instructor's presence while students are filling out the forms biases ratings upward.)

6) purpose of the evaluation (Students rate more generously if they believe their ratings will be used for personnel decisions than if they believe their ratings are only for instructor self-improvement.)

Improving Your Student Ratings

You might start by reviewing the statistical summaries and student comments from your previous evaluations and identify areas where you would like to improve. It is best to do this with your department chair, a trusted colleague, or a staff member from your institution's teaching center. This book, of course, presents a wealth of teaching formats and techniques that can enhance your ratings as well as your students' learning. However, it is wise to give a major innovation two or more terms to show positive results.

Secondly, consider getting student feedback far enough in advance of the official evaluation process to fine-tune your courses early in the term. You can write up, administer, and analyze your own midterm student evaluations, including items similar to those on your institution's or department's official student evaluation form, as well as others of concern to you. Alternatively you can ask your teaching center to conduct a small group instructional diagnosis in your course. Research shows that soliciting early student feedback and having an interpretive consultation result in significantly higher student evaluations at the end of the term (Cohen, 1980).

The Teaching Portfolio: Documenting Your Effectiveness

A teaching portfolio is a collection of materials that you assemble to highlight your major teaching strengths and achievements. It is comparable to your publications, grants, and scholarly honors in your research record (Seldin, 1991). It provides a comprehensive, factual base to develop self-assessment and improvement efforts and for faculty and administrators to make sound hiring, promotion, and tenure decisions. Your purpose will influence what you include and how you organize it.

At various times in your teaching career, you will be preparing a portfolio for your reviews. As the teaching evaluation literature cautions, student ratings alone, however valid and reliable, do not furnish a complete assessment of your teaching effectiveness. They should be supplemented with additional data and materials, and it is *your* responsibility to supply them.

To ensure objectivity in your selection of materials, it is best to prepare your portfolio in consultation with a mentor, a trusted colleague, your department chair, or teaching center consultant. Your objective partner can help you focus on the important questions: What is the purpose of the portfolio? What information will your audience find useful? Which teaching/learning areas best serve your purpose? What is the best way to present and analyze the information? What additional information do you need, and how can you obtain it?

Seldin (1991) suggests five steps to producing a good portfolio:

1) Summarize your teaching responsibilities. In two or three paragraphs, describe the types of courses you teach, your course objectives and design, your expectations for student progress, and your learning assessment tools.

2) Describe your criteria for teaching effectiveness and give reasons from your own experience for your choosing these criteria. They should reflect your own teaching style and coincide with your teaching responsibilities.

3) Prioritize your criteria according to your purpose. For instance, if you particularly want to demonstrate your improvement, then rank your participation in teaching workshops and seminars high.

4) Assemble and make a list of the materials and data that support your criteria. You might provide copies of student assignments, journals, test results, student evaluations, and the like while retaining the originals.

5) Incorporate the portfolio into your curriculum vita or attach it. A document of five to seven pages should be sufficient to document your teaching commitment and achievements.

Aside from a summary of your responsibilities, you might also in-

clude at least some of the following materials:

- A statement of your personal philosophy of teaching, including the specific formats and methods you use that reflect it.
- A statement of your teaching goals for the next five years.
- Selected course syllabi and information.
- A brief self-evaluation with your teaching improvement strategies and efforts.
- Descriptions of changes in your course assignments, materials, and activities.
- Professional activities related to teaching, such as instructional research, writing, or journal editing.
- Students you advise and student research projects you supervise.

As it is advisable to work with someone else, consider adding support materials from other sources, such as:

- Statements from supervisors or colleagues who have observed you in the classroom.
- Statements from colleagues who have reviewed your courses and materials.
- Student rating summaries that reflect improvement or overall satisfaction (aside from those automatically included in the review process).
- A statement from your chair or supervisor about your past and projected departmental contributions.
- Statements from your student advisees.
- Teaching awards, honors, and other types of recognition such as teaching committee appointments.
- Invitations to conduct teaching

workshops/programs.
- Involvement in teaching-related research.
- A full-period, classroom videotape.
- Student scores on standardized or your own tests.
- Samples of student work on graded assignments. It is wise to include samples of varying quality and your reasons for the grades you assigned.
- Records of student success in higher level courses following your course.
- Information on how you have influenced student career choices.

A good teaching portfolio cannot guarantee you a faculty position, tenure, or promotion. But teaching portfolios do make the academic reward system more responsive to teaching achievements (Seldin, 1991). Their use is gaining broad acceptance because they complement student evaluation data and fit easily into current hiring and review procedures. Perhaps most important, they motivate instructors and administrators to talk about teaching, thereby promoting instructional innovation and improvement.

Albright, Michael J. and David L. Graf, eds. 1992. *Teaching in the Information Age: The Role of Educational Technology.* New Directions for Teaching and Learning 51. San Francisco: Jossey-Bass.

Allen, Robert D. 1981. Intellectual development and the applications of William. *Journal of College Science Teaching* (November): 94-97.

Altman, Howard B. and William E. Cashin. 1992. Writing a syllabus. *Idea Paper* No. 27. Center for Faculty Evaluation and Development, Kansas State University.

Ambron, Joanna. 1987. Writing to improve learning in biology. *Journal of College Science Teaching* 16 (February): 263-66.

Angelo, Thomas A. 1991a. Introduction and overview: From classroom assessment to classroom research. In *Classroom Research: Early Lessons from Success,* edited by Thomas A. Angelo. New Directions in Teaching and Learning 46. San Francisco: Jossey-Bass.

_____. 1991b. Ten easy pieces: Assessing higher learning in four dimensions. In *Classroom Research: Early Lessons from Success,* edited by Thomas A. Angelo. New Directions in Teaching and Learning 46. San Francisco: Jossey-Bass.

Angelo, Thomas A. and K. Patricia Cross. 1993. *Classroom Assessment Techniques: A Handbook for College Teachers,* 2d ed. San Francisco: Jossey-Bass.

Astin, Alexander W. 1993. *What Matters in College: Four Critical Years Revisited.* San Francisco: Jossey-Bass.

Ballantine, Jeanne and Joanne Risacher. 1993. Coping with annoying classroom behaviors. Paper presented at the 13th Annual Lilly Conference on College Teaching, Oxford, OH. November 12.

Bandura, A. 1977. Self-efficacy: Toward a unifying theory of behavioral change. *Psychological Review* 84(2) (March): 191-215.

Barnett, David C. and Jon C. Dalton. 1981. Why college students cheat. *Journal of College Student Personnel* (November): 545-551.

Bartlett, Albert A. and Michael A. Thomason. 1983. Legibility in the lecture hall. *The Physics Teacher* (November): 531.

Belanoff, P. and M. Dickson. 1991. *Portfolios: Process and Product.* Portsmouth, NH: Boynton/Cook and Heinemann.

Bergman, Jerry. 1980. Peer evaluation of university faculty. *College Student Journal* 14 (3) (Fall): 1-21.

Bernhardt, Stephen A. 1992. Teaching English: Portfolio evaluation. *The Clearing House* 65 (6) (July/August): 333-334.

Black, B. and E. Axelson. 1991. Teaching students to solve problems. In *The University of Michigan TA Guidebook.* Ann Arbor: University of Michigan.

Bloom, Benjamin. 1956. *Taxonomy of Educational Objectives.* New York: David McKay.

Bodner, George. 1987. The role of algorithms in teaching problem solving. *Journal of Chemical Education* 64 (6) (June): 513-514.

Boling, Elizabeth and Gerald A. Sousa. 1993. Interface design issues in the future of business training. *Business Horizons* (November/December): 50-54.

Bonwell, Charles C. and James A. Eison. 1991. Active Learning: *Creating Excitement in the Classroom. ASHE-ERIC Higher Education Report* No. 1. Washington, D.C.: School of Education and Human Development, George Washington University.

Bourland, Julie. 1996. Hollywood hustle. *Parenting* (March): 53.

Bridges, Edwin M. with Philip Hallinger. 1992. *Problem-Based Learning for Administrators.* Eugene, OR: ERIC Clearinghouse on Educational Management.

Brookhart, Victoria. 1990. Problem solving in science. Unpublished manuscript, Teaching Assistant Development Program, University of California, Riverside.

Brooks, Robert P. 1987. Dealing with details in large classes. In *Teaching Large Classes Well,* edited by Maryellen G. Weimer. New Directions in Teaching and Learning 32. San Francisco: Jossey-Bass.

Browne, M. Neil and Stuart M. Keeley. 1986. *Asking the Right Questions: A Guide to Critical Thinking,* 2d ed. Englewood Cliffs, NJ: Prentice-Hall.

Burns, E. Bradford. 1993. *Liberating the Imagination for Intellectual Discoveries.* 89 minutes. Produced by Vanderbilt University Center for Teaching. Videocassette.

Cameron, Beverly J. 1993. *Teaching at the University of Manitoba.* Manitoba, Winnipeg, Canada: University of Manitoba Teaching Services.

Carrier, Carol A. 1983. Notetaking research implications for the classroom. *Journal of Instructional Development* 6 (3): 19-26.

Carroll, Raymonde. 1988. *Cultural Misunderstandings: The French-American Experience.* Translated by Carol Volk. Chicago: University of Chicago Press.

Cashin, William E. 1979. Motivating students. *IDEA Paper* No. 1. Center for Faculty Evaluation and Development, Kansas State University.

_____. 1988. Student ratings of teaching: A summary of the research. *IDEA Paper* No. 20. Center for Faculty Evaluation and Development, Kansas State University.

Cashin, William E. and B.M. Perrin. 1978. Description of a standard form data base. *IDEA Technical Report No. 4.* Center for Faculty Evaluation and Development, Kansas State University.

Centra, John A. 1975. Colleagues as raters of classroom instruction. *Journal of Higher Education* 46 (1) (May/June): 327-337.

Chiaramonte, Peter. 1994. The agony and the ecstasy of case teaching. *Reaching Through Teaching* 7 (2) (Winter): 1-2.

Clute, Pamela S., lecturer in mathematics and education. 1994. Telephone interview by author, February. University of California, Riverside.

Cohen, P.A. 1981. Student ratings of instruction and student achievement: A meta-analysis of multi-section validity studies. *Review of Educational Research* 51: 281-309.

Collison, Michele. 1990a. Apparent rise in students' cheating has college officials worried. *The Chronicle of Higher Education* (January 17): A33-34.

_____. 1990b. Survey at Rutgers suggests that cheating may be on the rise at large universities. *The Chronicle of Higher Education* (October 24): A31-32.

Cooper, J.L., P. Robinson, and M. McKinney. 1993. Cooperative learning in the classroom. In *Changing College Classrooms*, edited by Diane F. Halpern and associates. San Francisco: Jossey-Bass.

Crane, G. 1991. Hypermedia and the study of ancient culture. *IEEE Computer Graphics and Applications* 16: 45-51.

Cross, K. Patricia. 1988. In search of zippers. *AAHE Bulletin* (June): 3-7.

_____. 1992. Classroom assessment/classroom research: Four years into a hands-on movement. *The National Teaching & Learning Forum* 1 (6): 1-3.

Cross, K. Patricia and Thomas A. Angelo. 1988. *Classroom Assessment Techniques: A Handbook for Faculty.* Ann Arbor, MI: National Center for Research to Improve Postsecondary Teaching and Learning.

Crowley, Mary L. 1993. Student mathematics portfolio: More than a display case. *The Mathematics Teacher* 86 (7) (October): 544-547.

Daniel, J.S. 1975. Uses and abuses of slides in teaching. In *Teaching Aids in the College Classroom*, edited by L.P. Grayson and J.M. Biedenbach. Washington, D.C.: American Society for Engineering Education.

Davenport, G. and Harber, J.D. 1991. Numbers--a medium that counts. *IEEE Computer Graphics and Applications* 16: 39-44.

Day, R.S. 1980. Teaching from notes: Some cognitive consequences. In *Learning, Cognition, and College Teaching*, edited by W.J. McKeachie. New Directions for Teaching and Learning 2. San Francisco: Jossey-Bass.

Deming, W.E. 1993. *The New Economics for Industry, Government, and Education.* Cambridge, MA: MIT Center for Advanced Engineering Study.

Ellis, David B. 1985. *Becoming a Master Student.* Rapid City, SD: College Survival, Inc.

Ericksen, S.C. 1974. *Motivation for Learning: A Guide for the Teacher of the Young Adult.* Ann Arbor: University of Michigan Press.

Fagan, M.M. 1986. Do formal mentoring programs really mentor? In *Proceedings of the First International Conference on Mentoring* 2. Vancover, B.C.: International Association for Mentoring.

Feichtner, Susan Brown and Elaine Actis Davis. 1984-85. Why some groups fail: A survey of students' experiences with learning groups. *The Organizational Behavior Teaching Review* 9 (4): 58-73.

Ferris, William P. and Peter W. Hess. 1984-85. Peer evaluation of student interaction in organizational behavior and other courses. *The Organizational Behavior Teaching Review* 9 (4): 74-82.

Finkel, D.L. and G.S. Monk. 1983. Teachers and learning groups: Dissolution of the Atlas complex. In *Learning in Groups*, edited by C. Bouton and R.Y. Garth. New Directions for Teaching and Learning 14. San Francisco: Jossey-Bass.

Fleming, Neil D. and Colleen Mills. 1992. Not another inventory, rather a catalyst for reflection. *To Improve the Academy* 11: 137-155.

Fontana, L.A. 1991. The Civil War Interactive. *Instruction Delivery Systems* 5 (6): 5-9.

Frierson, H.T. 1986. Two intervention methods: Effects on groups of predominantly black nursing students' board scores. *Journal of Research and Development in Education* 19: 18-23.

Frymier, J.R. 1970. Motivation is what it's all about. *Motivation Quarterly* 1: 1-3.

Galbraith, John Kenneth. 1987. How I could have done much better. *The Journal of the Harvard-Danforth Center: On Teaching and Learning* 2 (January): 1-4.

Gale, Richard A. and John D.W. Andrews. 1989. *A Handbook for Teaching Assistants.* Center for Teaching Development, University of California, San Diego.

Gallupe, R. Brent and William H. Cooper. 1993. Brainstorming electronically. *Sloan Management Review* (Fall): 27-36.

Gigliotti, Richard J. and Donald R. Fitzpatrick. 1977. An investigation into the factors accounting for college student interest in courses. *Educational Research Quarterly* 2 (1) (Spring): 58-68.

Gogel, Howard K. 1985. Faculty office hours. *Journal of Medical Education* 60 (October).

Gordon, Larry. 1990. Study finds cheating joins 3 Rs as a basic college skill. *Los Angeles Times* (November 22).

Greenwood, Gordon E. and Howard J. Ramagli, Jr. 1980. Alternatives to student ratings of college teaching. *Journal of Higher Education* 51 (6): 673-684.

Gronlund, Norman E. 1985. *Stating Objectives for Classroom Instruction*, 3d ed. New York: Macmillan.

Grunert, Judith. 1997. *The Course Syllabus: A Learning-Centered Approach.* Bolton, MA: Anker Publishing.

Hall, Roberta M. and Sandler, Bernice Resnick. 1982. *The Classroom Climate: A Chilly One for Women?* Project on the Status and Education of Women. Washington, D.C.: Association of American Colleges.

Halpern, Diane F. and Associates. 1994. *Changing College Classrooms.* San Francisco: Jossey-Bass.

Hammons, James O. and Janice R. Barnsley. 1992. Everything you need to know about developing a grading plan for your course (well, almost). *Journal on Excellence in College Teaching* 3: 51-68.

Head, J.T. 1992. New directions in presentation graphics: Impact on teaching and learning. In *Teaching in the Information Age: The Role of Educational Technology*, edited by Michael J. Albright and David L. Graf. New Directions for Teaching and Learning 51. San Francisco: Jossey-Bass.

Hebert, Stephen W., M.D. 1984. A simple hypnotic approach to treat test anxiety in medical students and residents. *Journal of Medical Education* 59 (October): 841-842.

Heller, Patricia, Ronald Keith, and Scott Anderson. 1992. Teaching problem solving through cooperative grouping. Part 1: Group vs. individual problem solving.

Heller, Patricia and Mark Hollabaugh. 1992. Teaching problem solving through cooperative grouping. Part 2: Designing problems and structuring groups. *American Journal of Physics* 60 (7) (July): 637-644.

Herron, Carol. 1991. The garden path correction strategy in the foreign language classroom. *The French Review* 64, 6: 966-977.

Hinkle, S. and A. Hinkle. 1990. An experimental comparison of the effects of focused freewriting and other study strategies on lecture comprehension. *Teaching of Psychology* 17 (February): 31-35.

Howard, George S. and Scott E. Maxwell. 1980. The correlation between student satisfaction and grades: A case of mistaken causation? *Journal of Educational Psychology* 72 (6): 810-820.

_____. 1982. Do grades contaminate student evaluations of instruction? *Research in Higher Education* 16 (2): 175-188.

Hufford, Terry L. 1991. Increasing academic performance in an introductory biology course. *BioScience* 41 (2) (February): 107-108.

Hunter, Madeline. 1967. *Motivation Theory for Teachers.* El Segundo, CA: TIP Publications.

Hyman, Ronald T. 1978. *Simulation Gaming for Values Education: The Prisoner's Dilemma.* Washington, D.C.: University Press of America.

_____. 1981. Using simulation games in the college classroom. *Idea Paper* No. 5. Center for Faculty Evaluation and Development, Kansas State University.

Jalajas, David S, and Robert I. Sutton. 1984-85. Feuds in student groups: Coping with whiners, martyrs, saboteurs, bullies, and deadbeats. *The Organizational Behavior Teaching Review* 9 (4): 94-107.

Johnson, David, W. and others. 1981. Effects of cooperative, competitive, and individualistic goal structures on achievement: A meta-analysis. *Psychological Bulletin* 89: 47-62.

Johnson, David W. and Roger T. Johnson. 1989. *Cooperation and Competition: Theory and Research.* Edina, MN: Interaction Books.

Johnson, David W., Roger T. Johnson, and Karl A. Smith. 1991. *Active Learning: Cooperation in the College Classroom.* Edina, MN: Interaction Books.

Johnston, A.H. and W.Y. Su. 1994. Lectures--a learning experience? *Education in Chemistry* (May): 76-79.

Jonas, H., S. Etzel, and B. Barzansky. 1989. Undergraduate medical education. *JAMA* 262 (8) (August): 1011-1019.

Jordan, Dan. 1996. Copyright and multimedia. Session conducted at the 17th Annual Sharing Conference of the Southern Regional Faculty and Instructional Development Consortium, Baton Rouge, LA. February 4-6.

Kagan, Spencer. 1988. *Cooperative learning.* San Juan Capistrano, CA: Resources for Teachers.

Karraker, Meg Wilkes. 1993. Mock trials and critical thinking. *College Teaching* 41 (4) (Fall): 134-137.

Kaufman, A. 1985. *Implementing Problem-Based Medical Education.* New York: Springer Publishing Company.

Kaufman, A., et al. 1989. The New Mexico experiment: Educational innovation and institutional change. *Academic Medicine* (June Supplement): 285-294.

Kendall, Jane C. and Associates. 1990. *Combining Service and Learning: A Resource Book for Community and Public Service,* Vol I and II. Raleigh: National Society for Internships and Experiential Education.

Kibler, William L. 1992. Cheating: Institutions need a comprehensive plan for promoting academic integrity. *The Chronicle of Higher Education* (November 11): B1-2.

Kirby, P. 1989. The Trinity College mentor program. Unpublished manuscript, Trinity College, Washington, D.C.

Kirkpatrick, Larry D. and Adele S. Pittendrigh. 1984. A writing teacher in the physics classroom. *The Physics Teacher* 22 (March): 159-64.

Kloss, Robert J. 1994. A nudge is best: Helping students through the Perry schema of intellectual development. *College Teaching* 42 (4) (Fall): 151-158.

Knapper, C.K. 1982. Technology and teaching: Future prospects. In *Expanding Learning Through Communication Technologies,* edited by C.K. Knapper. New Directions for Teaching and Learning 9. San Francisco: Jossey-Bass.

Kolb, David A. 1984. *Experiential Learning: Experience as the Source of Learning and Development.* Englewood Cliffs, NJ: Prentice-Hall.

Krashen, Stephen. 1985. *The Input Hypothesis.* New York: Longman Press.

Krashen, Stephen and Tracy Terrell. 1983. *The Natural Approach.* Hayward, CA: Alemany.

Krashen, Stephen and H. White. 1991. Is spelling acquired or learned? A re-analysis of Rice (1897) and Cornman (1902). *Review of Applied Linguistics* I.T.L. 91-92: 1-48.

Krupnick, Catherine G. 1985. Women and men in the classroom: Inequality and its remedies. *The Journal of the Harvard-Danforth Center: On Teaching and Learning* 1 (May): 18-25.

Lacey-Casem, Merri Lynn. 1990. Testing students' learning and grading tests and papers. In *Teaching Techniques: A Handbook for TAs at UCR,* edited by Linda B. Nilson. Teaching Assistant Development Program, University of California, Riverside.

Lamb, Annette C. 1992. Multimedia and the teaching-learning process in higher education. *In Teaching in the Information Age: The Role of Educational Technology,* edited by Michael J. Albright and David L. Graf. New Directions for Teaching and Learning 51. San Francisco: Jossey-Bass.

Langer, Judith A. 1992. Speaking of knowing: Conceptions of understanding in academic disciplines. In *Writing, Teaching, and Learning in the Disciplines,* edited by Anne Herrington and Charles Moran. New York: Modern Language Association of America.

Langer, Judith A. and Arthur N. Applebee. 1987. *How Writing Shapes Thinking.* Urbana, IL: National Council of Teachers of English.

Lewis, R.J. and Wall, M. 1988. *Exploring Obstacles to Uses of Technology in Higher Education: A Discussion Paper.* Washington, D.C.: Academy for Educational Development.

Light, Richard J. 1990. *The Harvard Assessment Seminar, First Report: Explorations with Students and Faculty about Teaching, Learning, and Student Life.* Cambridge, MA: Harvard Graduate School of Education.

_____. 1992. *The Harvard Assessment Seminar, Second Report: Explorations with Students and Faculty about Teaching, Learning, and Student Life.* Cambridge, MA: Harvard Graduate School of Education.

Littlewood, William. 1991. *Teaching Oral Communication: A Methodological Framework.* Oxford: Blackwell Publishers.

Lowman, Joseph. 1987. Giving students feedback. In *Teaching Large Classes Well,* edited by Maryellen G. Weimer. New Directions for Teaching and Learning 32. San Francisco: Jossey-Bass.

Toulmin, Stephen, Richard Rieke, and Allan Janik. 1984. *An Introduction to Reasoning*. 2d ed. New York: Macmillan.

Treisman, P.U. 1986. A study of the mathematics performance of black students at the University of California, Berkeley. Doctoral dissertation. Berkeley: University of California.

Walvoord, Barbara E. and Lucille Parkinson McCarthy. 1991. *Thinking and Writing in College: A Naturalistic Study of Students in Four Disciplines*. Urbana, IL: National Council of Teachers of English.

Warmington, Eric H. and Philip G. Rouse, ed. 1984. *Great Dialogues of Plato*. Translated by W.H.D. Rouse. Markham, Ontario: Penguin Books.

Watson, David L. and Nancy A. Stockert. 1987. Ensuring teaching and learning effectiveness. *Thought and Action: The NEA Higher Education Journal* 3 (2): 91-104.

Wergin, Jon F. 1988. Basic issues and principles in classroom assessment. In *Assessing Students' Learning*, edited by James H. McMillan. New Directions for Teaching and Learning. San Francisco: Jossey-Bass.

Woods, Donald R. 1989. Developing students' problem-solving skills. *Journal of College Science Teaching* (November): 108-110.

Young, Art and Todd Fulwiler, eds. 1986. *Writing across the Disciplines: Research into Practice*. Upper Montclair, NJ: Boynton/Cook Publishers.

Zoller, Uri. 1987. The fostering of question-asking capacity. *Journal of Chemical Education* 64 (6) (June): 510-512.

INDEX